Feminist Praxis

Feminist social scientists often find that carrying feminism into practice in their research is neither easy nor straightforward. Designed precisely with feminist researchers in mind, *Feminist Praxis* gives detailed analytic accounts of particular examples of feminist research, showing how feminist epistemology can translate into concrete feminist research practices.

The contributors, all experts in their field, give practical examples of feminist research processes, covering colonialism, child-minding, gay men, feminist social work, cancer, working with young girls using drama, Marilyn Monroe, statistics – even the writing and reading of research accounts. These detailed accounts are located in relation to the position of feminism and of women generally in the academic world, and looked at in the light of discussions, debates, and controversies about feminist methodology across several disciplines.

Feminist Praxis is unique in combining theoretical discussion of feminist methodology with detailed accounts of practical research processes. This blend of the practical and the theoretical will make it an invaluable text for feminists carrying out research at all levels, and it will also appeal to those interested in the relationship between theory, method, and feminist epistemology.

The Editor

Now Senior Lecturer in Sociology at the University of Manchester, Liz Stanley has been teaching about feminist social science and its methodology since 1977, and has written widely on the subject.

Feminist Praxis

Research, Theory and Epistemology
in Feminist Sociology

Edited by

Liz Stanley

London and New York

First published 1990
by Routledge
11 New Fetter Lane, London EC4P 4EE

Simultaneously published in the USA and Canada
by Routledge
a division of Routledge, Chapman and Hall, Inc.
29 West 35th Street, New York, NY 10001

Typeset by LaserScript Limited, Mitcham, Surrey

Printed and bound in Great Britain by
Mackays of Chatham PLC, Chatham, Kent

British Library Cataloguing in Publication Data
Feminist praxis: research, theory and epistemology in feminist sociology
   1. Feminism
   I. Stanley, Liz, *1947–*
   305.4′2

Library of Congress Cataloging in Publication Data
Feminist praxis: research, theory, and epistemology in feminist sociology /
   (ed.), Liz Stanley.
   p. cm.
   Includes bibliographical references.
   1. Women's studies–Methodology. 2. Feminist–Research–Methodology.
   I. Stanley, Liz, 1947–
   HQ1180.F46 1990
   305.42′072–dc20   89–24200
                                       CIP

ISBN 0-415-04186-4
ISBN 0-415-04202-X (pbk)

What is a literary critic, a black woman critic, a black feminist literary critic? The adjectives mount up, defining, qualifying, the activity. How does one distinguish them? The need to articulate a theory, to categorize the activities is a good part of the activity itself to the point where I wonder how we ever get around to doing anything else. What do these categories tell anyone about my method? ... I'm irked, weighed down by Foucault's library as tiers of books written on epistemology, ontology and technique peer down at me. Can one theorize effectively about an evolving process? Are the labels informative or primarily a way of nipping the question in the bud? What are the philosophical assumptions behind my praxis? I think how the articulation of a theory is a gathering place, sometimes a point of rest as the process rushes on, insisting that you follow .... 'But I do have fun doing this,' ... though, humbled again by the terror of the blank page in front of me, it's a mystery to me why.

Barbara Christian (1985) *Black Feminist Criticism*, New York:
Pergamon, pp. x, xi and xv.

Contents

Contents

Brief biographies

Chung Yuen Kay is a Malaysian Chinese who lives in Singapore with her spouse. She has just finished her Ph.D. thesis, an ethnography of women workers in a high-technology factory in Singapore; and now considers herself to be 'freelancing'. She is an interpretive/ phenomenological sociologist who seeks always to understand how women themselves understand and handle domination/power in everyday lives and everyday ways. She is also interested in the development of feminist ethnography, women and work (all kinds of it), and the interaction of gender and ethnicity.

Denise Farran's first degree was in sociology at the University of Manchester, where she also completed an M.A. thesis dealing with biographies of Ruth Ellis and Marilyn Monroe. She is currently lecturing at Brunel University, and completing a Ph.D. thesis at Manchester on Ruth Ellis and other women murderers. Her research interests include textual analysis of research documents such as fieldwork notes, interview scripts and questionnaires. She lives in the countryside near Macclesfield. Her first baby, Adam, was born in summer 1989.

Clara Greed is a senior lecturer in the Department of Surveying at Bristol Polytechnic. She originally studied town planning in the late 1960s when there were relatively few women in the land-use professions. She was then employed in town planning in local government. She now teaches town planning, and more recently the social aspects of planning and development to surveying students. As a result of all these experiences she has sought to make sense of her life and discovered, in her thirties, that a feminist perspective contributes a great deal towards that objective. She continues to apply this new awareness to urban spatial issues, and is currently completing her doctorate on the position of women in surveying education and practice, and writing a book on the topic.

Vivienne Griffiths teaches in the Education Area at the University of Sussex, where she is co-ordinator for drama and educational issues on the teacher training course. Before this, she taught English and Drama in schools, and worked as an actor/teacher in drama-in-education groups. She is interested in feminist research methods and is currently completing some research on adolescent girls and their friends. She is also helping to evaluate an experiment in single-sex setting in Maths at a local comprehensive school, and is hoping to set up an action research project on gender in primary schools.

Jane Haggis. After some years travelling and working at a variety of jobs, Jane Haggis obtained a B.A. Honours degree from Adelaide University in Australia. She came to Britain in 1984 to take up doctoral studies. Now in the final stages, she hopes, of completing her Ph.D., she hopes to obtain a job which will allow her to develop her continuing interest in feminist methodology and colonialism.

Joyce Layland was born in the north east of England and now lives near Oldham. Her undergraduate career was as a mature student in the Sociology Department at Manchester University; she then worked for an M.A. dealing with the topic of researching masculinity. She has been involved in working with gay teenagers for a number of years. Since discovering she has multiple sclerosis, she has become increasingly aware of the political dimensions of people's responses to this experience.

Fiona Poland has spent most of her adult working life in Manchester exploring different ways of living and organising relationships within her everyday life and research. Formerly a research worker in a number of organisations, she is at present finishing her doctorate (which deals with different 'research methods') at Manchester University.

Anne Pugh decided that enough was enough after nine years as a research worker in the voluntary sector; a different sort of life has ensued, a gradual period of reorientation focussing on an aspiring athletics career and training in countryside management and horticulture. She tries to put feminist principles into practice in leading a gentle, pleasant sort of life with friends, the dog, cat and rabbit, with the occasional dabble in social research.

Liz Stanley. Working class by birth, a Northerner in England by choice, and a lesbian by luck, I have taught in the Sociology Department at Manchester University since 1977. Most recently my research interests have focussed on historical topics and issues and on feminist auto/ biography; and I am currently researching some aspects of the presence of Mass Observation in Bolton in the 1930s. Whatever the apparent diversity of my research topics, my central and abiding sociological and feminist concern is with the processes by which 'knowledge' is produced and contested.

Ann Tait has worked as a clinical nurse specialist, with women who have breast cancer, for several years and she now works in Bloomsbury Health Authority, London. She is presently Vice-Chairwoman of the Breast Care Nursing Forum at the Royal College of Nursing, and Chairwoman of the Council of the Breast Care and Mastectomy Association, UK, a registered charity which provides information and support to women with breast cancer. Ann became a feminist sociology student comparatively late in her life – but her enthusiasm for this subject is still increasing. She is married and has two sons and two daughters.

Sue Webb did her undergraduate degree at Leicester University and her M.A. at Manchester. She has taught Sociology and Women's Studies in a number of different educational organisations. She was a Research Fellow in the School of Education at the Open University. Most recently she has completed a funded project which examines the experiences of ACCESS-prepared students in higher education. In 1989 she joined Manchester Open College Federation, a regional accreditation unit in Greater Manchester and Cheshire, as a Development Officer. Her main research interests are in organisational behaviour and the sociology of gender. Her Ph.D. thesis, currently nearing completion, deals with an ethnography of a department store.

Anne Williams originally trained and worked as a nurse in Britain and then Canada. In Canada she later took an Anthropology degree. Following her return to Britain, she started the research outlined in her chapter, and which makes use of both of her areas of professional training. Her overall research interest is in the nature of ethnography; her current concern is with researching 'familiar settings' rather than those we come to as strangers, and her recently completed Ph.D. thesis dealt with this topic in detail. For the last few years she has been teaching in the Social Administration Department at Lancaster University.

Sue Wise has spent most of her adult life preoccupied with social work, sociology and feminist political struggle. As a social worker, she has been involved in formal and informal work, paid and unpaid, in residential day-care and fieldwork settings. As a sociologist she has contributed to a feminist understanding, especially in relation to research processes and practices. As a political activist she has endeavoured to foreground the political context of her practice in social work and in sociology, as well as being involved in various 'campaigns'. She is currently lecturer in social work at the University of Lancaster and is researching in the areas of child abuse, lesbian and gay issues in social welfare, and equal opportunities policies.

Acknowledgements

All books result from a collaborative process in which large numbers of people, among them 'the author/s', participate. This book results from a number of overlapping collaborative processes. I would like to acknowledge and thank the contributors to this particular volume, but also more generally contributors to the Studies in Sexual Politics series and its conferences, as well as its now many subscribers. British universities are beleaguered institutions in which increasing amounts of work are carried out by decreasing numbers of people; and I would like to thank members of the Multilith department for their crucial contribution to production of the SSP series. Sue Scott has been involved in the SSP series, as well as making the Manchester Department a better place to work – I hope permanently. David Morgan, a good friend and colleague, has provided interesting and useful comment on my own contributions to this volume, as well as welcome support for the Studies in Sexual Politics series. My grateful thanks to Jane Haggis for typing most of the papers herein and to Sue Wise for the others.

In memory of two good friends, Rupert Ray and Edgar Gray Doe.

Part one

Feminism and the Academic Mode

Chapter one

Feminist praxis and the academic mode of production
An editorial introduction

Liz Stanley

Feminist sociology of a 'Manchester School'

The chapters in this edited collection derive from a series of feminist working papers produced under the auspices of the Sociology Department at the University of Manchester, England. 'Studies in Sexual Politics' (SSP) was set up to give 'a voice' to feminist sociological work produced in the tradition of the Manchester Department. The series started in 1984, producing six titles a year; I have been its main editor throughout; and a full list of SSP titles appears as an appendix to this introduction. The tradition of the Manchester Department is one of detailed, particularly but not exclusively ethnographic, styles of research; and it derives from the 1940s and 1950s when the department was a joint Sociology and Anthropology one headed by Max Gluckman (see here Morgan 1981; also the introduction to Frankenberg 1982). Such a combination of detailed empirical work and theory, although not of a 'grand theory' kind, still characterises the work of the now separate Sociology Department, from interactionist occupational ethnographies to Marxist development studies to ethnomethodological conversational analysis and other strands. It is therefore no accident that much of the feminist research produced within it should show a similar determined concern with the close details of feminist sociological research processes.

This is not to argue that there is anything unique about this work compared with much feminist research produced elsewhere in Britain. What is perhaps unusual is such broadly based departmental support for qualitatively focussed empirical feminist research and theory; and, as a consequence of the long departmental tradition of producing and writing about this kind of research, the existence of a wide range of analytic skills to draw upon.

However, there is another difference, an altogether epistemologically more consequential one. This is the conscious reflexivity concerning the feminist research process explicitly encouraged by the SSP series.

Rather than simply acknowledging the researcher's active role, the SSP series encourages a close *analytic* attention to the details of that process. Rather than describing at a general level 'the research' before getting down to the serious business of discussing 'findings' and their relationship to 'theory', the intention has been to draw the *process* of knowledge production, in research and theorising, into its *product*, in the shape of written accounts of it. Thus 'feminist research' itself has been centred as a researchable topic.

This has happened because, from the start, the development of the SSP series has been located in a coherent set of ideas about knowledge production and a concomitant need for feminist researchers to avoid producing yet more 'alienated knowledge' (Rose 1983). This can usefully be explained in relation to ideas about an 'academic mode of production'.

The academic mode of production

The notion of an 'academic mode of production' has been discussed by a number of commentators, and in relation to feminist thinking in David Morgan's (1981) account of the combined production and use of 'masculinity' within the academic mode. I build on these ideas here.

A *mode of production* is characterised by a particular kind of relationship between the *relations* and *forces* of production; the following discussion locates academic work, research in particular, firmly within such a materialist analysis although the focus is on academic feminism (see also Kuhn and Wolpe 1978; Thompson 1983).

Within Marxist analyses of modes of production the emphasis is on the feudal, the transition to capitalist, and the capitalist modes. Nevertheless, the conceptual apparatus developed to analyse these is also pertinently applied to the academic production process, particularly in view of its combination of capitalist and patriarchal definitions and usages of 'knowledge' and 'science' in what is an effective denial of the labour processes involved in these. Thus it lends itself well to a feminist analysis of such features of the academic mode.

I am using this notion of a 'mode of production' as an *analytic* category in the same way that Marxist usages do, and with a similar recognition that, just as different societies will have more than one mode of production, so too will academic life (particularly, as now within academia, in periods of change). Similarly, as with other modes of production, so the academic mode too has a particular set of politics and ideology as part of the conditions of its existence, indeed as a defining feature of that existence. These politics centre, as Jürgen Habermas (1972, 1984) has argued in a number of wide-reaching works, on 'scientism' – that is, on essentially Cartesian ideas about 'science', 'knowledge', 'the research process', 'theory' and 'expertise'. And the existence of academic feminism – indeed academic feminism*s* – acts as a challenge to current expositions of these linked ideas (Stanley and Wise 1983a, 1983b; Harding 1987; *Resources for Feminist Research* 1987; Pateman and Gross 1986).

The *relations* of production are difficult to define with precision. However, as in the capitalist mode, production relations in the academic mode divide over who controls and has the capacity to possess the product and who does not. What is less clear is just how we are to assign different groups across that divide. To speak of two fundamental groups, whether of classes or men and women, is certainly insufficient.

Within the academic mode there are those who act as official and unofficial gatekeepers of academic inputs and outputs. Who these people are in terms of their sex, but also the academic politics and ideologies to which they subscribe, is consequential for feminists, indeed for women in general (Smith 1978; Spender 1981; Stanley 1984; Ward and Grant 1985; Cook and Fonow 1984, 1986). Publishers and publishers' readers; internal and external referees for research funds, books, journal articles, examinations and job applications; professors, heads of departments, deans and pro-vice-chancellors – all these act as gatekeepers. Moreover, in different times and places many of them are also subject to gatekeeping practices themselves. For at least the last twenty years one of the aims of academic feminism has been to join them; but another has also been to dismantle at least some of the sources and uses of their power over 'peers'.

The relations of production within the academic mode are further complicated by the organisational structure that surrounds written/ published academic outputs. There is an associated pedagogical process here, and there is also a hierarchical organisational structure across departments, faculties and whole institutions. This is composed by other professional groups, but also by secretaries, other office staff, cleaners, porters, refectory and cafeteria staff, building maintenance workers, security staff and others. Academic institutions are complex organisational structures indeed; and within them academic divisions are cross-cut, duplicated, under-cut and otherwise complicated by these other groups of necessary workers. It needs to be remembered at all times that without them academic staff could not function as academics.

This complexity is further demonstrated by discussing the *forces* of production in the academic mode. The 'materials worked on' and the 'tools of the trade' include not only blackboards, computers, blank sheets of paper, books, articles and conference papers in the making, but also people: as research subjects/objects, and also as students. And some of these people are located within and are an immediately identifiable part of the academy, while others just as clearly are not. The 'techniques of production' similarly range from those either at hand or learned within the organisation or a related one, and those necessarily learned outside the academy such as the ethnographic research method or the various clinical skills of medics, psychiatrists and others. And many of the specific techniques of social science research are themselves necessarily used in part outside of the organisation, in the 'production of data' of different kinds, as well as inside it in the analysis thereof.

Within the academic mode it is difficult to distinguish precisely between the 'classes' on either side of at least some of its production processes. For instance, are students at undergraduate but also at graduate levels commodities, raw materials, or co-producers? Perhaps the most sensible view is to suggest all three, depending on which part of the process an analysis is focussed on. Also the 'better' (but how to measure this? another by no means simple issue) the student, the less they are raw materials and the more co-producers (Rutenberg 1983; Coyner 1983; Smyth 1987; Minnich, O'Barr and Rosenfeld 1988). The notion of a labour theory of value in relation to the academic mode has its problems. Most research products and academic publications have either no monetary exchange value at all (for example, academic journal articles and conference papers), or are accorded an exchange value which has more symbolic than actual monetary value (for instance, advances and royalties for academic books rarely cover even the costs of typing and basic research expenses, let alone accord a monetary value to the labour time of either writing or researching).

In spite of this, it is clear that an academic *market* operates, albeit one with its own rather quirky characteristics. At its most basic a market is an 'area of exchange', where important activities of production and consumption are organised, as well as those of distribution and exchange. Moreover, this market (of job-seeking, funding applications, publication-seeking, promotion applications, applications for research studentships, the assessment of students, courses, departments and institutions) is operated by an overlapping variety of people, from academics to people employed in commercial capitalist organisations to government and related officials of various kinds and levels. The position of women in general, feminists in particular, in this market is a complex one closely related to the overlapping divisions of labour that exist within the academic mode, the sexual 'sedimentation' or hierarchicalisation of particular occupational groupings, the similar sexualised distribution of women/feminist students, but to an extent cross-cutting this the often more advantageous market position of feminist writings and thus of feminist researchers in publication terms.

I have already noted that some exchange values do not reflect the 'true value' of the commodities produced but are rather accorded symbolic payment. Often 'payment' is given actually in the form of *symbolic credit,* which can later be measured and 'expended' against jobs, promotions and so forth. Bourdieu (1977, 1984) has argued that those in power control the form that *culture* takes, and that they sustain their positions through *cultural reproduction* and the differential hierarchical distribution of accrued (inter-generationally as well as intragenerationally) *cultural capital* gained through the informal as well as formal educational system. Bourdieu's prime concern is with 'those in power' as an elite group in society generally. However, the same argument is made about the generation and accrual of cultural capital (what I referred to as 'symbolic credit') *within* the academic mode itself. Within the academic mode different and overlaid divisions of labour can be observed.

It has become conventional to note a *technical division of labour,* a division of tasks made on a technical basis; a *social division of labour,* in the form of sub-divisions of tasks into elements shared between people; and a *sexual division of labour.* To these I would add an *academic division of labour.*

The *technical division of labour* within the academic mode turns on what at first sight looks like divisions of qualification; but these in their turn come to rest on sex, race and class divisions and the intergenerational perpetuation of these through, among other factors, the educational system. To account fully for this claim requires an examination of the operations of both the educational system and of the job market, and cannot be undertaken here (but see Deem 1980 for an account of this in terms of sex/gender).

Within the academic mode a *social division of labour* exists which is in complex ways related to the specifics of the pedagogical process. 'Lectures' may be done by one person, 'tutorials' by another, and 'supervision' by yet another; but at its basis teaching is a relationship between two parties, 'a teacher' (who may be more than one in number) and 'the taught' (who may be one person or many). There is certainly also a *technical division of labour* within the pedagogical aspect of the academic mode (between teachers and other workers; between teachers divided in grades) but the specific activity of teaching by any one of these is a single interactional event that contains no division apart from that between the teacher and the student-commodities produced. Thus the division of labour that produces 'teachers' paradoxically contains an unseamed interactional act in the production of taught and qualified students. But then again – a further paradox – these students, or rather the best among them, are more autodidacts than the product of didactism.

The academic *sexual division of labour* and inequalities within it has received some attention from feminist researchers (for example, Acker and Warren Piper 1984). Women students and teaching staff alike are concentrated in particular disciplines and subjects, and at lower levels in whatever hierarchies exist. As in most other patriarchal capitalist organisations, women here too are concentrated in the worst-paid, worst-condition jobs, whether in teaching, research, secretarial and office work or catering and cleaning.

Within teaching in particular, women are many fewer in absolute terms than men in most disciplines, and are concentrated at lower points in the hierarchy (very few full professors, not many senior lecturers, more lecturers, more temporary lecturers). Alongside this, social science research work in Britain (Scott and Porter 1983, 1984) is not only scarce but also differentially employs over-qualified women as a source of cheap temporary labour which generates research materials, that are often later written up and published by and that add to the symbolic credit of other academics, particularly but not exclusively male.

I now want to sketch in some ideas about the *academic division of labour*. One key point is that academic divisions are overlaid by technical divisions and by sexual divisions. Another is that, as well as involving a division between those inside the academic mode as researchers, and those outside it as 'subjects' of various kinds, the academic mode involves technical divisions between different staff groups, but also separations, distinctions and hierarchies within academic staff groups. A third important aspect occurs in relation to the commodities it produces.

One of the sets of social science commodities produced by the academic mode – research and writing/publications (the other being the process and products of pedagogy) – depends for both its 'relations' and 'forces' of production on factors which lie outside the formal boundaries of 'the academy' but within its production process. These factors involve, on the one hand, the different organisations and institutions which compose 'publishing'; and, on the other, 'research objects' in the form of the people research is 'done on'. Of course a good deal of social science research in fact involves actual objects in the shape of documents and books and journal articles, and not 'people' in any direct sense at all. However, the specific concern here is with 'people research', although elsewhere the arguments apply to both.

The 'objects' of social science research are distinguished from those of the natural sciences by being subjects in their own right, indeed by producing their own understandings and theories of their independent experiences, but also those which involve researchers and their activities. Social science research is thus always and inevitably a social interaction in its own right, whether the 'moment' of interaction is in providing answers to survey questions for someone met only minutes before, or the building up of a relationship over months as part of an ethnographic process. Such 'research objects' are thus both 'forces' and 'relations' of production and a part of the academic labour process; and its object and external to it. They are also both objects and subjects in their own right; and also both commodities and co-producers.

Feminist researchers often make special claims about both the political basis and the consequences of such divisions, emphasising that 'research subjects' are disproportionately female but that male experiences form 'the norm' against which research outcomes are judged. In addition, it is often suggested (Eichler 1985; Cook and Fonow 1986) that almost a defining characteristic of feminist research is that feminist researchers and female subjects of their research are seen as located on the 'same critical plane'. However, this is clearly a complex matter. For example, Ann Oakley (1981) and Janet Finch (1984) discuss the power of feminist researchers in relation to interviewing women; while Stanley and Wise (1983a) suggest that it is the production of written texts that gives feminist researchers ultimate 'power'; however, a sharply contrary discussion of these views in relation to interviewing men is made by Carol Smart (1984).

The academic mode is highly characterised by an internal *sexual division of labour* (and including, as noted above, in relation to research subjects). Sexual divisions of labour occur not only between what has come to be called 'the public and the private' (Stacey 1981; Rose 1983; Gamarnikov *et al.* 1983), but also at different levels and occupations within the hierarchy of organisational employment. Such occupational groupings are sometimes referred to as forming a *dual labour market*, of related *primary* and *secondary* aspects. Primary labour markets are of full-time jobs with promotion prospects which are relatively secure and relatively highly paid; while secondary ones are of part-time or temporary jobs with few or no promotion prospects which are relatively insecure and relatively badly paid.

Many occupational groupings within the academic mode are 'secondary' in this way. Social science research work has already been noted as a prime example of 'secondary' employment for females. However, other occupational groupings within the academy, such as secretarial and other office work, provides full-time and relatively secure employment for women, but which is still characterised by low pay, poor or no promotion prospects and little work autonomy. Thus, as within the patriarchal capitalist mode more generally, a more appropriate term than 'dual' is 'segmented', which more accurately captures the fact that there are important differences between 'non-primary' occupations.

Thus the micro labour market that is 'the academy' is comprised by a number of inter-related but essentially non-competing sub-markets, some of which are sex-specific groupings, whilst others of which may contain often stark sexual divisions. And within each of them women are more likely to be found at the lower levels of such hierarchies and divisions, and white, middle-class men at higher.

Within classical and even recent Marxist accounts of the labour process, the spotlight is on *production*, while *consumption* is relegated to the shadows as but a mere dependent and theoretically unimportant sphere of activity. This is as true of Marxist feminist work, which has its own emphasis on production and social reproduction. However, for Marx himself, 'consumption is but a moment in production'; and while this can be taken to mean that only production in the narrow specific sense is important, this seems to me not what Marx intended.

Production defined so as to exclude consumption as a site of intellectual and political importance consequently removes concern from *exchange* as the massive area of interface between production and consumption. It is this site of connection, of interface, that is central to a sensible understanding of any mode of production. In the preceding account, exchange and consumption have been discussed in relation to the 'consumers' (in one sense; co-producers in another; raw materials in another; and commodities in yet another) of teaching; that is, students. I have also noted that the other major commodity produced by the academic mode, research and teaching, can become both an exchanged commodity in its own right in classrooms and in seminar and conference situations, but also a 'raw material', and a part of the 'forces' and of the 'relations' of production within journal and book publication.

Again, this demonstrates the complexities involved in separating out the constituent elements of the academic mode (and indeed all other modes, once these are examined in any detail). It also highlights the importance of exchange relations to 'production' in the specific, narrow sense. That is, it is exchange and consumption that forms the motor-force that provides the organisational apparatus of 'the academy' with both its dynamic and its legitimation. It is by this means that there is a demonstrable measurable 'throughput': of students, research funding, reports, articles, conference papers and books. This exchange process also serves to demarcate time and activity within the academic year and the academic mode (Martins 1974).

So far, I have said nothing about 'knowledge' as *the* commodity produced by the academic mode and which, as Dorothy Smith (1987) emphasises, is constitutive of relations of *ruling* as well as of relations of *knowing*. It is this which forms the central practical rationale and legitimation for the academic mode.

As Alvin Gouldner (1971) pointed out, in his critique of western institutionalised sociology (and see Bauman 1988 for a more recent discussion of similar features), the discipline came into existence as a 'provider of facts' to help political rulers rule. It laid claim to scientific status on a par with the natural sciences, for an indivisible 'Science'. And thus a place for its practitioners as *fundable* by government and its direct and indirect institutional apparatus was claimed. Scientism has thus been at the heart of the social science academic mode: grounded in Cartesian dualisms, in flight from the assumed nightmarish chaos of 'nature' and its relativisms and to the assumed security of science and the foundationalism of its ways and means of knowing (Bordo 1986).

Its dominating motifs are of the separations between knowers and what/who is known, subjectivity and objectivity, science and nature. Feminists have argued these rest ultimately on the division male/subject and female/object. And, as many feminist commentators on the role of science within the academic mode foreground assert in their analyses (Keller 1985; Bleier 1986; Fee 1986; Rose 1983, 1986), 'cancelling out' the actual *act of knowing* and thus of *labour* within the social science research process is immensely consequential. By constructing 'what is known' at a conceptual and categorical level, even if reference is made to 'research findings', then how these are known to be such is rendered invisible. Their indexical properties are denied, their contextually specific meaning glossed in universalist terms. The result is *alienated knowledge*, a product apparently complete, bearing no apparent trace of the conditions of its production and the social relations that gave rise to this. It is, no more and no less, as much an alienated commodity produced within patriarchal capitalism as any other alienated capitalist commodity.

I have been arguing a case for taking seriously at an intellectual and analytical level the academic mode of production: for taking seriously the research and writing process within the social sciences generally, and within feminist social science in particular. Feminist social science (although many of the arguments apply equally within the arts and humanities) has a foot in each of two traditions, two ways of 'being in the world'. The first is the tradition of the academic mode and its production of alienated knowledge out of a denied labour process; and within this tradition at least one of its major products, teaching, has been largely denied importance as a central means of measuring output from its production process. The second is the tradition (I do not think it too soon to term it such) of feminist insistence on the determined conjoining of dichotomies, a refusal to accept that such divisions exist within the world of experience. For feminists, the known are also knowers, re-search objects are their own subjects; objectivity is a set of intellectual practices for separating people from knowledge of their own subject-ivity.

Within this feminist tradition, divisions between students and teach-ers, the researched and researchers, ancillary staff and academics are seen as neither simple nor absolute, nor denoting that teachers –

11

researchers–academics have any monopoly over understanding, analysis, theorising, consciousness, political commitment. More than this, feminism outside of the academic mode has insisted on the crucial need for useful knowledge, theory and research as practice, on committed understanding as a form of praxis ('understand the world and then change it'), and also on an unalienated knowledge. For the purposes of this present discussion, the most pertinent dimensions of an 'unalienated knowledge' in feminist terms are where:

- the researcher/theorist is grounded as an actual person in a concrete setting;
- understanding and theorising are located and treated as material activities and not as unanalysable metaphysical 'transcendent' ones different in kind from those of 'mere people'; and
- the 'act of knowing' is examined as the crucial determiner of 'what is known'.

Succinctly, academic feminist unalienated knowledge is that which concretely and analytically locates the product of the academic feminist labour process within a concrete analysis of the process of production itself. The chapters which follow exemplify this argument.

Feminist sociological research processes

The chapters in this collection can be read in at least two ways. One is as a series of substantive examples of academic feminist ideas about 'research' as part of the academic labour process. Another is to disregard this unity of activity, to see the collection as a whole as an exposition on *difference*.

In earlier discussions of feminist research processes (Stanley and Wise 1979, 1983a, 1983b) Sue Wise and I argued that there is no one set of methods or techniques, nor even a broad category of types of method ('qualitative'), which should be seen as distinctly feminist. Feminists should use any and every means available for investigating the 'condition of women in sexist society'. To this we added the qualifier: written accounts of feminist research should locate the feminist researcher firmly within the activities of her research as an essential feature of what is 'feminist' about it.

What unifies the chapters in this collection is that they do indeed do this. However, there are clear differences in the feminist framework (socialist feminist, radical feminist, liberal feminist, Marxist feminist or others) in which the researcher positions herself, the topic she sets out to investigate, the 'method/s' or 'technique/s used', the purposes of the research, the form and style it is written in. Thus, in so far as this collection is concerned with 'feminist methodology', this is interpreted in the broad sense identified by Judith Cook and Mary Fonow (1986) and also described in the three postulates outlined above for the production of 'unalienated knowledge'. There are no prescriptions herein concerning either method (in the sense of 'technique') or methodology (in the sense of 'frame-work').

Methods manuals abound in the social sciences. Soon feminist alternatives will proliferate also. This collection should not be seen as offering 'research advice' of the manual variety. Rather, it should be used as a kind of cookbook: read the recipes; try out those you like but modifying, as good cooks always do, the ingredients and their proportions; jettison those you don't like; pass on those you do. But do so always in the spirit of what Lisa Heldke (1988) calls the 'co-responsible option'. That is, do not treat these discussions of feminist research processes prescriptively and/or proscriptively, but rather as accounts for readers to relate to variously and discriminatingly.

The chapters which form the collection have in the main been taken from longer pieces of work, which are located within current relevant research and theory. Thus behind these edited chapters lie a number of related methodological, theoretical and epistemological debates which, for space reasons, have not been discussed and referenced in full. The intention has been, not to produce another mainly theoretical collection, but rather to focus on the details of the research production process, for it is this that is a comparative rarity in academic feminist published work.

On reading the original version of one of these chapters, a friend remarked that although he could see what made it interesting, good research, he was hard-pressed to discern what was distinctively 'feminist' about it, such that it could have been produced by no other kind of person. What is distinctly feminist in research terms is difficult to pin down, but I will hazard some possible responses.

One of the preconditions for 'good research' is that it should account for the conditions of its own production; that is, it has to be 'unalienated knowledge'. I do not mean that only feminists can produce unalienated knowledge. Certainly it is an available option for all social researchers, and certainly some who are not feminist have chosen it. However, I doubt that many social scientists share the epistemological or political premises of this option, as witnessed by the generally negative and/or uncomprehending responses to similar propositions within early statements of the Ethnomethodological project (see here Sharrock and Anderson 1986:39-47 for a discussion of such responses and their origins). I also doubt there are many who are willing to accept the risks associated with adopting such a position: the professional vulnerability it occasions, particularly that it becomes possible for other academics to dismiss it *ad feminam* or *ad hominem* rather than in terms of its theoretical and methodological strengths and weaknesses.

In a way this first response – 'feminist research is that which produces unalienated knowledge; but so can other research processes' – elides the question, then. My second response focusses on what is constitutive of 'the conditions of its own production'. I would argue that a focus on feminist research labour processes shifts the epistemological basis of the completed research: it proposes a different kind of 'knowledge' than that proposed by Cartesian scientism. But as I am quite willing to acknowledge, various male sociologists and sociological perspectives other than feminism propose similar epistemological projects. My third and final response, then, is that the basis of what is distinctive about feminist expositions lies in the relation between epistemology and ontology.

That is, 'feminism' is not merely a 'perspective', a way of seeing; nor even this plus an epistemology, a way of knowing; it is also an ontology, or a way of being in the world. What is distinctively 'feminist' about a concern with research processes is that this constitutes an invitation to explore the conditions and circumstances of a feminist ontology, with all its slips and contradictions certainly, but a feminist ontology none the less.

Am I swimming in the murky waters of essentialism here, as some commentators on 'feminist methodology' (Barrett 1987) have suggested? My answer is a decided and unequivocal 'no'. For one thing, I am referring to a specifically *feminist* ontology, not an ontology attached to the category '(all) women'. I make no claims that 'women' will share this state of being; patently, most do not. For another, such an ontological state comes into existence, not in relation to something essentially female, but rather the facts of the present social construction of 'women' as this is seen, understood and acted upon (however imperfectly, and with whatever backsliding) by those who call themselves feminist; *and* who name this present social construction of women *as oppressive*. That is, it is the experience of and acting against perceived oppression that gives rise to a distinctive feminist ontology; and it is the analytic exploration of the parameters of this in the research process that gives expression to a distinctive feminist epistemology.

The argument that a distinct feminist epistemological position exists has been misrepresented as an argument in favour of a form of disguised methodological separatism. A fuller response to this appears in the following chapter. However (and briefly): Any social scientist concerned with questions of methodology and epistemology needs to consider the relationship between what is after all an 'ontological separatism' that we *all* share as a condition of human existence (for each of us is ultimately alone inside our minds) but which as competent social actors we negotiate and manage satisfactorily as an actual inter-actional inter-subjectivity. My concern is with the conditions under which some classes of people, but not others, are treated as, or come to feel they are treated as, 'other'; and consequently construct a (shared, social) epistemology of that distinctly defined ontological position. There is nothing 'separatist' about such a concern, any more than there is with an exploration of, for example, the theoretical and substantive dimensions of Mannheim's (1952) concern with a distinctively *sociological* epistemology. There is also nothing about the acknowledgement of 'difference' that precludes discussion, debate and a mutual learning process.

So what of 'praxis'? This word is used in the title of this collection to accomplish three interconnected things. The first is to stress that the notion of praxis cannot and should not be reduced to a gloss for any one particular feminist position (for example, Lather 1988 reserves it for a feminist variant on action research only). Its use here is rather an indication of a continuing shared feminist commitment to a political position in which 'knowledge' is not simply defined as 'knowledge *what*' but also as 'knowledge *for*'. Succinctly the point is to change the world, not only to study it. The second is that the chapters in this collection, whatever their undoubted differences, are united in a social science endeavour which rejects the 'theory/research' divide, seeing these as united manual and intellectual activities which are symbiotically related (for all theorising requires 'research' of some form or another). The third is that each of the chapters in their different ways centres on methodological/epistemological concerns. Instead of seeing 'method' as a relatively insignificant matter, the well-known problems in which can be sorted out after the important questions of theory have been settled, each insists on the primacy of 'how'. Or rather they insist that 'how' and 'what' are indissolubly interconnected and that the shape and nature of the 'what' will be a product of the 'how' of its investigation.

© 1990 Liz Stanley

Appendix: SSP titles

Sue Scott has helped to edit the SSP series, while those papers that appear in this book have been my responsibility alone.

No.1, *Looking Back: Essays from the 1986 'Gender and Society' Conference*, Sue Webb and Clive Pearson (eds).
No.2, *Feminist Experience in Feminist Research*, Olivia Butler (ed.).
No.3, *At The Palace: Work, Ethnicity and Gender in a Chinese Restaurant*,

Chung Yuen Kay.

No.4, *Breaking the Rules: Assessing the Assessment of a Girls' Project*, Fiona Poland.

No.5, *Counter Arguments: an Ethnographic Look at 'Women and Class'*, Sue Webb.

No.6, *Becoming a Feminist Social Worker*, Sue Wise.

No.7, *Undergraduate Feminist Essays*, Sally Brett, Elaine Hewitt, Julia Horn, Rae Potter and Emma Simmonds (eds).

No.8, *Feminism and Friendship: Two Essays on Olive Schreiner*, Liz Stanley.

No.9, *Using Drama to Get at Gender*, Vivienne Griffiths.

No.10, *The Mastectomy Experience*, Ann Tait.

No.11, *On Researching the Topic of 'Care'*, Social Care and Research Seminar (ed.).

No.12, *'Leisure': Some Practical Feminist Considerations*, Denise Farran.

Nos.13/14, *Writing Feminist Biography*, Denise Farran, Sue Scott and Liz Stanley (eds).

No.15, *The Difference of Women's Writing*, Celia Lury.

No.16, *Feminist Research Processes*, Feminist Research Seminar.

No.17, *'It Will Make a Man of You': Notes on National Service, Masculinity and Autobiography*, David Morgan.

No.18, *Essays on Women's Work and Leisure*, Liz Stanley.

No.19, *Writing Feminist Biography 2: the Use of Life Histories*, Vivienne Griffiths, Maggie Humm, Rebecca O'Rourke, Janet Batsleer, Fiona Poland and Sue Wise.

No.20, *'More in Hope than Anticipation': Fatalism and Fortune Telling Amongst Women Factory Workers*, Kate Purcell.

No.21, *Doing Feminist Social Work: an Annotated Bibliography and Introductory Essay*, Sue Wise.

No.22, *Feminist Research in Rochdale*, Fiona Poland and Liz Stanley.

No.23, *'Negotiating Target': an Ethnographic Exploration of Women and Work in a High-Technology Factory in Singapore*, Chung Yuen Kay.

No.24, *The Trial of Ruth Ellis*, Denise Farran.

No.25, *Women and Colonialism: Untold Stories and Conceptual Absences*, Jane Haggis.

Nos.26/27, *The Writing I, the Seeing Eye: Papers from Two 'Writing Feminist Biography' Conferences*.

No.28, *'Not Drowning, but Waving': Reading Nineteenth Century Whaling Women's Diaries*, Marilyn Porter.

No.29, *Reflections on the Making of an Ethnographic Text*, Anne Williams.

No.30, *Anti/Depression Dialogue: Theory as Rough Working*, Teresa Iles.

References

Acker, Sandra and Warren Piper, David (eds) (1984) *Is Higher Education Fair To Women?* London: Nelson.

Barrett, Michele (1987) The Concept of "Difference"', *Feminist Review* 26:29–41.

Bauman, Zygmunt (1988) 'Is There a Postmodern Sociology?' *Theory, Culture and Society* 5:217–37.

Bleier, Ruth (ed.) (1986) *Feminist Approaches to Science*, New York: Pergamon Press.

Bordo, Susan (1986) 'The Cartesian Masculinization of Thought', *Signs* 11:439–56.

Bourdieu, Pierre (1977) *Reproduction in Education, Society and Culture*, London: Sage.

——(1984) *Distinction*, London: Routledge & Kegan Paul.

Cook, Judith and Fonow, Mary (1984) 'Am I my Sister's Gatekeeper? Cautionary Tales from the Academic Hierarchy', *Humanity and Society* 8:442–52.

——(1986) 'Knowledge and Women's Interests: Issues of Epistemology and Methodology in Feminist Sociological Research', *Sociological Inquiry* 56:2–29.

Coyner, Sandra (1983) 'Women's Studies as an Academic Discipline: Why and How to Do It', in Gloria Bowles, and Renate D. Klein (eds), *Theories of Women's Studies*, London: Routledge & Kegan Paul, pp.46–71.

Deem, Rosemary (ed.) (1980) *Schooling for Women's Work*, London: Routledge & Kegan Paul.

Eichler, Margrit (1985) 'And the Work Never Ends: Feminist Contributions', *Canadian Review of Sociology and Anthropology* 22: 619–44.

Fee, Elizabeth (1986) 'Critiques of Modern Science: the Relationship of Feminism to Other Radical Epistemologies', in Ruth Bleier (ed.), *Feminist Approaches to Science*, New York: Pergamon Press, pp. 42–56.

Finch, Janet (1984) 'It's Great to Have Someone to Talk to': the Ethics and Politics of Interviewing Women', in Colin Bell and Helen Roberts (eds), *Social Researching: Politics, Problems, Practice*, London: Routledge & Kegan Paul, pp. 70–87.

Frankenberg, Ronald (1982) *Custom and Conflict in British Society*, Manchester: Manchester University Press.

Gamarnikov, Eva, Morgan, David, Purvis, June and Taylorson, Daphne (eds) (1983) *The Public and the Private*, London: Heinemann.

Gouldner, Alvin (1971) *The Coming Crisis of Western Sociology*, New York: Basic Books.

Habermas, Jürgen (1972) *Knowledge and Human Interest*, London: Heinemann.

——(1984) *Reason and the Rationalisation of Society*, London: Heinemann.

Harding, Sandra (ed.) (1987) *Feminism and Methodology*, Milton Keynes: Open University Press.

Heldke, Lisa (1988) 'Recipes for Theory Making', *Hypatia* 3:15–29.

Keller, Evelyn Fox (1985) *Reflections on Gender and Science*, New Haven, CT: Yale University Press.

Kuhn, Annette and Wolpe, Ann-Marie (eds) (1978) *Feminism and Materialism: Women and Modes of Production*, London: Routledge & Kegan Paul.

Lather, Patti (1988) 'Feminist Perspectives on Empowering Research Methodologies', *Women's Studies International Forum* 11:569–81.

Mannheim, Karl (1952) *Essays on the Sociology of Knowledge*, London: Routledge & Kegan Paul.

Martins, Herminio (1974) 'Time and Theory in Sociology', in John Rex (ed.), *Approaches to Sociology*, London: Routledge & Kegan Paul, pp. 246–94.

Minnich, Elizabeth, O'Barr, Jean and Rosenfeld, Rachel (eds) (1988) *Reconstructing the Academy: Women's Education and Women's Studies*, Chicago: University of Chicago Press (papers from *Signs* 1978–88).

Morgan, David (1981) 'Men, Masculinity and the Process of Sociological Enquiry', in Helen Roberts (ed.) *Doing Feminist Research*, London: Routledge & Kegan Paul, pp. 83–113.

Oakley, Ann (1981) 'Interviewing Women: a Contradiction in Terms', in Helen Roberts (ed.), *Doing Feminist Research*, London: Routledge & Kegan Paul, pp. 30–61.

Pateman, Carole and Gross, Elizabeth (eds) (1986) *Feminist Challenges: Social and Political Theory*, Sydney: Allen & Unwin.

Resources for Feminist Research (1987) 16:3 (special issue on *Women and Philosophy*).

Rose, Hilary (1983) 'Hand, Brain and Heart: a Feminist Epistemology for the Natural Sciences', *Signs* 9:73–90.

——(1986) 'Beyond Masculinist Realities: a Feminist Epistemology for the Sciences', in Ruth Bleier (ed.), *Feminist Approaches to Science*, New York: Pergamon Press, pp. 57–76.

Rutenberg, Tally (1983) 'Learning Women's Studies', in Gloria Bowles and Renate D. Klein (eds), *Theories of Women's Studies*, London: Routledge & Kegan Paul, pp. 72–8.

Scott, Sue and Porter, Mary (1983) 'On the Bottom Rung: a Discussion of Women's Work in Sociology', *Women's Studies International Forum* 6:211–22.

——(1984) 'The double Marginalisation of Women in Research', in Sandra Acker and David Warren Piper (eds), *Is Higher Education Fair To Women?*, London: Nelson, pp. 180–6.

Sharrock, Wes and Anderson, Bob (1986) *The Ethnomethodologists*, London: Tavistock.

Smart, Carol (1984) 'Researching Prostitution: Some Problems for Feminist Research', *Humanity and Society* 8:407–13.

Smith, Dorothy (1978) 'A Peculiar Eclipsing: Women's Exclusion from Men's Culture', *Women's Studies International Quarterly* 1:281–96.

——(1987) *The Everyday World as Problematic: a Feminist Sociology*, Northeastern University Press, Milton Keynes: Open University Press.

Smyth, Ailbhe (1987) 'All Change or Small Change? Reflections on Women's Studies', *Women's Studies Forum Working Paper* No.5, University College, Dublin.

Spender, Dale (1981) 'The Gatekeepers: a Feminist Critique of Academic Publishing', in Helen Roberts (ed.), *Doing Feminist Research*, London: Routledge & Kegan Paul, pp. 186–202.

Stacey, Margaret (1981) 'The Division of Labour Revisited or Overcoming the Two Adams', in Philip Abrams, Rosemary Deem, Janet Finch and Paul Rock (eds), *Practice and Progress: British Sociology 1950–80*, London: Allen and Unwin, pp. 172–90.

Stanley, Liz (1984) 'How the Social Science Research Process Discriminates against Women', in Sandra Acker and David Warren Piper (eds), *Is Higher Education Fair to Women?*, London: Nelson, pp. 189–209.

Stanley, Liz and Wise, Sue (1979) 'Feminist Research, Feminist Consciousness and Experiences of Sexism', *Women's Studies International Quarterly* 2:359–74.

——(1983a) *Breaking Out: Feminist Consciousness and Feminist Research*, London: Routledge & Kegan Paul.

——(1983b) '"Back into the Personal" or: Our Attempt to Construct "Feminist Research"', in Gloria Bowles and Renate D. Klein (eds), *Theories of Women's Studies*, London: Routledge & Kegan Paul, pp. 192–209.

Thompson, Paul (1983) *The Nature of Work: an Introduction to Debates on the Labour Process*, London: Macmillan.

Ward, Kathryn and Grant, Linda (1985) 'The Feminist Critique and a Decade of Published Research in Sociology Journals', *Sociological Quarterly* 26: 139–57.

Chapter two

Method, methodology and epistemology in feminist research processes

Liz Stanley and Sue Wise

Introduction

This chapter discusses six closely related aspects of recent feminist debates concerning method, methodology and epistemology in the social sciences and humanities. The first section, 'Feminist consciousness and feminist research', reviews the main relevant arguments and ideas in *Breaking Out*, a book we wrote together, published in 1983. This is followed, in 'Feminist method, methodology or epistemology?', by a discussion of Sandra Harding's account of feminist epistemological positions and in particular the 'successor science' and 'feminist standpoint' positions. Other feminist standpoint epistemologies are discussed in the third section, on 'Silenced feminist standpoints', while the fourth, 'The feminist standpoint revisited', looks at complexities in the work of one of the 'successor science' writers, Dorothy Smith.

'Experience, research and theory in academic feminism', the fifth section, reviews arguments across a wider body of academic feminist writing concerned with methodology and epistemology and their relationship to, on the one hand, feminist theory, and, on the other, the possibilities and status of feminism within existing academic disciplines. The sixth and final section, on 'Establishing feminist hegemony', suggests some of the consequences of present ways of arguing and evaluating which academic feminism has incorporated from malestream disciplines.

Lastly but by no means least, an extensive bibliography on method, methodology and epistemology follows the chapter. Readers are referred to it to establish the wider feminist context and parameters of the arguments and discussion that appear here.

Feminist consciousness and feminist research

We first wrote about the 'feminist research process' within the social sciences (Stanley and Wise 1979) when the prevailing concerns were with the 'feminist critique' of existing methodology. The feminist critique came in various formulations (see Bernard 1973 for an important contribution; also Ward and Grant 1985) but generally contained one or more of the following propositions. First, 'feminist research' was defined as a focus *on* women, in research carried out *by* women who were feminist, *for* other women. Second, there was a perceived distinction between 'male' quantitative methods and feminist qualitative ones. And third, feminist research was overtly political in its purpose and committed to changing women's lives.

The feminist critique was a reaction against existing sexist bias within the social sciences, with the emphasis on exposing male-dominated disciplines and research behaviours (Spender 1981), and relatively little attention to problematising the research process *for feminists ourselves*. Succinctly, the view was that 'they' had 'bias' while we feminists did not.

We discussed problems with such a narrowly limited construction of feminist research in *Breaking Out* (Stanley and Wise 1983a; also see Roberts 1981b), outlining a number of arguments for an alternative view (and see also Stanley and Wise 1983b; Wise and Stanley 1984, 1987; Stanley 1984a).

Challenging monoliths

Feminist social science writing of the time relied on over-generalised and under-researched categories such as 'woman', 'gender', 'structure'. While accepting that these analytic categories were important and useful to feminism, we felt the ways they were used unexplicated failed to unpack the assumptions and generalisations embedded within them. Relatedly, the category 'feminism' itself was used in monolithic terms, without fully exploring the *academic* implications of the political, ethical and epistemological differences that existed 'within feminism' as 'between women'.

The categories of 'woman' and 'oppression'

A defining assumption of feminism is that 'woman' is a necessary and valid category because all women share, by virtue of being women, a set of common experiences. These shared experiences derive, not causally from supposed 'biological facts' but women's common experience of oppression. That is, 'woman' is a socially and politically constructed category, the ontological basis of which lies in a set of experiences rooted in the material world.

However, to say that women share 'experiences of oppression' is not to say that we share the *same* experiences. The social contexts within which different kinds of women live, work, struggle and make sense of their lives differ widely across the world and between different groupings of women. We argued that the experience of 'women' is ontologically fractured and complex because we do not all share one single and unseamed material reality. We also suggested that the category 'woman' used in academic feminist writing then (and, to an extent, now) actually reflected the experiences and analyses of white, middle-class, heterosexual, First World women only, yet treated these as universals.

Relatedly, we were concerned that such analyses saw 'women's oppression' as single, determined, and a state in which 'women' almost by definition have no power. In contrast, we argued that 'oppression' should be seen as an extraordinarily complex process in which women are only rarely and *in extremis* totally powerless and in which, ordinarily, women utilise a range of resources – verbal, interactional and other – in order to 'fight back' (Wise and Stanley 1984, 1987).

The nature of knowledge

Our concern with feminist consciousness and feminist research queried the basis of knowledge – or rather knowledges – within feminism. That is, we turned attention towards epistemological issues within feminist research and theorising. Earlier (Stanley and Wise 1979) we had expressed serious reservations with dichotomised understandings of the relationship between research and theory, glossed as either 'deduct-ivism' or 'inductivism'. Deductivism treats experience as a 'test' of previously specified theoretical hypotheses; and so within it theory precedes both experience and research, and these latter two are in a sense predicated upon theory. In apparent contrast, inductivism specifies a model of research in which theory is derived from research experience and is often referred to as 'grounded theory'.

As ideal types these models have analytic validity; however, neither model has experiential validity as an actual description of how research is conducted and knowledge produced. Researchers cannot have 'empty heads', in the way that inductivism proposes; nor is it possible that theory is untainted by material experiences in the heads of theoreticians in the way that deductivism proposes. In producing feminist research, what is needed is not adherence to one of the existing dichotomised models, but instead detailed descriptions of actual feminist research processes sited around an explication of 'feminist consciousness' (and for alternative and complementary views to this, see Bartky 1977; Kasper 1986; Stone 1975).

Defining feminist research

Definitions of 'epistemology' as, for example, 'the nature of knowledge, its scope, and the assessment of the reliability or degree of warrant of "knowledge claims"' (Phillips 1987:203), tell little about what this looks like translated into practical sets of research behaviours. 'Feminism', we argued, should be present in positive ways within the research process, as feminist epistemological principles underpinning behaviour and analysis both; and we outlined five related sites of these:

- in the researcher–researched relationship;
- in emotion as a research experience;
- in the intellectual autobiography of researchers; therefore
- in how to manage the differing 'realities' and understandings of researchers and researched; and thus
- in the complex question of power in research and writing.

These principles should be located in research behaviour but also in written research reports by explicating the analytic processes involved in understanding 'what is going on here': something we later referred to as an analytic concern with 'intellectual autobiography' (Stanley 1984a). *Breaking Out* suggested that ethnomethodology and other variants of phenomenological sociology offered feminists, if used in a discriminating way, useful tools for unpacking such analytical processes, because these approaches share a concern with methodological issues as well as those of theory.

One implication of treating 'women' as a monolithic category, and 'researcher' as another and opposing one, is that the researcher's notion of 'the truth', in feminist terms a true or raised consciousness, may be seen as preferable on 'scientific' grounds. In contrast, we argued that researchers' understandings are necessarily temporally, intellectually, politically and emotionally grounded and are thus as contextually specific as those of 'the researched'. This was not to propose that researchers' analyses are individualist or incapable of producing generalisations. The argument was philosophically more subtle: First, all research analyses and theories are inevitably grounded in the material experiences of researchers/theorists. Second, a key problem of social science is how to understand 'inter-subjectivity' – the fact that in spite of our ontological distinctness none the less we assume we can, and indeed we *do*, 'share experiences' such that we recognise ourselves in others and they in us and can speak of 'common experiences'. And third, because inter-subjectivity is possible, we *all* produce theoretical descriptions of the social world which can be tested out against it. This raises central questions concerning the nature of 'theory' within feminist research.

23

Theory

Various extraordinarily powerful feminist writings (such as Millett 1969; Firestone 1970; and Mitchell 1971 amongst others) have more recently been succeeded by a plethora of academic feminist writings. The focus has turned to the relationship between analytic categories – 'women', 'patriarchy', 'capitalism', 'race' and 'class' among them. However, the inconvenient fact that much human behaviour cannot be described, let alone understood, in unexplicated categorical terms is largely ignored, or rather 'resolved' by treating people's experiences as faulty versions of the theoretician's categories.

This is theory with a capital T, one produced by theorists who are supposed experts on the relationship between categories and thus on the 'real meaning' of social experience and behaviour. Here 'academic feminism' becomes the legitimation for a new form of expertise, that of feminist theoreticians over 'mere women'. Whether as an intended or unintended consequence, feminist social scientists working with such assumptions necessarily position themselves as experts on and over other women's experiences.

We argued against this as strongly as possible and in favour of a style of theorising which was grounded, but not in the over-simplistic sense of a feminist version of inductivism. We defined 'feminist theory' as:

- theory derived from experience analytically entered into by enquiring feminists;
- continually subject to revision in the light of that experience;
- thus reflexive and self-reflexive and accessible to everyone (not just to theoreticians as a 'special' kind of person); and
- certainly not to be treated as sacrosanct and enshrined in 'texts' to be endlessly pored over like chicken entrails.

Subsequent developments

The central concern of *Breaking Out* was to raise major ontological and epistemological questions concerning the nature of feminist knowledge and its relationship to the nature of feminist consciousness, whilst insisting that the category 'women' is socially constructed and internally fractured in ways that should be welcomed and explored in depth. At the time it was written there was no 'name' for the position we allied ourselves with, no 'ism' or 'ology' to belong to. There were also remarkably few other published feminist discussions of epistemology and its relevance for substantive research in the social sciences. The closest to our position was the work of Canadian sociologist Dorothy Smith, whose work we followed with interest. However, apart from this we felt alone.

Retrospectively, the position outlined above can be characterised as a variant expression of what has come to be called a 'feminist standpoint' epistemology. That is, it argues for a feminist research not only located in, but proceeding from, the grounded analysis of women's material realities. We also proposed the deconstruction of any notion of 'a feminist standpoint', or even 'women's experience'; and thus also reached towards what has become known as 'deconstructionism'. However, at the time there was no available feminist conceptual language to describe these ideas. But subsequently there have been a number of consequential developments within academic feminism, and there is now a sophisticated conceptual language with which many more feminists are conversant.

This language has been adapted from a number of sources: from the now much more widely published writings of feminist philosophy, in particular the synthesising work of Sandra Harding (Harding and Hintikka 1983; Harding 1986a, 1987a); but also from years of feminist academics struggling with the densely packed terminology of French feminist theoretical writings, and more recently with the 'post-structuralist' propounding of deconstructionist and postmodernist theoretical writings. Moreover, this conceptual language is no longer the prerogative of philosophers and those working in the sociology of knowledge. It has been assimilated into and used by, in increasingly sophisticated ways, feminist philosophy (Code *et al.* 1987; Fraser and Nicholson 1988; Frye 1983; Grimshaw 1986) but also feminist literary criticism (Christian 1988; de Lauretis 1986a; Showalter 1986), history (Alexander 1984; Daniels 1985; Fox-Genovese 1982; Riley 1987) and anthropology (Moore 1988; Strathern 1988), with feminist sociology a relative laggard here. It has thus become possible to give names to various of the ideas concerned with feminist epistemology and ontology which *Breaking Out* described but was unable to gloss using phrases such as 'feminist standpoint arguments' or 'feminist deconstructionism'.

Thus the major developments in feminist ideas concerning the 'feminist research process' can be summarised as: the present availability of a conceptual language of wide currency that centres discussions of epistemology; the location and use of this in a much wider group of disciplines; the 'naming' of a 'feminist standpoint' epistemology; and the important synthesising work of feminist philosophy. There is also the existence of a now voluminous literature on 'feminist standpoint' and other ideas concerning the relationship between method, methodology and epistemology in feminist research processes.

We have noted the importance of the synthesising work of feminist philosophy. For many people, in Britain as well as America, Sandra

Harding's work, although Americanocentric, has been the most available and accessible exposition of this. At this point it is therefore appropriate to discuss it more directly.

Feminist method, methodology or epistemology?

Feminists within sociology have variously denied the existence of a feminist methodology (Clegg 1985); argued that those promoting it have 'hijacked' feminism within the discipline (Barrett 1986); and described matter-of-factly its basic principles as generally accepted by all academic feminists (Cook and Fonow 1986). Such startlingly divergent views on the very existence and the acceptability of 'feminist methodology' should alert us to a semantic problem, the possibility that these commentators are referring to rather different things whilst using the same technical term, 'methodology'.

Sandra Harding (1987b) suggests that the preoccupation with 'method' has hidden more interesting aspects of feminist research processes, in particular the differences between 'method', 'methodology' and 'epistemology'. Indeed, we found that many - both positive and negative – assessments of *Breaking Out* treated it as a discourse on either method or methodology, while it was produced as a discussion of epistemology. Like Harding and other philosophers, we see 'method' as 'techniques' or specific sets of research practices, such as surveys, interviews, ethnography and the like. 'Methodology', however, is a 'perspective' or very broad theoretically informed framework, such as symbolic interactionism or functionalism within sociology, and which may or may not specify its own particular 'appropriate' research method/s or technique/s. And 'epistemology' is a theory of knowledge which addresses central questions such as: who can be a 'knower', what can be known, what constitutes and validates knowledge, and what the relationship is or should be between knowing and being (that is, between epistemology and ontology).

Sandra Harding (1986a, 1986b, 1987b, 1987c) focusses upon epistemology as the foundation for method and methodology. She examines various materialist feminist writings and identifies two distinct 'transitional epistemologies': feminist empiricism and feminist standpoint. 'Feminist empiricism' is identified as the main feminist response to the biases and problems of traditional disciplines. It also contains 'inner tensions' which hold the promise of something more radical by acknowledging that: the 'context of discovery' of research is as important in constructing knowledge as research products or theories; 'scientific method' is insufficient as a means of eliminating overt sexism and covert androcentrism; and 'research norms' for supposedly good practice actually contribute to feminist research problems.

Alongside this, 'feminist standpoint' epistemology, as exemplified in the work of Hilary Rose (1983, 1986), Nancy Hartsock (1983, 1987), Jane Flax (1983) and Dorothy Smith (1979, 1981), is described as more radical. Here knowledge based on a feminist standpoint is identified as scientifically preferable since it is more complete and less distorted. Its knowledge is derived from a committed feminist exploration of women's experiences of oppression. It is thus a practical achievement, not an abstract 'stance':

> To achieve a feminist standpoint one must engage in the intellectual and political struggle necessary to see natural and social life from the point of view of that disdained activity which produces women's social experiences instead of from the partial and perverse perspective available from the 'ruling gender' experience of men.
>
> (Harding 1987b:185)

Harding argues that feminist standpoint epistemology still produces a 'successor science'. It accepts the basic premises of 'scientific endeavour' just as feminist empiricism does, for it still accepts the existence of 'true reality' and the methods of science as the means to establish it. Thus neither feminist empiricism nor the feminist standpoint are 'relativist' epistemologies: both specify feminist knowledge as *better* or *truer* because derived from 'outsiders' who can see the relations of domination and suppression for what they truly and objectively are. This is what makes them successor *sciences*.

The first 'inner tension' of the feminist standpoint position derives from its Marxist paternal discourse's emphasis on class and economy to the exclusion of sex and patriarchy. Its second and more crucial tension is that, once one 'feminist standpoint' is admitted to exist, then other and alternative standpoints become possible, and this in turn problematises the truth-claims of feminist standpoint as a 'successor science'.

The existence of tensions within and between feminist empiricism and feminist standpoint epistemologies, Harding suggests, reveals their 'transitional' status. Existing alongside them, but in an as yet less well-developed form, is a 'feminist postmodernist' epistemology. This has its origins in, first, a feminist scepticism of all universalising claims, derived from semiotics, deconstructionism and psychoanalysis and their rejection of any notion of a 'more authentic self'; and, second, in the rejection by black feminists in particular that all women do 'share experiences'. Feminist postmodernism 'creates troubles' for the two 'successor science' epistemologies because it rejects universalism and consequently sees 'science' as a doomed project. It also relativises 'experience' by locating it within a micro-politics which is highly localised but organised through meta-narratives and more grounded ideological discourses.

Harding (1986b) notes that feminist postmodernism makes visible in a strong form the tension present in a weaker form in the feminist standpoint position: once one standpoint is recognised, this then admits the possibility of a range of different but equally valid feminist standpoints. We are driven to recognise the existence of not only 'a' feminist standpoint but also those of black women, working-class women, lesbian women, and other 'minority' women, and also those women who combine these oppressions. Once we admit the existence of feminist stand*points* there can be no a priori reason for placing these in any kind of a hierarchy; each has *epistemological* validity because each has *ontological* validity. Here we have contextually grounded *truths*.

In a perceptive review of Sandra Harding's *The Science Question in Feminism* (1986a), Jacquelyn Zita (1988) notes its strengths, but also makes three major critical comments. First, Harding's specification of 'feminist standpoint' as only those positions which theorise out of a sexual division of labour in society ignores the sexualisation of women's experiences, and also the widespread existence of sexual and other violence and the threat of violence towards women. Second, Zita describes Harding's remarks on feminist postmodernism as half-hearted, given she is a proponent of the position of a materialist feminist successor science standpoint. Third and most crucially, Harding's account cannot theorise feminist pluralism satisfactorily: she effectively denies the existence of a radical feminist epistemological perspective, looking at the proponents of the materialist feminist standpoint alone.

Zita's argument, then, is that Harding's account is not the impartial review of epistemological possibilities it appears to be. It suppresses the existence of an actual feminist pluralism, of feminist stand*points*, by discussing only one variant within this. A clue as to why lies in Sandra Harding's (1980) review of Mary Daly's *Gyn/Ecology*. Here, while acknowledging some strengths in Daly's book, Harding uses it to criticise all radical feminist writing: 'She, like they [that is, all other radical feminists], thinks it is *wrong ideas* which fundamentally *cause* the actual history of women's oppression' (Harding 1980:458). In supposed contrast, Harding specifies materialist feminism as proposing that it is 'the concrete, "material", social relations of reproduction which are responsible for men's generally pre-conscious psychological needs to dominate others rationally' and in which 'the ideas which direct and justify "culture" are only the reflection of this underlying concrete social dynamic' (Harding 1980:458). It is clear she sees no problem in dismissing the totality of radical feminist thinking, writing and political practice by dismissing the work of Mary Daly. Harding's approach is tantamount to, for instance, dismissing all feminist history because of disagreeing with Gerda Lerner's (1979) account of black American women's history.

Sandra Harding is not alone in expressing reservations about what are seen (we think mis-seen) as the propensity of radical feminism to analyse at the level of 'ideology' rather than the level of 'material reality'. What is so surprising about her account (in Harding 1986a, 1987b and 1987c) is that it silences, removes from existence within academic feminist discourse, radical feminist and other 'Other' feminist standpoint perspectives, associating 'academic' more or less exclusively with materialist feminism.

One instance of this is that when Harding (1986a) considers the notion of 'other Others', the existence of 'fractured identities', we expected her to provide a fuller account of the plurality of feminist epistemologies. In common with Zita, we found Harding's actual discussion of representations of African identities a perplexing one. Certainly Harding's slightly later work recognises the increasing definition of their position in ontological and epistemological terms by black feminists. Thus one source of perplexity is her failure to give more detailed attention to black feminism in America and elsewhere. Another is that the same failure to give space to 'differences in being', to ontology, which silences black feminism, also silences other states of being. In the following section ontological issues related to epistemology are discussed in relation to a black feminist standpoint and a lesbian feminist standpoint, as two examples of the many that could have been explored.

Silenced feminist standpoints

The two 'silences' discussed here are those of a black feminist and a lesbian feminist epistemology. Our search in the literature suggests that the weight of discussion around both standpoints rests upon classroom practices and ways in which 'knowledge' can be critiqued and re-organised using classroom practice and good feminist interaction between teachers and taught as its focus (see for example Hull, Scott and Smith 1982; and Cruikshank 1982). Readers should keep this relative emphasis on pedagogy in black and lesbian feminist approaches to knowledge in mind in the following discussion.

The writings of black feminists as of black liberationists before them centre the related ideas of wearing 'masks' to seem 'other than you are' – of disclosure to one's own but silence to others – and of passing. However, for feminists there are additional components – a recognition and valuing of 'difference', the centring of both 'black' and 'feminism', and knowledge as a shared process – within the development of a black feminist epistemology.

Sondra O'Neale (1986) emphasises the importance of the 'mask' metaphor in black literature and poetry, but also in life. Black people in oppressor countries may appear tamed reflections of whites, but beneath the mask lies . . . perhaps the 'duplicity' of black people, perhaps the fears of whites. Knowledge about this 'double facedness' is not confined to black people: it is something whites worry about the existence of, indeed fear. Its 'origins' are those of oppression: super-ordinates fear that some secret knowledge, some secret selves, have escaped their control; while subordinates need secret knowledge and secret selves to survive, both physically and psychically. With different names, the same 'double-facedness' has been described as a component of the ontology of women, of lesbians and gay men, and also of children. This notion of 'false' and 'true' selves has no essentialist basis, but rather derives from the material and everyday circumstances of being a member of an oppressed group. There are other material products of ontological and epistemological importance within oppression.

To be a black woman and a feminist is to be 'different', for to be black is to stand outside of white racist society, while to be a feminist is to make oneself 'Other' to black (male and other non-feminist) society. Patricia Hill Collins (1986b) describes this as being a 'stranger' who is *in* and yet not *of* 'normal social life'. Many people have noted that being 'Other' brings with it the possession of knowledge concerning 'rulers' and their ways, but also the different and subversive knowledge that accrues to the 'ruled', as a consequence of seeing the 'underside' of oppression and oppressors both. For Patricia Hill Collins, what should follow is the theoretical and analytical development of this knowledge that to be a black feminist is to inhabit an ontologically distinct set of experiences. She argues that this knowledge should be trusted as providing access to a valid viewpoint on social life and thus should be used as the basis of a black feminist standpoint (Collins 1986b).

Black feminists are more readily aware than white that the onto-logical experience of 'women' is multiply characterised by difference, by different although overlapping contextually grounded material experiences of oppression (see, for instance, hooks 1981, 1984, 1989; Lorde 1984; Christian 1985, 1988; as well as Collins 1986a, 1986b). Throughout her writing, Audre Lorde (1984) emphasises the existence of difference, insists on the need for feminists to centre their analyses and lives on coming to terms with difference. Unlike many other people, Lorde discusses not only race, sex and class as sites of difference, but *age*, noting both the young that we all were and the old we hopefully may become (Lorde 1984:114-23, 72-80), and also dis-ablebodiedness (Lorde 1985).

Such a determined black feminist insistence on the experiential, political *and* academic importance of difference has other consequences. Thus Barbara Christian (1988) emphasises her rejection of invitations to create generalised 'grand theory' on behalf of all black women, to write authoritative statements constitutive of 'black feminist literary criticism', because she recognises the complexity of black women's experiences (like other black feminists such as Cherrie Moraga and Gloria Anzaldua 1981; Audre Lorde 1984; and bell hooks 1981 and 1984). Instead she insists on theorising in a different and contextually specific way, out of her awareness of the multiplicity of black women's experiences. She thus rejects what she terms the 'race for theory'.

For these black feminists, 'theory' comes most decidedly with a small and not a capital T. It speaks to contextually grounded experiences and recognises difference and complexity. The 'ethnocentrism' of *white* feminist theory is not their problem, although its claims for general applicability is undoubtedly a source of justifiable anger. Indeed, as Sheila Radford-Hill (1986) insists, to become concerned with the ethnocentrism/racism of 'feminist thinking' implicitly accepts not only the evaluation of this as 'general feminist thought', but also that the priority of black feminists is to change both 'it' and 'them', the white feminists who speak in other women's names while denying these other women's experiences. A similar refusal of 'changing (white) feminist thinking' seems to be the basis of Caroline Ramazanoglu's (1986) insistence that the problem is not that white feminist theory needs to include notions of ethnocentrism, but rather that white feminism actually exists in relations of power over black.

In a comparable way lesbian feminist theorists have long insisted that to be a lesbian is to be ontologically 'Other' within heterosexual society (Radicalesbians 1972; Johnston 1973; Abbott and Love 1973). Two interesting discussions of this in epistemological terms are by Monique Wittig and by Marilyn Frye, whose arguments share some assumptions but sharply diverge in others (on Wittig's ideas, see Shaktini 1982; and on Frye's, Card 1986).

The starting point for Wittig is 'heterosexuality' as the dominant meta-narrative of all societies and in which 'woman' is defined in terms of social, economic, physical or any other personal dependency on a man. Thus for Wittig (1980, 1981) 'lesbian' does not exist; rather, this does not exist in the sense that the category 'woman' (which she sees as a politically and socially constructed class, not as a biological or any other essentialism) is defined as existing *in terms of heterosexuality*. This is not an argument that lesbians are 'really' defined in terms of a rejection of or exclusion from men. Rather, her concern is with how the dominant definition of such categories is formulated and used as a material oppression in discourses which colonise women's experiences.

31

Marilyn Frye (1983) takes something like this for granted, or rather her concern is less with the ontological origins of 'lesbian' as outsider than with the epistemological consequences of such an ontological status. In an extended metaphor, Marilyn Frye likens the position of lesbians in heterosexual society to members of an audience, a small and highly particular audience watching a performance on a stage. On the foreground of the stage are the men, the actors, highly aware of themselves and of the performances their fellow actors are giving. In the background of the stage are the women, who are the backcloth itself and also the 'small scurryings to and fro' of stage hands and the like. The men are aware of the comforting regularities that are the activities of and the movements in the backcloth, and also of each other.

Lesbians are 'Other' to the performance, outsiders looking on, but in particular looking at the women who are the backcloth. Marilyn Frye describes men's ontological insecurity as arising from an awareness not only that the lesbian onlooker is looking at the women immersed in supporting men's performances, but also because of their half-awareness that for the lesbian 'seers' the performance is *the backcloth*, is constituted by the activities and indeed by the presence or being or ontology of the *women* present. The lesbian seer foregrounds women. The consequent anxiety for men is that women may become aware of the lesbians who see them, and thereby become aware of and 'see' their own activities as foreground, rather than those of men.

Lesbian epistemology in the work of these and other writers (for example, Jeffner Allen 1986; Hoagland 1988) is composed of a number of elements: of silences and closures, but also of determined mis-namings of the ontological basis of lesbian existence; and, in addition, of a conscious and deliberate withdrawal of energy and material support from men to women on the part of lesbian women. It is out of these elements that comes a combination of contradictory responses. Shame and pride, humiliation and anger, and self-oppression and political awareness, underpin lesbian ontology: 'oppression' and 'liberation' mingle here. A black feminist epistemology derives from comparably fractured or contradictory ontological parameters, but there are many more intrusions and misnamings here than in relation to lesbian ontology because of the greater 'visibility' of black women. Most lesbians can and often do 'pass'; black women can only very rarely do so, and this has enormous ontological significance.

Frye argues that she wants heterosexual women to become continu-ally aware that they are heterosexual and also for them to recognise the privileges of their ontological state, one privilege of which is not to notice that it is privileged. But precisely how should heterosexual women become aware of their heterosexuality as an ontology in this way? Surely not by the means Frye herself envisages, through moral conviction or a changed 'state of mind'. Changed *consciousness* requires a changed *material* reality, a changed social context within which heterosexual women must come to move. A distinct lesbian standpoint or epistemology is composed not by any 'essence' (whether biological or psychological or cultural), but rather out of *oppression*. What gives rise to something distinctively ontologically 'lesbian' is precisely the material experience of those silences, closures, intrusions, misnamings and withdrawals specified above as the contradictory parameters of a lesbian feminist standpoint. Lesbians are women who are continually jolted back out of 'everyday routine' into a grounded experience of ourselves as 'different'. Denise Riley (1987) discusses this happening to all women: usually we are 'ourselves', 'just a person'; but then some sexist intrusion forces us back into a sense of ourselves as *Other*. To be a lesbian woman, however, is to be an 'other Other'.

Similar problems exist with Marilyn Frye's analysis of whiteness and racism. Frye's discussion, although illuminating on a number of levels, poses an 'effort of mind' route out of whiteness. Her proposal is that we 'resist whiteness' in the same way that men can struggle to resist masculinity. This is insufficient if one takes seriously, as surely Frye intends us to, her insistence that maleness, heterosexuality and whiteness all 'work' ontologically by being states of *unawareness* in which the key privilege of the privileged group is not to notice that they are such. And in contrast, as noted above, she argues that a lesbian feminist epistemology is brought into existence out of an explicit consciousness of oppression, out of silences, intrusions, misnamings.

It is surely a massive paradox in Frye's argument that she sees the ontology of the oppressed in such concrete and material terms, but expects members of dominant groups to come to true consciousness purely at the level of mind, of effort of will. More in keeping with Frye's basic position concerning the materiality of epistemology is Minnie Pratt's discussion of her immersion as a white woman in a 'black area' and the ways in which this continually problematised herself as a white-raced woman (Bulkin, Pratt and Smith 1984). That is, Pratt was located in an immediate social context in which she was made 'Other', in a situation in which the original and oppressed 'other' becomes in a sense the norm. Of course she could always leave, de-race herself, in a way that black people in western societies never can; none the less her account is a suggestive one.

We have argued, then, that the notion of 'feminist standpoint' is considerably wider than Sandra Harding's account implies and in particular that it needs to incorporate a number of feminisms, including black and lesbian standpoints. Succinctly, a range of feminist epistemologies exists. The cornerstone of our argument is the differences that exist between women, such that the category 'women' needs deconstructing in order to focus on ontological separations as well as similarities.

In addition, even taking into account the characterisation of feminist standpoint epistemologies in materialist feminist terms, what is being argued by the named proponents of this position (Rose, Hartsock, Flax and Smith) is in fact more complex than Sandra Harding's account of their work suggests. In particular, we will argue that the work of at least one of these proponents – Dorothy Smith – contains within it, indeed is predicated upon, a detailed consideration of some of the features which Harding assigns to radical feminism and thus to silence.

The feminist standpoint revisited

We have been appreciative readers of Dorothy Smith's writing since 1977, not least because of her complex use of ideas and analyses drawn from feminism, Marxism and ethnomethodology (see here Stanley and Wise 1983a: 162-6; but Yeatman 1986 for a very different view). Thus we argue for the greater complexity of the base-line feminist standpoint epistemology using Dorothy Smith's work, in particular *The Everyday World as Problematic* (Smith 1987), which contains essays published over a number of years but also three synthesising essays on a feminist 'institutional ethnography'.

Dorothy Smith's 'project' is to participate in the construction of a 'sociology for women', in which feminist research practice should never lose sight of women as actively *constructing*, as well as interpreting, the social processes and social relations which constitute their everyday realities. Smith's feminist sociologist inhabits the same critical plane as the women whose 'everyday world' she investigates. While Smith is aware that women are involved in each of the 'levels' or contexts of social and institutional relations, her choice is to research from 'the standpoint of women' who are on the receiving end of the 'textually mediated relations of knowing and ruling' she is centrally concerned with.

For Smith 'text' is constituted not only by written but also by verbal bodies of acknowledged knowledge. In turn, these are constituted in and by, and indeed are constitutive of, institutions. The term 'institution' brings together more than one relational organisational mode: a discourse and constitutive material practices that cross specific organisational boundaries. Her concern is thus with the ways in which organisational frameworks and relevancies (including those of disciplines and indeed of radical discourses) alienate people from their experiences: their experiences are institutionally specified, named, theorised, organised and so colonised.

Sociology and other social science disciplines constitute key elements of institutional *textually mediated* relations of ruling. Their statements provide the authority and legitimation of 'science' for this alienated knowledge, but also provide its material grounding in everyday institutional practices. Smith sees 'ideology' as sets of grounded practices which come to act as frameworks for materially and temporally structuring and so understanding experience. The ideological and the material are symbiotically related; and her work emphasises that a materialist feminism must take as centrally important the ways in which ideological practices colonise material realities.

Smith outlines the dangers of assimilation for Marxism and feminism as radical discourses. Indeed, she argues their presently institutionalised forms adopt the same concerns as other institutionalised and theoretically based discourses:

> The importance of 'theory' to feminists has been, it seems, the importance of creating the terms that will 'run' discourse from a standpoint independent of that of particular individuals speaking to one another. The 'structural' metaphor captures precisely this development of a discursive process, the statements of which are its properties rather than the expressions of subjects....To participate in such a discourse, we take on its methods of speaking and writing texts. We stand outside the world in which we live and in which that discourse, its texts, and its statements are brought into being.
>
> (Smith 1987:221)

Invoking and using a radical discourse has no political force as such; and Smith notes this is a problem for her own work as much as any other. Of course this is a problem for *all* feminist theorising, not only academic varieties; and although some materialist feminists specify 'the answer' as a feminist form of action research (Nava 1982; Acker, Barry and Esseveld 1983; Mies 1983; Currie and Kazi 1987; Lather 1988), in its own ways this is at least equally problematic.

Dorothy Smith is certainly a materialist feminist, but one crucially concerned with a materialist feminist analysis which operates at the level of 'ideas', at the level of 'ideology' which, like Marx and Engels (1970), she identifies as ideas embedded in material institutional practices. Her analysis proceeds from a sexual division of labour, but one concerned with 'social relations' *in toto* and in particular with all the work that women do. This includes not just employment, nor employment plus domestic labour and caring work, but rather the complete range of women's 'service' activities within patriarchal capitalism. Thus Smith's notion of a division of labour encompasses the sexualisation of women and male sexual and other violence towards women.

Dorothy Smith's is a detailed attempt to come to grips with epistemological elements involved in developing a feminist sociology. Given the nature of the discipline, she has necessarily had to tackle how epistemology can be put into practice *methodologically*, as a perspective, and how this in turn relates to the practical use of different research *techniques*. This differentiates her project from feminist philosophers, who by virtue of differences in the nature of their discipline can both 'do research' *and* remain at the level of 'epistemology'. However, her work is not 'successor science' in quite the way Harding implies. Smith's feminist sociologist locates herself on the same critical plane of understanding as the women she is carrying out a 'sociology for women' for. She does not derive from women's standpoint some transcendent and superior understanding; rather, her job is to carry out a set of activities which move between different standpoints, different contexts; and there is no necessary reason in Smith's account why 'women' cannot carry out similar work to that done by professional feminist sociologists.

We are not arguing that Dorothy Smith's work is problem-free. However, the problems we discern are not a constitutive part of the terms and framework of her own work, but derive from our somewhat different but related epistemological and sociological project. First, Smith's feminist sociologist proceeds from the standpoint of women who are 'like her', who are located similarly in relation to particular kinds of institutional material practices. We wonder how she would – or indeed if she could – specify a feminist standpoint project for women who are unlike: who embody a standpoint she could not share, like black women; or whom she would morally or politically disagree with, like women abusers of children. Relatedly, Smith's feminist standpoint proceeds from the viewpoint of *women*, whereas much of our work focusses on the activities and the 'work' (in the wide sense Smith uses) of men, as obscene telephone callers, as sexual murderers and as sexual harassers in everyday life. Second, Smith's work is concerned with specifying a 'pre-textual' feminist research process, but uses a heavily textually influenced epistemological account. There is no easy route out of this problematic, however, for the basic problem is whether *anything* can be said to be pre-textual.

Dorothy Smith's work constitutes a complex 'feminist standpoint' position, which contains within it the capacity to recognise other standpoints and thus analytically grapple with those features assigned in Harding's account to feminist postmodernism. Additionally and revealingly, Smith's feminist standpoint, while a materialist feminist one, also centrally locates 'ideology', a feature which Harding's account assigns to a dismissed and supposedly 'inadequate' radical feminism.

Experience, research and theory in academic feminism

The increasing discussion of a 'feminist standpoint' has been an important step in the development of distinctly feminist epistemologies. Succinctly, feminist theorists have moved from the 'reactive' stance of the feminist critique of social science, and into the realms of exploring what 'feminist knowledge' could conceivably look like.

As might be expected, such a development is surrounded by lively controversy, contributed to by proponents of alternative feminist epistemological positions, and by feminists who object to the very idea that 'knowledge' comes in distinctly feminist forms as well as by proponents of 'standpoint' arguments. We now consider samples of this literature through discussing a number of propositional statements. These have been made as criticism or praise of ideas concerned with 'feminism and methodology', and they are a useful route into this growing body of feminist writing. Readers are additionally referred to the bibliography on feminist method, methodology and epistemology in feminist research, which covers a wider range of British, Irish, Australasian and North American material.

'Feminist methodology' is separatist

Marilyn Frye (1983) uses the notion of 'separatism' as an indication of the radical nature of theories, concepts and practices rather than their reformism. She is not thereby saying that feminist theorists and practitioners have to be 'separatist' from men in all ways, nor that epistemological separatism necessarily entails separatist academic locations and research practices, but rather that 'separatism' is a statement of 'women-identified' purpose. In contrast, Michele Barrett (1986) insists that proponents of feminist methodology have not only 'hijacked feminism' in the name of separatism, but are thereby responsible for the rest of the discipline of sociology failing to 'take gender seriously'. In a related discussion (Barrett 1987), she outlines a linked 'package' of essentialism, methodological separatism and relativism as the fault-line of this mistaken feminism. Here 'separatism' is presented as an epistemological position which necessarily translates into entirely different 'male' and 'feminist' methods (that is, separatism at the level of research technique) and thus entails a completely bifurcated discipline.

Relatedly, Sue Clegg (1985) is clear that feminist methodology does not exist and that proponents of it are completely misguided. Her reasons are less clear than her evident rejection of the idea. In spite of invocations of the word 'epistemology', her dismissal of 'feminist methodology' is actually a reference to *method* as the product of a different feminist perspective from the one she favours. This is surprising, given her statements in favour of 'reflexivity' in feminist accounts of the research process, described as feminism's major contribution to social science thinking. More than this, Clegg describes such a feminist reflexivity similarly to Stanley and Wise (1979), whilst condemning this specific piece of writing as an obviously misguided example of 'feminist methodology', in her terms starkly different from 'feminist research reflexivity'.

A very different approach by Judith Cook and Mary Fonow (1986; Cook 1983) argues that five basic epistemological propositions of 'feminist methodology' are found within the broad run of feminist accounts of the research process, rather than being the prerogative of one kind or type of feminism. These are: a reflexive concern with gender as all-pervasive; consciousness-raising as a 'way of seeing' and a 'methodological tool'; challenging 'objectivity' by refusing to treat it as separate from subjectivity and refusing to see experience as 'un-scientific'; a concern with ethics and in particular not treating women as research objects (on ethics see also Andolsen *et al.* 1985; Bristow and Esper 1984; *Humanity and Society* 1984; Sherin 1987; Wise 1987); and seeing research as a political activity.

In similar terms Margrit Eichler (1985) derives four epistemological propositions for feminist research from the basic postulates of the sociology of knowledge. She treats these (as we do) as a 'base-line' for all feminist research, with which all feminist researchers might be expected to agree. Eichler's four propositions are that: all knowledge is socially constructed; the dominant ideology is that of the ruling group; there is no such thing as value-free science and the social sciences so far have served and reflected men's interests; and because people's perspective varies systematically with their position in society, the perspectives of men and women differ.

There are other accounts of 'feminist methodology' (such as Rein-harz 1979, 1983; Mies 1983; Smart 1984a, 1984b; Stacey 1988; Wil-kinson 1986a, 1986c) that could be added to the discussion. However, the basic arguments are those sketched out here. They encompass a widely and sometimes wildly different definition of basic terms, with critics by and large confusing methodology with method. They also reveal a division of feminist opinion as to whether an 'intellectual separatism' is a good or a bad thing. This latter debate is a rather odd one, for what critics leave unexamined is the epistemological status of existing social science understandings of knowledge, knowers and the process of knowing.

That is, the 'anti-feminist methodology' position seemingly takes for granted that 'feminist standpoint' represents a new departure from what is presently a neutral 'discipline standpoint' subject to sexist intrusions.

Our position is that *all* knowledge, necessarily, results from the conditions of its production, is contextually located, and irrevocably bears the marks of its origins in the minds and intellectual practices of those lay and professional theorists and researchers who give voice to it. The existing discipline of sociology is neither neutral nor impartial; it reflects the practices and knowledge of groups of highly particular white, middle-class, heterosexual men while seemingly reflecting universalisms. Its sexism is no 'intrusion' or 'mistake'.

For Cartesians (including feminist neo-Cartesians) this is a problem: for them knowledge is, or rather ought to and can be, independent of the conditions of production, and including of the minds and concrete research and theorising practices of the people who are knowledge-producers (and see here Bordo 1986 for an interesting discussion of the origins of Cartesian ideas). But our view is that knowledge is actually a crucial part of 'textually mediated relations of ruling'. It is political knowledge through and through, because it necessarily derives from the world-views, assumptions and frameworks concerning knowledge (that is, the epistemologies) of its producers; and these are typically highly particular groups of men who give voice/text to the social world as seen, understood and colonised by men like themselves.

Thus to argue for a 'feminist standpoint epistemology' is *not* to argue in favour of female separatism. It is rather to propose *to remove an existing methodological separatism*, one which understands and researches the social world through an assimilationist and textually mediated alienated knowledge which proceeds by measuring social life against pre-existent theoretically (that is, ideologically) derived categories. This existing 'malestream' (by which we do not mean that only men do it or adhere to such a viewpoint) methodological separatism by and large ignores, because it silences, because it almost literally cannot 'see', the social world from women's standpoint. And indeed it has precisely the same alienating and colonising relationship to the social world from many men's standpoints too.

'Feminist standpoint' relies on essentialist thinking

One clear statement of 'essentialist' criticisms of feminist standpoint arguments is to be found in Michele Barrett's (1987) packaging together of essentialism, intellectual separatism and relativism. Denise Riley's (1987) extended and most interesting discussion/deconstruction of the category 'women' in history is the clearest and most sophisticated rejection of 'essentialist' views we have read. She insists that effectively *any* invocation of the category 'women' *necessarily* trades on essentialist thinking; and argues that the prime need for feminism is to escape the political impasse this creates. Riley's 'answer' is both continually to refuse to play the 'women are...' game and always to deconstruct the term, and to recognise that politically 'women' are made to exist.

We agree with almost the entirety of Denise Riley's argument. We part company, first, in insisting that the category 'men' requires an active deconstructionism too. Unlike her, we are convinced that theorisations of 'women' thereby necessarily theorise 'men' even if this is seemingly 'invisible'. Second, we refuse to buy the 'if you say "women" you necessarily say "essentialism"' argument. We cannot speak concerning Riley's discipline of history; however, we take it as axiomatic that within sociology *all* categories are social constructions, as indeed are all invocations of 'biology' or 'psychology' themselves (Stanley 1984a). Our concern, as that of others (Gatens 1986; Gross 1986b; Wilkinson 1986c), is to unpack the elements which go into referencing biology and psychology in discourses constitutive of both 'women' and 'men', whilst also recognising that actual people, who identify themselves as sexed as well as gendered persons, 'inhabit' these categories.

Denise Riley's discussion is a most useful and convincing one, but it operates at the level of 'theory', at the level of a perspective with pointers to a particular – feminist postmodernist or feminist deconstructionist – epistemology (it is also usefully compared with Alcoff 1988; Poovey 1988; and Scott 1988; who propose rather different versions of feminist deconstruction). This kind of feminist history offers few clues as to how a substantive feminist research process concerned with actual living, breathing, thinking theorising people should proceed at the level of methodology translated into method. Similarly, the rather different statements of a 'feminist history' by Gerda Lerner (1979) and of Judith Allen (1986) propose revolutionary changes to the discipline but also 'stick' at the level of epistemology. Allen's exemplary account, for instance, swingeingly criticises the positivist and empiricist framework of malestream history, but her own methodological proposals are for reading old sources with an enquiring feminist eye, and introducing new and more appropriate sources. However, for those of us located in social science disciplines concerned at least in part with substantive research involving living people (for instance, Cook 1983; Cook and Fonow 1986; Eichler 1985; Finch 1984, 1987; Geiger 1986; Graham 1983, 1984; Griffin 1986; Gurney 1985; McRobbie 1982; Marshall 1986; Nicholson 1986; Oakley 1981; Smart 1984b; Stacey 1988; Stanley and Wise 1979; Warren 1988), there is a need for a research praxis which discusses with greater precision just what the 'feminist research process' consists of.

Feminist standpoint arguments lead to relativism

The term 'relativism' is used in a number of contradictory ways, sometimes even within the same discussion. The most common (mis)usage is
to portray it in terms of a 'radical relativism' which denies not only the
existence of 'the truth', but also the existence of any external material
reality. In contrast, we define 'relativism' as an insistence that, although
there is 'truth', judgements of truth are always and necessarily made
relative to the particular framework or context of the knower (while its
perceived opposite, 'foundationalism', is an insistence that 'the truth',
rather than a number of truths, exists inde- pendently of the knower and
that it is the job of science and scientists of all kinds to find, describe and
analyse this).

Some critics of a purportedly 'essentialist' feminist standpoint
position reject what they negatively characterise as its 'radical relativism' (and see here Barrett 1986; Currie and Kazi 1987; Currie 1988).
However, other feminists (such as Alcoff 1988; Poovey 1988; Scott
1988) argue that it is the *rejection* of essentialism which leads to an (in
their eyes) positively valued relativism within a basically decon-
structionist/postmodernist framework. And confusingly, at least some
critics of essentialism/relativism (such as Barrett 1986) welcome
deconstructionist ideas without seeming to notice their strong relativist
impulse.

Part of the problem is that many discussions rely on a dichotomised
understanding of the positions available: one has to be *either* relativist
or foundationalist. In thinking through such confusions, it is useful to
refer to discussions which refuse dichotomised models of theorising.
Lisa Heldke (1988), for instance, refuses to play the 'if it's not
foundationalist then it must be relativist' game. There are other
theoretical options made available through a serious investigation of the
conditions and practices of theorising in everyday life. She argues for
the 'co-responsible option', in which theory is not treated as 'Theory',
but rather as akin to *recipes* for practice, modest in their claims for
applicability in contexts and for persons other than those who originate
them. She suggests we treat theory 'co-responsibly': as something to be
collected and not used, or used at some point, or used in a changed or
modified form, or scrapped as inapplicable.

Elizabeth Gross (1987) also suggests an alternative to the 'foun-
dationalist/relativist' dichotomy. Her option for a 'middle ground' is a
proposal in favour of a 'fractured foundationalism' (although she does
not use this phrase herself). Her argument is that there are truths, which
speak to the existence of different, overlapping but not coterminous
material realities. This is precisely our view of relativism (not the
'radical relativism' referred to above). However, we are perfectly happy

with the notion of fractured foundationalism, for neither we nor other academic feminists argue against the existence of a material objective reality 'out there', independent of individual constructions of it. In this sense we are all Durkheimians. But of course what is at dispute here is how to understand and analyse the material social world; our preference is to begin by insisting upon the indivisibility of the ideological and the material.

Experience is 'raw' and needs critical theorising

Dawn Currie (1988) characterises our approach in Stanley and Wise (1979) as a rejection of deductivism which is ignorant of the existence of inductivism; and here and in a related discussion (Currie and Kazi 1987) describes us as necessarily remaining immersed within a pretheoretical 'experience' which condemns us to an apolitical or even anti-feminist and anti-radical individualist relativism. For instance, she ascribes to us (erroneously) use of the term 'raw experience' and sees this as a kind of pre-theoretical chaos much like the 'pool of tears' the animals and birds in *Alice In Wonderland* dejectedly swim around in. Accompanying this is an almost unrecognisable account of phenomenological philosophy, portrayed as an inward-looking concern with 'experience' as a, by definition, pre-theoretical state. Consequently feminist phenomenologists (among whom we are cast) are criticised for a theoretically denuded approach which remains immersed in mere experience rather than using it as a springboard into theory.

Paradoxically, what Dawn Currie and Hamida Kazi (1987; Currie 1988) argue in favour of is very close to Alfred Schutz's (1964) position concerning the 'natural attitude' and the 'scientific attitude', to the differences he perceived between 'lay' and 'scientific' theorising. Phenomenological sociologies proceed from the position that experience is never 'raw', always constitutive of a lay 'first-order' theorising. Schutz himself insists on unmistakable and rather stark differences between this and 'scientific' second-order theorising. Similarly, Currie and Kazi criticise feminist standpoint positions from the viewpoint that the feminist researcher is a theoretician who carries out activities *different in kind* from those engaged in by ordinary women. There is no suggestion of being on the 'same critical plane' here. Relatedly, claims that phenomenologically informed approaches necessarily reject political commitment (Farganis 1986; Marshall 1988) are connected to their perceived failure to develop a 'transcendent' theoretical style.

Sandra Farganis (1986) argues the need, also specified by Barbara Marshall (1988), for welding together feminist structural analysis with a 'critical theory' account of 'social action', one allied to its critique of positivism and political commitment to theoretical discourse as praxis.

However, the version of critical theory referenced is a theoretical concern with 'structuration' processes and their implications for social action. The project in hand is to clean up theoretical inadequacies *at the level of theory*, then to turn to small, carefully presented snippets of life to exemplify the success of the theoretical project.

These and related discussions are concerned with marking out a privileged role for feminist researchers in the production of 'Theory' (with a decidedly capital T) as a transcendent and so privileged account of the realities of other women's lives (see also Evans 1982). This is a feminist project for which we have little sympathy, as readers will by now be aware.

Feminist standpoint entails methodological individualism, and this is a death-blow to the social science disciplines

A feminist standpoint concern with 'women's experience' has been criticised as exploration of individual and merely subjective sets of experience: a kind of phenomenological version of the psyche. This is structural sociological criticism of 'methodological individualism' re-made by feminists. Relatedly, our concern with the knowledge-gaining process of feminist researchers (earlier termed the researcher's 'intellectual autobiography' and in the previous chapter the 'research labour process') has been entirely erroneously characterised as methodological individualism with a vengeance (for example, in Hollway 1989:106).

Mainstream social sciences pride themselves on being generalising disciplines, dealing in categories and collectivities, not single individuals. Yet feminist critics of feminist standpoint's 'individualism' disbelieve the basic social science premise that we are social beings through and through: they assume that a focus on less than large collectivities or categories means staying in a pre- or non-social sphere (and the influence of psychoanalytic ideas on them can perhaps be detected here). Along with other social scientists who reject scientific dualisms (theory *or* experience, structure *or* process, mind *or* body...), we insist on two propositions. One is that 'individuals' do not exist except as socially located beings; thus social structures and categories can be 'recovered' by analysing the accounts of particular people in particular material circumstances (and see here Cline 1984 for a powerful exposition of this). The other is that patterned social structural phenomenon can be recovered and analysed from the 'intellectual autobiographies' of researchers (see Smith 1978a for a feminist and Wieder 1974 for an ethnomethodological exposition of some of the forms this can take). We categorically reject the depiction of this as methodological individualism, seeing this labelling as a failure to understand sociological fundamentals. It is also a failure to take the work of other feminists seriously, a point to which we return.

A focus on 'women' and not on 'gender' will ghettoise academic feminism as a sub-discipline

The arguments in Michele Barrett (1986) can be read in at least two ways, one of which we made earlier; but a second and more generous reading is to see it as a concern with ghettoisation, an effective end to feminism's revolutionary aspirations for the totality of academic life. A similar argument appears in Henrietta Moore's (1988:1–11) discussion of the relationship between feminism and anthropology, in which she suggests that feminism necessarily insists on the commonality, at some level, of all women's experiences; while feminism as a collectivity has increasingly been forced to recognise the existence of difference – that 'women' is in actuality a multiply fractured category. Alongside this, Moore describes successive stages of the feminist presence in anthropology, in which anxieties about ghettoisation and marginalisation have led to a feminist anthropology concerned not with 'the study of women' but rather with 'the study of gender'.

We have sympathy with these expressions of concern about the desirable route for feminism within the social science disciplines, but also important reservations. Feminists should beware such an easy dubbing of the 'mainstream' of disciplines as the only mainstream possible and which, almost without question, is assumed to be worth joining (and as re-reading Bernard 1973 amply confirms). Also it is worth considering that revolution is best practised precisely from the margins, rather than from the mainstream where the temptations of assimilation, of keeping one's head down and 'getting on', are so much greater. 'Mainstreams' in disciplines are best seen as 'malestreams' (Spender 1981), and feminists should subject even half-desires to join them to careful scrutiny.

Most importantly, it is a misreading of feminist standpoint positions to see these as proffering any simple 'focus on women': a kind of Rolls-Royce version of the earlier feminist model-T Ford 'the anthropology/sociology/etc. of women'. Women do not inhabit a single-sexed universe; the real world involves not only 'actual men', but also the ideologically founded but materially practised discourses by which some men, individually and collectively, actively construct the category 'woman/women' and also and thereby construct the category 'man/men' as well. In investigating the textually mediated, institutionally located social relations of ruling, there is no way in which a focus on men can be excluded; but it should be included so as to deconstruct the notion of any transcendent, always all-powerful, patriarchal 'Man' (and an extended version of this argument appears in Wise and Stanley 1987).

So where does this leave 'the study of gender'? A poor second, for we see the study of gender as a de-politicised version of feminism akin to studying 'race relations' rather than racism and colonialism. However, this is an estimation *for us*; we have no wish to impose our academic feminist project on to other feminists. What we aim and hope for are coexistent feminisms inside and outside of the academic arena, different and often disagreeing but also mutually appreciating and supporting. The main barrier to this, as we see it, is not a censoring malestream establishment. Rather it is that some versions of feminism, or rather particular proponents of these, appear to be in the process of trying to establish a hegemonic position *vis-à-vis* 'Other' feminisms.

Establishing feminist hegemony

At a number of points reference has been made to 'reading generously' or ungenerously the work of others. This idea and that of 'fair play for theorists' is borrowed from Bob Anderson, John Hughes and Wes Sharrock's (1985:51–73) discussion of the form which theoretical uncharitableness takes and some of its consequences in sociology, although their remarks have considerably wider applicability than this one discipline.

We provided a 'generous reading' of Dorothy Smith's work, treating it 'on its own terms'. We assumed that, being a sensible, clever and well-intentioned woman, Dorothy Smith is likely to have thought through and provided satisfactory (in her terms) answers to 'knowledge problematics' such as the problems of idealism, of determinism, of agency and so forth. In other words, we treated her as being (at least) as sensible and clever and well-meaning as we are. This can be contrasted with our reading of Sandra Harding's work, to which we assigned 'ill-meaning' in the form of exclusionary and unfair practices with regard to contrary feminist positions to her own. The gaps and awkwardnesses of Harding's work were stressed rather than seeking from inside it ways of repairing these problems. However, this repair work *could* have been done by reading more generously. For instance, we could have pointed out that there are no radical feminist writers on epistemology concerned with grounded feminist research processes, and thus with methodology and method, who are well known in the USA; and could have emphasised that her concern was not exhaustively to describe the feminist standpoint position, but rather account for 'the science question in feminism'.

One impressive feature of the work of both Smith and Harding is that they say what they have to say, using the work of other feminists where they can in support of their ideas and arguments. Neither works by criticising other feminists' (or indeed anyone else's) work; or by 'describing' it as ill-thought-out and inadequate and thereby providing a basis for their own; nor through setting up this 'bad "other"' to present their work as both 'superior' and that with which the reader should identify. This 'uncharitable academic three-step' seems to us to characterise what has become a central academic means of producing published work.

Philosophers of social science have discussed a number of ways of constructing theories and making knowledge-claims. These specify who are knowers and what conditions are constitutive of 'knowledge' rather than mere 'belief', and also specify how to deal with competing knowledge-claims. The main means is simply to judge 'other' against 'self' and find it wanting because it *is* 'other': 'white is good; if it is not white then it must be not-good: not-white is bad; black is bad'. The alternative, which we find intellectually as well as ethically preferable, is to assess what is being said in its *own* terms, against *its own* specification of 'knowledge', 'truth' and so forth. Whether it is good, or at least adequate, in its own terms should be the bench-mark against which it is measured.

There are severe dangers for feminism in adopting conventional academic means of dealing with 'intellectual others': through the 'uncharitable academic three-step', underpinned by judging contrary opinions as necessarily wrong. This formulates feminism as unreconstructed academic assimilationism.

Any piece of writing can have different readings made of it. More and less generous readings are always readings made in *relation to*, or even *against*, those of other positions and arguments and accounts. As Anderson, Hughes and Sharrock (1985) point out neatly through contrastive readings of the work of Max Weber and Karl Marx, it is possible to read them so that they differ in major and consequential ways but only by denying one or both of them 'good sense' about what we earlier termed 'knowledge problematics'. However, a more generous reading which assumes the good sense of both men produces an account which points up the closeness of the trajectories of analysis, but also notes that their overall projects differ importantly.

To read the work of other theorists, writers or researchers in this 'generous' sense is not usual in academic work. Academic social science, including feminist social science, is increasingly characterised by the uncharitable academic three-step and the dismissal of contrary opinion. This way of operating requires the sharp separation between the researcher/writer and an 'Other', *for without this 'other' the author would have little to say*. Her work cannot stand alone, has to draw upon, expend, the substance of some other work. We suggest readers read

published work with this description of an academic feminist assimilationist mode of arguing, discussing and apparently 'describing' in
mind, to distinguish between work which does and which does not use
such practices in the creation and damnation of 'other' and the
promotion of 'self'.

Whether such a way of working is an intentional or an accidental
by-product of what is taken to be the 'proper' way to produce academic
feminist work does not affect its consequentiality. These consequences
are, first, to construct false difference and disagreement within feminism where these do not exist, or do not exist in the form suggested;
and, second, effectively to begin the business of constructing feminist
orthodoxy, hegemony, by crediting one form of academic feminism
alone with having intellectually respectable responses to the 'knowledge problematics'.

The discussion in this chapter has been a motivated one, grounded in
our own epistemological position. We ally ourselves with a decon-
structed and reconstructed feminist standpoint epistemology, one which
rejects the 'successor-science' label and insists on the existence of
feminist stand*points*. We emphasise that there is no need for feminists to
assign ourselves to one 'end' or another of the dichotomies 'foundationalism v. relativism', 'idealism v. materialism' and 'methodological
individualism v. collectivism' which have resurfaced in feminist discussions of methodology. We reject the disguised hegemonic claims of
some forms of feminism, and actively promote academic feminist
pluralism.

In a discussion of 'tensions' within the feminist epistemologies she
describes, Sandra Harding poses what seems to us a particularly crucial
question. She wonders whether the existence of such internal and
relational tensions is actually the means of preventing epistemological
(and thus political) hegemony within feminism; that is, a way of
avoiding any one feminism setting itself up as a 'dominant discourse'.
Our answer to this question is an unequivocal *yes*.

© 1990 Liz Stanley and Sue Wise

References and extended bibliography

Abbott, Sidney and Love, Barbara (1973) *Sappho was a Right-on Woman*, New
York: Stein & Day.
Acker, Joan, Barry, Kate and Esseveld, Joke (1983) 'Objectivity and Truth:
Problems in Doing Feminist Research', *Women's Studies International
Forum* 6:423–35.
Alcoff, Linda (1988) 'Cultural Feminism versus Post-structuralism: the Identity
Crisis in Feminist Theory', *Signs* 13:405–36.
Alexander, Sally (1984) 'Women, Class and Sexual Difference in the 1830s and

1840s: Some Reflections on the Writing of a Feminist History', *History Workshop* 17:125–49.

Allen, Jeffner (1986) *Lesbian Philosophy: Explorations*, Institute of Lesbian Studies, Palo Alto, Cal.

Allen, Judith (1986) 'Evidence and Silence: Feminism and the Limits of History', in Carole Pateman and Elizabeth Gross (eds), *Feminist Challenges: Social and Political Theory*, Sydney: Allen & Unwin, pp.173–89.

Anderson, Robert, Hughes, John and Sharrock, Wesley (1985) *The Sociology Game: an Introduction to Sociological Reasoning*, London: Longman.

Andolsen, Barbara Hilkert, Gudorf, Christine and Pellauer, Mary (eds) (1985) *Women's Consciousness, Women's Conscience: a Reader in Feminist Ethics*, San Francisco: Harper & Row.

Armstrong, Patricia and Hamilton, Roberta (1988) 'Feminist Scholarship: Introduction', *Canadian Review of Sociology and Anthropology* 25:157–62 (special issue).

Atkinson, Ti-Grace (1974) *Amazon Odyssey*, New York: Links Books.

Barrett, Michele (1986) 'The Soapbox', *Network* (British Sociological Association newsletter) 35:20.

——(1987) 'The Concept of "Difference"', *Feminist Review* 26:29–41.

——(1988 2nd edn), *Women's Oppression Today*, London: Verso.

Barrett, Michele and McIntosh, Mary (1985) 'Ethnocentrism and Socialist-Feminist Theory', *Feminist Review* 20:23–47.

Bartky, Sandra (1977) 'Toward a Phenomenology of Feminist Consciousness', in Mary Vetterling-Braggin, Frederick Elliston and Jane English (eds), *Feminism and Philosophy*, Totowa, NJ: Littlefield, Adams & Co., pp.22–37.

Bartlett, Elizabeth (1986) 'Liberty, Equality and Sorority: Contradiction and Integrity in Feminist Thought and Practice', *Women's Studies International Forum* 5:521–9.

Belenky, Mary, Clinchy, Blythe, Goldberger, Nancy and Tarule, Jill (eds) (1986) *Women's Ways of Knowing: the Development of Self, Voice and Mind*, New York: Basic Books.

Bell, Colin and Roberts, Helen (1984) 'Introduction', in Colin Bell and Helen Roberts (eds), *Social Researching: Politics, Problems, Practice*, London: Routledge & Kegan Paul, pp.1–13.

Bernard, Jessie (1973) 'My Four Revolutions: an Autobiographical History of the ASA', *American Journal of Sociology* 78:773–801.

Bleier, Ruth (ed.) (1986) *Feminist Approaches to Science*, New York: Pergamon Press.

Bordo, Susan (1986) 'The Cartesian Masculinization of Thought', *Signs* 11:439–56.

Bowles, Gloria (1984) 'The Uses of Hermeneutics for Feminist Scholarship', *Women's Studies International Forum* 7:185–8.

Bowles, Gloria and Klein, Renate D. (eds) (1983) *Theories of Women's Studies*, London: Routledge & Kegan Paul.

Bristow, Ann and Esper, Jody (1984) 'A Feminist Research Ethos', *Humanity and Society* 8:489–96.

Brock, Deborah (1987) 'The Sex Debates: Toward a Feminist Epistemology and Ontology', *Atlantis* 13:98–110.

Bulkin, Elly, Pratt, Minnie Bruce and Smith, Barbara (1984) *Yours in Struggle:*

Three Feminist Perspectives on Anti-Semitism and Racism, New York: Long Haul Press.

Burden, Dianne and Gottlieb, Naomi (eds) (1987) *The Woman Client: Providing Human Services in a Changing World*, London: Tavistock.

Canadian Review of Sociology and Anthropology (1988) 25:2 (special issue on *Feminist Scholarship*).

Card, Claudia (1986) 'Oppression and Resistance: Frye's Politics of Reality', *Hypatia* 1:149–64.

Christian, Barbara (1985) *Black Feminist Criticism*, New York: Pergamon Press.

——(1988) 'The Race for Theory', *Feminist Studies* 14:67–79.

Clegg, Sue (1985) 'Feminist Methodology – Fact or Fiction?' *Quality and Quantity* 19:83–97.

Cline, Sally (1984) 'The Case of Beatrice: an Analysis of the Word "Lesbian" and the Power of Language to Control Women', in Olivia Butler (ed.), *Feminist Experience in Feminist Research*, Studies in Sexual Politics No. 2, University of Manchester, pp. 5-32.

Code, Lorraine, Mullett, Sheila and Overall, Christine (eds) (1987) *Feminist Perspectives: Philosophical Essays on Method and Morals*, Toronto: University of Toronto Press.

Collins, Patricia Hill (1986a) 'Learning from the Outsider Within: the Sociological Significance of Black Feminist Thought', *Social Problems* 33:14–32.

——(1986b) 'The Emerging Theory and Pedagogy of Black Women's Studies', *Feminist Issues* 6:3–17.

Cook, Judith (1983) 'An Interdisciplinary Look at Feminist Methodology: Ideas and Practice in Sociology, History and Anthropology', *Humboldt Journal of Social Relations* 10:127–52.

Cook, Judith and Fonow, Mary (1984) 'Am I My Sister's Gatekeeper? Cautionary Tales from the Academic Hierarchy', *Humanity and Society* 8:442–52.

——(1986) 'Knowledge and Women's Interests: Issues of Epistemology and Methodology in Feminist Sociological Research', *Sociological Inquiry* 56:2–29.

Cruikshank, Margaret (ed.) (1982) *Lesbian Studies: Present and Future*, New York: The Feminist Press.

Cummerton, Joan M. (1986) 'A Feminist Perspective on Research: What Does It Help Us See?' in Nan Van Den Berg and Lynn B. Cooper (eds), *Feminist Visions for Social Work*, Silver Spring, Md: National Association for Social Work, pp. 80–100.

Currie, Dawn (1988) 'Re-thinking What We Do and How We Do It: a Study of Reproductive Decisions', *Canadian Review of Sociology and Anthropology* 25:231–53.

Currie, Dawn and Kazi, Hamida (1987) 'Academic Feminism and the Process of De-radicalisation: Re-examining the Issues', *Feminist Review* 25: 77–98.

Daniels, Arlene (1975) 'Feminist Perspectives on Sociological Research', in Rosabeth Kanter and Marcia Millman (eds), *In Another Voice*, New York: Anchor, pp. 340–80.

Daniels, Kay (1985) 'Feminism and Social History', *Australian Feminist Studies* 1:27–40.

Davis, Angela (1982) *Women, Race and Class*, London: The Women's Press.

Du Bois, Barbara (1983) 'Passionate Scholarship: Notes on Values, Knowing and Method in Feminist Social Science', in Gloria Bowles and Renate D. Klein (eds), *Theories of Women's Studies*, London: Routledge & Kegan Paul, pp. 105–16.

Easton, Susan (1983) *Humanist Marxism and Wittgensteinian Social Philosophy*, Manchester: Manchester University Press.

Eichler, Margrit (1980) *The Double Standard: a Feminist Critique of Feminist Social Science*, London: Croom Helm.

——(1985) 'And the Work Never Ends: Feminist Contributions', *Canadian Review of Sociology and Anthropology* 22:619–44.

——(1988) *Non-Sexist Research Methods*, London: Allen & Unwin.

Eisenstein, Hester (1983) *Contemporary Feminist Thought*, Boston: Hall & Co.

Eisenstein, Hester and Jardine, A. (eds) (1985) *The Future of Difference*, New Brunswick, NJ: Rutgers University Press.

Evans, Mary (1982) 'In Praise of Theory: the Case for Women's Studies', *Feminist Review* 10:61–74.

Farganis, Sandra (1986) 'Social Theory and Feminist Theory: the Need for Dialogue', *Sociological Inquiry* 56:50–68.

Fee, Elizabeth (1986) 'Critiques of Modern Science: the Relationship of Feminism to Other Radical Epistemologies', in Ruth Bleier (ed.), *Feminist Approaches to Science*, New York: Pergamon Press, pp. 42–56.

Feminist Studies (1988) 14:1 (special issue on 'Deconstructionism').

Ferguson, Ann, Zita, Jacquelyn and Addelson, Kathryn (1981) 'On "Compulsory Heterosexuality and Lesbian Existence": Defining the Issues', *Signs* 7:158–99.

Fildes, Sarah (1984) 'The Inevitability of Theory', *Feminist Review* 14:62–76.

Finch, Janet (1984) '"It's great to have someone to talk to": the Ethics and Politics of Interviewing Women', in Colin Bell and Helen Roberts (eds), *Social Researching: Politics, Problems, Practice*, London: Routledge & Kegan Paul, pp. 70–87.

——(1987) 'The Vignette Technique in Survey Research', *Sociology* 21: 105–14.

Firestone, Shulamith (1970) *The Dialectic of Sex*, St Albans: Paladin.

Fisher, Berenice (1984) 'Guilt and Shame in the Women's Movement: the Radical Ideal of Action and Its Meaning for Feminist Intellectuals', *Feminist Studies* 10:185–212.

Flax, Jane (1983) 'Political Philosophy and the Patriarchal Unconscious: a Psychoanalytic Perspective on Epistemology and Metaphysics', in Sandra Harding and Merrill Hintikka (eds), *Discovering Reality: Feminist Perspectives on Epistemology, Metaphysics, Methodology and Philosophy of Science*, Dordrecht and Boston: Reidel Publishing Co., pp. 245–81.

——(1987) 'Postmodernism and Gender Relations in Feminist Theory', *Signs* 12:621–43.

Fox, Bonnie (1988) 'Conceptualising Patriarchy', *Canadian Review of Sociology and Anthropology* 25:163–82.

Fox-Genovese, Elizabeth (1982) 'Placing Women's History in History', *New Left Review* 133:5–29.

Fraser, Nancy and Nicholson, Linda (1988) 'Social Criticism Without Philosophy: an Encounter Between Feminism and Postmodernism', *Theory,*

Culture and Society 5:373–94.

Frye, Marilyn (1978) 'Some Thoughts on Separatism and Power', *Sinister Wisdom* 6:30–9.

——(1981) 'To Be and Be Seen: Metaphysical Misogyny', *Sinister Wisdom* 17:57–71.

——(1983) *The Politics of Reality: Essays in Feminist Theory*, New York: Crossing Press.

Gardiner Judith Kegan (1987) 'Self-Psychology as Feminist Theory', *Signs* 12:761–80.

Gardiner, Judith Kegan, Bulkin, Elly, Patterson, Rena Grasso and Kolodny, Annette (1982) 'An Interchange on Feminist Criticism: on "Dancing Through the Minefield"', *Feminist Studies* 8:629–75.

Gatens, Moira (1986) 'Feminism, Philosophy and Riddles Without Answers', in Carole Pateman and Elizabeth Gross (eds), *Feminist Challenges: Social and Political Theory*, Sydney: Allen & Unwin, pp. 13–29.

Geiger, Susan (1986) 'Women's Life Histories: Method and Content', *Signs* 11:334–51.

Gilligan, Carol (1982) *In a Different Voice: Psychological Theory and Women's Development*, Cambridge, MA: Harvard University Press.

Gottlieb, Naomi (1987) 'Dilemmas and Strategies in Research on Women', in Dianne Burden and Naomi Gottlieb (eds), *The Woman Client: Providing Human Services in a Changing World*, London: Tavistock, pp.53–66.

Gould, Meredith (1980) 'The New Sociology', *Signs* 5:459–68.

Graham, Hilary (1983) 'Do Her Answers Fit His Questions? Women and the Survey Method', in Eva Gamarnikov, June Purvis, Daphne Taylorson and David Morgan (eds), *The Public and the Private*, London: Heinemann, pp. 132–46.

——(1984) 'Surveying Through Stories', in Colin Bell and Helen Roberts (eds), *Social Researching: Politics, Problems, Practice*, London: Routledge & Kegan Paul, pp.104–24.

Griffin, Christine (1986) 'Qualitative Methods and Feminist Experience: Young Women from School to the Job Market', in Sue Wilkinson (ed.), *Feminist Social Psychology: Developing Theory and Practice*, Milton Keynes: Open University Press, pp. 173–92.

Grimshaw, Jean (1986) *Feminist Philosophers*, Brighton: Wheatsheaf.

Gross, Elizabeth (1986a) 'Philosophy, Subjectivity and the Body: Kristeva and Irigaray', in Carole Pateman and Elizabeth Gross (eds), *Feminist Challenges: Social and Political Theory*, Sydney: Allen & Unwin, pp. 125–43.

——(1986b) 'What Is Feminist Theory?' in Carole Pateman and Elizabeth Gross (eds), *Feminist Challenges: Social and Political Theory*, Sydney: Allen & Unwin, pp. 190–204.

——(1987) 'Feminist Theory and the Challenge to Knowledges', *Women's Studies International Forum* 10:475–80.

Gurney, Joan Neff (1985) 'Not One of the Guys: the Female Researcher in a Male-Dominated Setting', *Qualitative Sociology* 8:42–62.

Harding, Sandra (1980) 'Review of *Gyn/Ecology*', *Women's Studies International Quarterly* 3:456–8.

——(1983) 'Why Has the Sex/Gender System Become Visible Only Now?' in Sandra Harding and Merrill Hintikka (eds), *Discovering Reality: Feminist*

Perspectives on Epistemology, Metaphysics, Methodology and Philosophy of Science, Dordrecht and Boston: Reidel Publishing Co., pp. 311–24.
——(1986a) *The Science Question in Feminism*, Milton Keynes: Open University Press.
——(1986b) 'The Instability of the Analytical Categories of Feminist Theory', *Signs* 11:645–64.
——(ed.) (1987a) *Feminism and Methodology*, Milton Keynes: Open University Press.
——(1987b) 'Introduction: Is There a Feminist Methodology?' in Sandra Harding (ed.), *Feminism and Methodology*, Milton Keynes: Open University Press, pp. 1–14.
——(1987c) 'Conclusion: Epistemological Questions', in Sandra Harding (ed.), *Feminism and Methodology*, Milton Keynes: Open University Press, pp. 181–90.
Harding, Sandra and Hintikka, Merrill (eds) (1983) *Discovering Reality: Feminist Perspectives on Epistemology, Metaphysics, Methodology and Philosophy of Science*, Dordrecht and Boston: Reidel Publishing Co.
Hartsock, Nancy (1983) *Money, Sex and Power: Towards a Feminist Historical Materialism*, New York: Longman.
——(1987) 'The Feminist Standpoint: Developing the Ground for a Specifically Feminist Historical Materialism', in Sandra Harding (ed.), *Feminism and Methodology*, Milton Keynes: Open University Press, pp. 157–80.
Heldke, Lisa (1988) 'Recipes for Theory Making', *Hypatia* 3:15–29.
Hoagland, Sarah Lucia (1988) 'Lesbian Ethics: Beginning Remarks', *Women's Studies International Forum* 11:531–44.
Hollway, Wendy (1989) *Subjectivity and Method in Psychology*, London: Sage Publications.
hooks, bell (1981) *Ain't I A Woman: Black Women and Feminism*, Boston: South End Press.
——(1984) *Feminist Theory: From Margin to Center*, Boston: South End Press.
——(1989) *Talking Back: Thinking Feminist, Thinking Black*, London: Sheba Feminist Publishers.
Hull, Gloria, Scott, Patricia Bell and Smith, Barbara (eds) (1982) *All the Women are White, All the Men are Black, but Some of Us are Brave: Black Women's Studies*, New York: The Feminist Press.
Humanity and Society (1984) 8:4 (special issue on *Feminist Ethics and Social Science Research*).
Hurstfield, Jennifer and Phillips, Eileen (1983) '"Teaching Feminism" – a Contradiction in Terms?' *Feminist Review* 15:94–8.
Jayaratne, Toby Epstein (1983) 'The Value of Quantitative Methodology for Feminist Research', in Gloria Bowles and Renate D. Klein (eds), *Theories of Women's Studies*, London: Routledge & Kegan Paul, pp. 140–61.
Johnston, Jill (1973) *Lesbian Nation: the Feminist Solution*, New York: Touchstone Books.
Kanter, Rosabeth and Millman, Marcia (eds) (1975) *Another Voice*, New York: Anchor.
Kaplan, E. Ann (ed.) (1988) *Postmodernism and Its Discontents*, London: Verso.

Kasper, Anne (1986) 'Consciousness Re-evaluated: Interpretive Theory and Feminist Scholarship', *Sociological Inquiry* 56:30–49.

Keller, Evelyn Fox (1985) *Reflections on Gender and Science*, New Haven, CT: Yale University Press.

Keller, Evelyn Fox and Moglen, Helen (1987) 'Competition and Feminism: Conflicts for Academic Women', *Signs* 12:493–511.

Kelly, Alison (1978) 'Feminism and Research', *Women's Studies International Quarterly* 1:225–32.

Kelly, Liz and Pearson, Ruth (1983) 'Women's Studies: Women Studying or Studying Women?' *Feminist Review* 15:76–80.

Kerber, Linda, Greenow, Catherine, Maccoby, Eleanor, Luria, Zella, Stack, Carol and Gilligan, Carol (1986) 'On "In a Different Voice": an Interdisciplinary Forum', *Signs* 11:304–33.

Klein, Renate D. (1983) 'How to Do What We Want to Do: Thoughts about Feminist Methodology', in Gloria Bowles and Renate D. Klein (eds), *Theories of Women's Studies*, London: Routledge & Kegan Paul, pp. 88–104.

Kolodny, Annette (1980) 'Dancing Through the Minefield: Some Observations on the Theory, Practice and Politics of a Feminist Literary Theory', *Feminist Studies* 1980:1–25; also in Dale Spender (ed.), *Men's Studies Modified*, Oxford: Pergamon Press, pp. 23–42.

Krieger, Susan (1982) 'Lesbian Identity and Community: Recent Social Science Literature', *Signs* 8:91–108.

Lather, Patti (1988) 'Feminist Perspectives on Empowering Research Methodologies', *Women's Studies International Forum* 11:569–81.

Lauretis, Teresa de (1984) *Alice Doesn't: Feminism, Semiotics, Cinema*, Indianapolis: Indiana University Press.

——(ed.) (1986a) *Feminist Studies/Critical Studies*, Indianapolis: Indiana University Press.

——(1986b) 'Feminist Studies/Critical Studies: Issues, Terms and Contexts', in Teresa de Lauretis (ed.), *Feminist Studies/Critical Studies*, Indianapolis: Indiana University Press, pp. 1–19.

Lerner, Gerda (1979) *The Majority Finds Its Past: Placing Women in History*, Oxford: Oxford University Press.

Longino, Helen (1981) 'Scientific Objectivity and Feminist Theorizing', *Liberal Education* 67:187–95.

Lorde, Audre (1982) *Zami, a New Spelling of My Name*, MA.: Persephone Press.

——(1984) *Sister Outsider*, New York: Crossing Press.

——(1985) *The Cancer Journals*, London: Sheba Feminist Press.

Lowe, Marian and Benston, Margaret Lowe (1984) 'The Uneasy Alliance of Feminism and Academia', *Women's Studies International Forum* 7:177–84.

Lugones, Maria and Spelman, Elizabeth (1983) 'Have We Got a Theory for You! Feminist Theory, Cultural Imperialism and the Demand for "the Women's Voice"', *Women's Studies International Forum* 6:573–82.

McCormack, Thelma (1981) 'Good Theory or Just Theory? Toward a Feminist Philosophy of Social Science', *Women's Studies International Quarterly* 4:1–12.

McFadden, Maggie (1984) 'Anatomy of Difference: Toward a Classification of Feminist Theory', *Women's Studies International Forum* 7:495–504.

McRobbie, Angela (1982) 'The Politics of Feminist Research: Between Talk, Text and Action', *Feminist Review* 12:46–58.

Marchant, Helen and Wearing, Betsy (eds) (1986) *Gender Reclaimed: Women in Social Work*, Sydney: Hale & Iremonger.

Marks, Eleanor and de Courtrivon, Isobel (1981) *New French Feminisms*, Brighton: Harvester.

Marshall, Barbara (1988) 'Feminist Theory and Critical Theory', *Canadian Review of Sociology and Anthropology* 25:208–30.

Marshall, Judi (1986) 'Exploring the Experiences of Women Managers', in Sue Wilkinson (ed.), *Feminist Social Psychology: Developing Theory and Practice*, Milton Keynes: Open University Press, pp. 193–210.

Martin, Biddy and Mohanty, Chandra Talpade (1986) 'Feminist Politics: What's Home Got to Do With It?' in Teresa de Lauretis (ed.), *Feminist Studies/Critical Studies*, Indianapolis: Indiana University Press, pp. 191–212.

Marx, Karl and Engels, Frederick (1970) *The German Ideology*, London: Lawrence & Wishart.

Matthews, Sarah (1982) 'Rethinking Sociology Through a Feminist Perspective', *The American Sociologist* 17:29–35.

Mazhotra, Valerie (1984) 'Research as Critical Reflection: a Study of Self, Time and Communicative Competency', *Humanity and Society* 8: 468–77.

Messer-Davidow, Ellen (1985) 'Knowers, Knowing, Knowledge: Feminist Theory and Education', *Journal of Thought* 20:8–24.

Mies, Maria (1983) 'Towards a Methodology for Feminist Research', in Gloria Bowles and Renate D. Klein (eds), *Theories of Women's Studies*, London: Routledge & Kegan Paul, pp. 117–39.

Miles, Angela and Finn, Geraldine (eds) *Feminism in Canada*, Montreal: Black Rose Press.

Miller, Nancy (1986) 'Changing the Subject: Authorship, Writing and the Reader', in Teresa de Lauretis (ed.), *Feminist Studies/Critical Studies*, Indianapolis: Indiana University Press, pp.102–20.

Millett, Kate (1969) *Sexual Politics*, London: Abacus.

Minnich, Elizabeth, O'Barr, Jean and Rosenfeld, Rachel (eds) (1988) *Reconstructing the Academy: Women's Education and Women's Studies*, Chicago: University of Chicago Press (papers from *Signs* 1978–88).

Mitchell, Juliet (1971) *Women's Estate*, Harmondsworth: Penguin.

Modleski, Tania (1986) 'Feminism and the Power of Interpretation: Some Critical Readings', in Teresa de Lauretis (ed.), *Feminist Studies/Critical Studies*, Indianapolis: Indiana University Press, pp. 121–38.

Moi, Toril (1985) *Sexual/Textual Politics: Feminist Literary Theory*, London: Methuen.

Moore, Henrietta (1988) *Feminism and Anthropology*, Oxford: Polity Press.

Moraga, Cherrie and Anzaldua, Gloria (eds) (1981, 1983) *This Bridge Called My Back: Writings by Radical Women of Color*, New York: Kitchen Table: Women of Color Press.

Morgan, Kathryn Pauly (1987a) 'The Perils and Paradoxes of Feminist Pedagogy', *Resources for Feminist Research* 16 (3):49–52.

——(1987b) 'Bibliography of Feminist Philosophy and Theory', *Resources for Feminist Research* 16 (3):89–103.

Morris, Meaghan (1988) *Feminism, Reading, Postmodernism: the Pirate's Fiancée*, London: Verso.

Nava, Mica (1982) "'Everybody's Views were Just Broadened'": A Girls' Project and Some Responses to Lesbianism', *Feminist Review* 10:37–59.

Nebraska Feminist Collective (1983) 'A Feminist Ethic for Social Science Research', *Women's Studies International Forum* 6:535–44.

Nicholson, Paula (1986) 'Developing a Feminist Approach to Depression Following Childbirth', in Sue Wilkinson (ed.), *Feminist Social Psychology: Developing Theory and Practice*, Milton Keynes: Open University Press, pp. 135–50.

Nye, Andrea (1986) 'Preparing the Way for a Feminist Praxis', *Hypatia* 1:101–16.

——(1988) *Feminist Theory and the Philosophies of Man*, Beckenham, Kent: Croom Helm; see chap. 7, 'The Theory of Feminism', pp. 229–33.

Oakley, Ann (1981) 'Interviewing Women: a Contradiction in Terms', in Helen Roberts (ed.), *Doing Feminist Research*, London: Routledge & Kegan Paul, pp.30–61.

——(1987) 'Comment on Malseed', *Sociology* 21:633.

Oakley, Ann and Oakley, Robin (1979) in John Irvine, Ian Miles and Jeff Evans (eds), *Demystifying Social Statistics*, London: Pluto Press, pp. 172–89.

O'Neale, Sondra (1986) 'Inhibiting Midwives, Usurping Creators: the Struggling Emergence of Black Women in American Fiction', in Teresa de Lauretis (ed.), *Feminist Studies/Critical Studies*, Indianapolis: Indiana University Press, pp. 139–56.

Patai, Daphne (1983) 'Beyond Defensiveness: Feminist Research Strategies', *Women's Studies International Forum* 6:177–90.

Pateman, Carole (1986) 'The Theoretical Subversiveness of Feminism', in Carole Pateman and Elizabeth Gross (eds), *Feminist Challenges: Social and Political Theory*, Sydney: Allen & Unwin, pp. 1–10.

Pateman, Carole and Gross, Elizabeth (eds) (1986) *Feminist Challenges: Social and Political Theory*, Sydney: Allen & Unwin.

Pheterson, Gail (1982) 'The Struggle of an Academic Feminist: Elitism versus Excellence', *Women's Studies International Forum* 5:83–6.

Phillips, Damien (1987) *Philosophy, Science, and Social Inquiry: Contemporary Methodological Controversies in Social Science and Related Applied Fields of Research*, Oxford: Pergamon Press.

Poovey, Mary (1988) 'Feminism and Deconstruction', *Feminist Studies* 14: 51–66.

Radicalesbians (1972) 'Woman-identified Woman', in Karla Jay and Alan Young (eds), *Out of the Closets*, New York: Douglas, pp. 172–7.

Radford-Hill, Sheila (1986) 'Considering Feminism as a Model for Social Change', in Teresa de Lauretis (ed.), *Feminist Studies/Critical Studies*, Indianapolis: Indiana University Press, pp. 157–72.

Ramazanoglu, Caroline (1986) 'Ethnocentrism and Socialist-feminist Theory: a Response to Barrett and McIntosh', *Feminist Review* 22:83–86.

Reed, Evelyn (1978) *Sexism and Science*, New York: Pathfinder Press.

Reinharz, Shulamit (1979) *On Becoming a Social Scientist*, San Francisco: Jossey-Bass.

——(1983) 'Experiential Research: a Contribution to Feminist Research', in Gloria Bowles and Renate D. Klein (eds), *Theories of Women's Studies*, London: Routledge & Kegan Paul, pp. 162–91.

Reinharz, Shulamit, Bombyk, Marti and Wright, Janet (1983) 'Methodological Issues in Feminist Research: a Bibliography of Literature in Women's Studies, Sociology and Psychology', *Women's Studies International Forum* 6:437–54.

Reinharz, Shulamit and Davidman, Lynn (eds) (1989) *Social Science Methods: Feminist Voices*, New York: Pergamon Press.

Resources for Feminist Research (1987) 16:3 (special issue on *Women and Philosophy*).

Rich, Adrienne (1980) 'Compulsory Heterosexuality and Lesbian Existence', *Signs* 5:631–60.

Riley, Denise (1987) *Am I That Name? Feminism and the Category of 'Women' in History*, London: Macmillan.

Roberts, Helen (1981a) 'Some of the Boys Won't Play Anymore: the Impact of Feminism on Sociology', in Dale Spender (ed.), *Men's Studies Modified*, Oxford: Pergamon Press, pp. 73–81.

——(ed.) (1981b) *Doing Feminist Research*, London: Routledge & Kegan Paul.

Roff, Deborah (1985) 'Feminism Flies Too: the Principles of a Feminist Epistemology', *Resources for Feminist Research* 14 (3):6–8.

Rose, Hilary (1983) 'Hand, Brain and Heart: a Feminist Epistemology for the Natural Sciences', *Signs* 9:73–90.

——(1986) 'Beyond Masculinist Realities: a Feminist Epistemology for the Sciences', in Ruth Bleier (ed.), *Feminist Approaches to Science*, New York: Pergamon Press, pp. 57–76.

Rosenfelt, Deborah and Stacey, Judith (1987) 'Second Thoughts on the Second Wave', *Feminist Studies* 13:341–61.

Rosser, Sue (1986) *Teaching Science and Health from a Feminist Perspective*, New York: Pergamon Press; see esp. chap. 1, 'Feminist Perspectives on Science: is Reconceptualization Possible?', pp. 3–19.

Rosser, Sue (1988) 'Good Science, Can It Ever Be Gender Free?' *Women's Studies International Forum* 11:13–20.

Saarinen, Aino (1988) 'Feminist Research: In Search of a New Paradigm?' *Acta Sociologica* 31:35–51.

Sawicki, Jana (1986) 'Foucault and Feminism: Toward a Politics of Difference', *Hypatia* 3:23–36.

Sayers, Janet (1987) 'Feminism and Science – Reason and Passion', *Women's Studies International Forum* 10:171–80.

Schutz, Alfred (1964) *Collected Papers II: Studies in Social Theory*, The Hague: Martinus Nijhoff.

Scott, Joan (1988) 'Deconstructing Equality-Versus-Difference: Or, the Uses of Post-structuralist Theory for Feminism', *Feminist Studies* 14:33–50.

Scott, Sue (1984) 'The Personable and the Powerful: Gender and Status in Sociological Research', in Colin Bell and Helen Roberts (eds), *Social Researching: Politics, Problems, Practice*, London: Routledge & Kegan Paul, pp. 165–78.

——(1985) 'Feminist Research and Qualitative Methods: a Discussion of Some of the Issues', in Robert Burgess (ed.), *Issues in Educational Research*, Brighton: Falmer Press, pp. 67–85.

Scott, Sue and Porter, Mary (1983) 'On the Bottom Rung: a Discussion of Women's Work in Sociology', *Women's Studies International Forum* 6:211–22.

——(1984) 'The Double Marginalisation of Women in Research', in Sandra Acker and David Warren Piper (eds), *Is Higher Education Fair to Women?* London: Nelson, pp.180–6.

Shaktini, Namascar (1982) 'Displacing the Phallic Subject: Wittig's Lesbian Writing', *Signs* 8:29–44.

Sheridan, Susan (1986) 'From Margin to Mainstream: Situating Women's Studies', *Australian Feminist Studies* 2:1–14.

Sherin, Susan (1987) 'A Feminist Approach to Ethics', *Resources for Feminist Research* 16 (3):25–8.

Sherman, Julia and Beck, Evelyn (eds) (1979) *The Prism of Sex: Essays in the Sociology of Knowledge*, Madison: University of Wisconsin Press.

Showalter, Elaine (ed.) (1986) *The New Feminist Criticism*, London: Virago and New York: Pantheon.

Signs (1987) 12:2 (special issue on *Reconstructing the Academy*).

Smart, Carol (1984a) *The Ties that Bind: Law, Marriage and the Reproduction of Patriarchal Relations*, London: Routledge & Kegan Paul.

——(1984b) 'Researching Prostitution: Some Problems for Feminist Research', *Humanity and Society* 8:407–13.

Smith, Brenda and Noble-Spruell, Carolyn (1986) 'An Overview of Feminist Research Perspectives', in Helen Marchant and Betsy Wearing (eds), *Gender Reclaimed: Women in Social Work*, Sydney: Hale & Iremonger, pp. 134–46.

Smith, Dorothy (1974a) 'The Ideological Practice of Sociology', *Catalyst* 8:39–54.

——(1974b) 'Theorising as Ideology', in Roy Turner (ed.), *Ethnomethodology*, Harmondsworth: Penguin, pp. 39–54.

——(1974c) 'The Social Construction of Documentary Reality', *Sociological Inquiry* 44:257–68.

——(1974d) 'Women's Perspective as a Radical Critique of Sociology', *Sociological Quarterly* 44:7–13.

——(1978a) 'A Peculiar Eclipsing: Women's Exclusion from Men's Culture', *Women's Studies International Quarterly* 1:281–96.

——(1978b) 'K is Mentally Ill', *Sociology* 12:23–53.

——(1979) 'A Sociology for Women', in Julia Sherman and Evelyn Beck (eds), *The Prism of Sex: Essays in the Sociology of Knowledge*, Madison: University of Wisconsin Press, pp. 135–87.

——(1981) 'The Experienced World as Problematic: a Feminist Method', Sorokin Lecture no. 12, University of Saskatchewan Saskatoon.

——(1983) 'No One Commits Suicide: Textual Analysis of Ideological Practices', *Human Studies* 6:309–59.

——(1984) 'The Deep Structure of Gender Antithesis', *Humanity and Society* 8:395–402.

——(1987) *The Everyday World as Problematic: a Feminist Sociology*, Boston,

Mass.: Northeastern University Press, Milton Keynes: Open University Press.

Smith, Hilda (1976) 'Feminism and the Methodology of Women's Histories', in Bernice Carroll (ed.), *Liberating Women's History*, Evanston; Ill.: University of Illinois, pp. 368–84.

Smith-Rosenberg, Carroll (1986) 'Writing History: Language, Class and Gender', in Teresa de Lauretis (ed.), *Feminist Studies/Critical Studies*, Indianapolis: Indiana University Press, pp.31–54.

Smyth, Ailbhe (1987) 'All Change or Small Change? Reflections on Women's Studies', *Women's Studies Forum Working Paper* No.5, University College, Dublin.

Sociological Inquiry (1986) 56:1 (special issue on *Gender Roles and Women's Issues*).

Spender, Dale (ed.) (1981) *Men's Studies Modified*, Oxford: Pergamon.

Stacey, Judith (1988) 'Can There Be a Feminist Ethnography?' *Women's Studies International Forum* 11:21–7.

Stacey, Judith and Thorne, Barrie (1985) 'The Missing Revolution in Sociology', *Social Problems* 32:301–16.

Stacey, Margaret (1981) 'The Division of Labour Revisited or Overcoming the Two Adams', in Philip Abrams, Rosemary Deem, Janet Finch and Paul Rock (eds), *Practice and Progress: British Sociology 1950–80*, London: Allen & Unwin, pp. 172–90.

Stanley, Liz (1984a) 'How the Social Science Research Process Discriminates Against Women', in Sandra Acker and David Warren Piper (eds), *Is Higher Education Fair to Women?* London: Nelson, pp. 189–209.

——(1984b) 'Should "Sex" Really Be "Gender" or "Gender" really be "Sex"', in Robert Anderson and Wesley Sharrock (eds), *Applied Perspectives in Sociology*, London: Allen & Unwin, pp. 1–20.

Stanley, Liz and Wise, Sue (1979) 'Feminist Research, Feminist Consciousness and Experiences of Sexism', *Women's Studies International Quarterly* 2:359–74.

——(1983a) *Breaking Out: Feminist Consciousness and Feminist Research*, London: Routledge & Kegan Paul.

——(1983b) '"Back into the Personal" or: Our Attempt to Construct "Feminist Research"', in Gloria Bowles and Renate D. Klein (eds), *Theories of Women's Studies*, London: Routledge & Kegan Paul, pp. 192–209.

Stone, Pauline Terrelonge (1975) 'Feminist Consciousness and Black Women', in Jo Freeman (ed.), *Women: a Feminist Perspective*, Palo Alto, Cal.: Mayfield, pp. 575–88.

Strathern, Marilyn (1985) 'Dislodging a World View: Challenge and Counterchallenge in the Relationship Between Feminism and Anthropology', *Australian Feminist Studies* 1:1–25.

——(1987) 'An Awkward Relationship: the Case of Feminism and Anthropology', *Signs* 12: 276–92.

——(1988) 'Between Things: a Melanesianist's Comment on Deconstructive Feminism', unpublished paper, Social Anthropology Department, University of Manchester.

Sydie, R.A. (1987) *Natural Women: Cultured Men: a Feminist Perspective on Sociological Theory*, Milton Keynes: Open University Press.

Vetterling-Braggin, Mary, Elliston, Frederick and English, Jane (eds) (1982) *Feminism and Philosophy*, Totowa, NJ: Littlefield, Adams & Co.

Vickers, Jill (1987) 'Memoirs of an Ontological Exile: the Methodological Rebellions of Feminist Research', in Angela Miles and Geraldine Finn (eds), *Feminism in Canada*, Montreal: Black Rose Press, pp. 27–46.

Wallace, Michele (1979) *Black Macho and the Myth of the Superwoman*, London: John Calder.

Ward, Kathryn and Grant, Linda (1985) 'The Feminist Critique and a Decade of Published Research in Sociology Journals', *Sociological Quarterly* 26: 139–57.

Warren, Carol (1988) *Gender Issues in Field Research*, Beverly Hills, Cal.: Sage.

Waugh, Patricia (1989) *Feminine Fictions, Revisiting the Postmodern*, London: Routledge.

Westkott, Marcia (1979) 'Feminist Criticism of the Social Sciences', *Harvard Educational Review* 49:422–30.

Whyte, Karen (1988) 'Can We Learn This? We're Just Girls. Feminists and Science – Visions and Strategy', *Resources for Feminist Research* 17: 6–9.

Wieder, D. Laurie (1974) 'Telling the Code', in Roy Turner (ed.) *Ethnomethodology*, Harmondsworth: Penguin, pp. 144–72.

Wilkinson, Sue (ed.) (1986a) *Feminist Social Psychology: Developing Theory and Practice*, Milton Keynes: Open University Press.

——(1986b) 'Introduction', in Sue Wilkinson (ed.), *Feminist Social Psychology: Developing Theory and Practice*, Milton Keynes: Open University Press, pp. 1–6.

——(1986c) 'Sighting Possibilities: Diversity and Commonality in Feminist Research', in Sue Wilkinson (ed.), *Feminist Social Psychology: Developing Theory and Practice*, Milton Keynes: Open University Press, pp. 7–24.

——(1988) 'The Role of Reflexivity in Feminist Psychology', *Women's Studies International Forum* 11:493–502.

Winant, Terry (1987) 'The Feminist Standpoint: a Matter of Language', *Hypatia* 2:123–48.

Wise, Sue (1987) 'A Framework for Discussing Ethical Issues in Feminist Research: a Review of the Literature', *Writing Feminist Biography 2*, Studies in Sexual Politics No. 19, University of Manchester, pp. 47–88.

Wise, Sue and Stanley, Liz (eds) (1984) *Men and Sex: a Case Study in Sexual Politics*, a special issue of *Women's Studies International Forum* 7:1.

——(1987) *Georgie Porgie: Sexual Harassment in Everyday Life*, London: Pandora Press.

Wittig, Monique (1980) 'The Straight Mind', *Feminist Issues* 1(1):103–11.

——(1981) 'One is Not Born a Woman', *Feminist Issues* 1 (2):47–54.

Women's Studies International Forum (1983) 6:1 (special issue on *Women's Studies in the UK*).

Wylie, Alison and Okruhlik, Kathleen (1987) 'Philosophical Feminism: Challenges to Science', *Resources for Feminist Research* 16(3):12–15.

Yeatman, Anna (1986) 'Women, Domestic Life and Sociology', in Carole Pateman and Elizabeth Gross (eds), *Feminist Challenges: Social and Political Theory*, Sydney: Allen & Unwin, pp.157–72.

Zimmerman, Bonnie (1981) 'What Has Never Been: an Overview of Lesbian Feminist Literary Criticism', *Feminist Studies* 7:451–75.
Zita, Jacquelyn (1988) 'Review Essay: a Critical Analysis of Sandra Harding's "The Science Question in Feminism"', *Hypatia* 3:157–68.

Part two
Feminist Research Processes

Chapter three

Introduction

The two chapters in Part One have 'set the scene' for those in Part Two, by locating ideas about 'feminist research' firmly within a social context: within an academic mode of production which has its own distinctive features as well a those shared with other modes that typify capitalist patriarchy; and within as feminist intellectual market in which 'ideas' are produced, distributed, shared, consumed, modified and in relation to which all academic feminists locate themselves. The chapters in Part Two are each discussions of particular substantive feminist research processes, and they look in detail at the dynamics by which knowledge is produced through these. They can thus each be read in (at least) two ways: as exemplifications of particular aspects of feminist research processes; and as contributions to knowledge about the particular topic investigated.

The five section headings of Part Two ask that their composing chapters be read as exemplars of 'beginning and finishing research', 'demolishing the "quantitative v. qualitative" divide', 'recognising the role of auto/biography', 'analytically using experience' and 'analysing written and visual texts'. In a fairly loose way, this arrangement of the chapters takes readers from defining and starting a research topic, through analysing the resultant research materials, to analysing the end products, in the form of written and visual texts, of knowledge-generating research processes. As the introductory chapter points out, there is much difference in approach and intention between the chapters in this book; but each of them shares the firm conviction that knowledge-products should not be divorced from research labour processes.

Although dealing with research, theory and epistemology across conventional discipline boundaries, the contributors to this book do so from the vantage points of feminist sociologists. The particular substantive topics of the chapters are thus each located in two overlapping sets of debates. Fully to account for these debates would have shifted the emphasis of the collection away from discussions of feminist *research* and towards a more conventional version of feminist *theory*. This does not mean that these chapters are atheoretical; far from it. However, each in different ways sees theory as context-specific and thus as grounded in particular investigative procedures and processes, and rejects the conventional and abstracted notion of 'theory' as knowledge of a different order from that substantively generated. But what it does mean is that readers in search of guides to and discussions of 'the literature' in relation to the substantive focus of each chapter should seek these elsewhere, for the purpose of these contributions is a different one.

'Reading', as itself one form of research process, remains a largely neglected topic of investigation by feminist sociologists. Similarly 'research' and 'theory' remain largely unexplicated terms, but which social science education and training encourages us to treat as dichotomous activities/products. Among other purposes, this collection contributes to that impulse fundamental to contemporary feminism which refuses such dichotomies and which indeed sees ideas/theory as necessarily predicated upon experience/research. Consequently each of the chapters in Part Two should be read as insisting upon the symbiosis of research and theory.

Section A

Beginning and Finishing Research

Chapter four

The feminist research process – defining a topic

Jane Haggis

Introduction

This chapter describes the 'making' of one feminist research topic. In the process it not only describes a personal intellectual journey, but also illustrates the content of a 'feminist research methodology' as a distinct approach to the production of academic knowledge. Some concluding remarks will address the interrelations between the research path, feminist method and western social science generally.

The specific research topic I am pursuing is that of women's experiences within colonial social transformations. This encapsulates a set of exclusions expressed in the following research hypotheses:

1 women's experiences have not yet been described, identified or included within the study of colonialism;
2 this omission is the result of a series of exclusionary practices operating at various levels within western academic knowledge;
3 the task is not simply a matter of inclusion but of major analytical and methodological reconceptualisation of the tools at hand;
4 this task is of considerable contemporary relevance.

The identification of such exclusionary practices raises questions about how research methods contribute directly to exclusions, what is recognised as 'knowledge' and who it is that produces it, and where the researcher herself fits into these ways of producing 'knowledge'.

A personal voyage

Before discussing the formal exclusions preventing women's experiences from being included in the study of colonial social change, I briefly outline how I became aware of this. Such an account is important because it was in the conjuncture between my particular social experiences as a woman, and my educational career, that my research topic became 'visible' to me. A series of personal experiences informed an awareness of a whole series of exclusions operating within the production of academic knowledge. It is a major point of this chapter that such conjunctures, and the self-conscious awareness of their determining impact on the conduct of research, is a principal characteristic of feminist research.

At the most personal level, as someone from a working-class environment and culture, my encounter with university 'knowledge' brought the discovery that working-class people were not 'there' within the academy as participants or subjects but as 'others', as 'ordinary people' to be studied and observed. Even a somewhat more congenial socialist milieu within the university did not overcome this exclusion. An implicit judgemental attitude of 'we know' ensured that 'the working class' remained a category for study and not participants in the making of socialist knowledge. Little space was accorded the common-sense knowledge and logic which I knew operated sensibly to inform the ways in which people conducted their lives. Even less space or recognition was given to the distinct presences and realities of working-class women.

The second related awareness of exclusions developed out of studying politics in Australia. In particular, the failure of theorists of the crisis of western capitalism to include even a cursury mention of Third World economies seemed puzzling, especially to an Australian whose society often seems to straddle the First/Third World divide. At the time (the early 1980s), the export of manufacturing jobs to South-east Asia, and the ensuing unemployment and re-emergence of working-class racism in Australia, made such interconnections very visible.

In an endeavour to integrate these two aspects of contemporary reality, the study of developing societies seemed appropriate. I found in much of the literature that the 'peasant' character of many such societies was taken as indicative of their backwardness. This was expressive of underlying assumptions about the nature of capitalist development: implicit in most models of development was the belief that rationality and organisation along capitalist lines could not occur in non-western forms. At the same time, my study of colonial social protest made it increasingly difficult to ignore the exclusion of women, especially in the examples I came across concerning morality, dress and family organisation. While the subject matter seemed to indicate the centrality of women's presence, they were not 'there' in the historical accounts and analyses, certainly not as actors.

This work fuelled my awareness of the neglect of women in the study of colonialism and my dissatisfaction with ways of viewing the Third World and colonialism within social science. My personal voyage was thus informed by two strands of critical thought within western social science: feminist work; and the sociology of colonialism, which has related the analyses of colonialism directly to the contemporary problems of Third World societies. At this stage, neither of these two areas have fully recognised each other. What I have to say is very much in dialogue with both approaches, in a long-term endeavour to utilise both productively in my research while also acknowledging their places within the exclusionary discourse of western social science.

Social science and vanishing genders

Since the late 1960s a major historical undertaking has begun to be outlined by many western feminists: to identify the obscuring of women's historical experiences and participations by historians. In the process of this essentially descriptive task, feminist writers have begun to allude to more subtle processes of exclusion at work, not least in the very definition of what is considered history and hence worthy of record and comment, indicating broader dimensions of the exclusion of women in western academic and intellectual discourses (for example, Rowbotham 1973; Hartmann and Banner 1976; Fox-Genovese 1982; Taylor 1983).

Language has been an important element in both the nature and quality of women's conceptual presence in knowledge. A wide-ranging critique by feminists from a variety of disciplines has developed on the impact of the indiscriminate use of generic terms such as 'man' and 'humanity' on major areas of western intellectual thought (Moller-Ohlin 1979; Smith 1979; Spender 1981; Silveira 1980). Some of the most basic concepts of our socio-political vocabulary, such as citizenship, equality, representation, have in fact been predicated on the a priori exclusion of women from 'civil society'.

This invisibility has been ignored or denied because of the use of, and rationale for, the generic language in which such exclusions are couched. In broad terms, this means that what in effect are 'Men's Studies' (Spender 1981) can systematically misrepresent in their empirical documentation of 'human' society, leaving half of the participants of that process with the task of having to 'read' themselves into the story as 'other' than its 'real' content.

Such invisibility is compounded by a second aspect of the western conceptual heritage, its overwhelming emphasis on happenings in the 'public' sphere of social life. The failure to recognise and include actions within the non-formal, private areas of social life automatically severely discriminates against the principal arenas of operation of most women, as well as excluding large and significant areas of men's experiences and operations. This 'public' focus is reflected in most research topics and in the nature of the questions asked of historical materials. The places and type of archival material considered as potential sources of, or suitable for, historical analysis still remain firmly pinned to a conception of the 'public' sphere of formal – and predominantly male – activity and procedure.

These two areas of feminist criticism of western intellectual knowledge – generic language and the emphasis on the 'public' domain – provide a background against which to set the lack of empirical and analytical attention expended to date on women's experiences within colonial social change. This stems not so much from an overt determination to exclude or ignore women, as from a failure even to pose the conceptual presence of women in the problematic or historical epoch being examined. This is partly imposed on the researcher by – usually his – presence within an existing body of conceptualisations and language inheritance (Smith 1979; Bourque and Warren 1981:45-6). How this happens can be traced by considering some key assumptions and practices incorporated within sociological and anthropological discourses. I focus especially on anthropology because it is the discipline which most sees itself as concerned with the study of non-western societies; as such, it is the academic area in which feminists and non-feminists have begun to consider various of the issues with which I am concerned.

While it is true that much anthropological energy is expended on describing and comprehending the private realms of household and personal relations in local communities of non-western societies, this has not meant a concomitantly greater inclusion of, or focus on, the specificities of women's participations and roles in either public or private spheres. This happens largely because of the conceptual baggage of its western intellectual heritage; assumptions are built into the conceptual methods of anthropology which automatically involve the exclusion, relegation and reification of women's place in the societies that anthropologists study (Bourque and Warren 1981:46).

A fundamental assumption running through much anthropological work has been that women's subordination is both universal and natural. It has occurred to few researchers to ask why women might be subordinate. Where anthropologists have, more recently, asked questions about the reasons for and nature of women's historical subjection, there has been a tendency to reify the reproductive functions of women as the sole and ultimate cause of any inequalities in relations between men and women as social actors; while in reality these are new clothes for a very old model of 'biology as destiny' (Leacock 1979; Etienne and Leacock 1980).

Such views are not isolated or eccentric, but consist of the usually unacknowledged attitudes brought to the study of non-western societies by most anthropologists. This is a 'reading in' to non-western social relations the assumptions about women's social positions and practices of western society (Rogers 1980; Sacks 1979).

This is reinforced by the 'ethnographic present' – the practice of assuming that the observable social practices, beliefs and everyday behaviours of non-industrialised and non-western societies are accurate representations of the substance of past social realities, structures and organisations of such societies (Leacock 1983). This poses a static conception of the history of non-industrialised societies, and it automatically devalues and obscures the colonial dimensions of the near-past of most such societies, further mitigating the development of a truly non-ethnocentric depiction of colonial impacts on them.

By such means not only were women in such societies considered automatically subordinate to their male counterparts, but in a contradictory and superficial conceptualisation noticeable or extreme examples of the 'subjugation' of women, such as genital mutilation and suttee, were seen as purely derivative of the continuing 'traditional' nature of the society (for critiques of these approaches see El Saadawi 1980; Jeffery 1979; Etienne and Leacock 1980). Thus a kind of vicious circle was drawn for ethnographic case studies: all societies were conceived as illustrating the western definition of women as subordinate to men, yet the more uncomfortable examples of these were assigned to the 'traditional' nature of these communities, for such practice could not be conceived as co-existing with western social mores.

Such assumptions inform the fieldwork operations of many practising anthropologists. The failure to acknowledge women's roles, activities and rituals as significant has resulted in a definite informational bias. Bourque and Warren argue that a 'double bias' ensues, consisting of 'our biased assumptions and expectations combined with the male-centric biases of many informants in the societies we study'; moreover, 'Biases need not be conscious' and hence are all the more difficult to identify and prevent (Bourque and Warren 1981:47).

Colonialism – a double-edged sword

From this awareness of the underlying ethnocentrism imbuing western cognition of other societies, I have found it essential to rethink the existing sociological models of colonialism. I suggest a somewhat different model, extending the established critique of colonialism and neo-colonialism as positive influences on non-western societies to argue that this critique is itself enmeshed in the ethnocentrism of western social science.

'Colonialism' usually describes a particular epoch (or series of epochs) during which certain nations of western Europe (and latterly the USA) were involved in political, economic and military imposition and domination. These relations of domination engendered far-reaching changes within colonised societies. The most prevalent view has seen the benefits of colonialism passing to the metropolitan society as economic rewards, while disadvantages were reserved for the colonies, which reaped the full costs of neglect, deprivation and dependency (Frank 1969; Higgot 1983; Alavi 1983). Although this view is, in my opinion, a fairly accurate assessment of the overall effects of the colonial economic endeavour, it does not allow for the full complexities of colonial social processes and transformations to be elaborated and investigated. While in no way wishing to undermine or belittle the full extent of the devastations and inimical social changes foisted upon colonial societies, such a single-stranded view of the colonial relationship usurps from the colonial society any autonomy or dynamism in response, and limits its role to that of passive victim.

The obvious, but rarely appreciated, point about the social facts of colonialism is that they inevitably involve a 'meeting' between two social formations: the indigenous society and the colonial power. This 'meeting' or interaction is not between two homogeneous units but occurs between different social groups on many levels, and in many permutations, according to the various social constructions, circumstances and dynamics operating in both the indigenous society and the colonising power. It needs to be recognised analytically that the colonised society is not a passive object of imposition, but, albeit in ultimately dominated forms, actively participates not only in moulding the colonising process and its overall social impact, but also in setting definite limits to the shape and aims of colonisation. Neither the indigenous society nor the colonising society can be accurately conceptualised as a social formation without acknowledging the other's reality and the specific relations of interaction in which they are involved. Not only were the colonised people profoundly affected by their colonial rulers, but the existence of the colonies, and the experiences of the colonisers in that society, were translated and transferred back to the metropolitan society where they played complicated and multi-dimensional roles in the on-going social, cultural as well as economic changes in imperial countries.

It is within such hypotheses about the colonial relationship that the topic of women's experiences of colonialism is extended to include both women as *colonised* and women as *colonisers*. This extension of the topic allows a fuller elaboration of the two-way channels of influence and change between the colonised society and the colonising one, especially in relation to the important changes in the definition of, and social relations enmeshing, western women during the heyday of the British colonial era, the nineteenth century.

By including the interrelations between women – both colonised and colonisers – the intention is also to highlight the need to develop feminist theory. Feminism, although able to generate a critique of the gender bias inherent in western social science, does not itself operate outside of western discourse on non-western societies (Carby 1982; Amos and Parmar 1984; hooks 1984).

A major intention of my research is to formulate suggestions and questions which will inform the fuller integration of post-colonial women's historical and contemporary situations and realities into the construction of a feminist sociological understanding of the social processes of change informing our contemporary world. I do not wish to diminish the importance and priority of identifying and addressing the inclusion of post-colonial realities into the dominant representations of social life, but the task is not simply one of inclusion. A primary reason for the comparative neglect of women from studies of colonialism has been the limitations and biases of the conceptual and cognitive approaches available to consider social life, both historical and contemporary. A study of women and colonialism will, perforce, involve not only a critique, but the construction of a new conceptual apparatus, because of the particular blinkers constricting current western social science.

The beginnings of my project

The preceding discussion is preliminary to the development of a concrete research agenda. The following summary of my initial research agenda permits illustration both of the points made above and of the difficulties involved in constructing 'feminist research'.

The particular historical study I am developing attempts to visualise colonialism – in this case the colonial relations between Britain and India – in a specific way. I conceptualise colonialism as a dialectic complexity of 'meetings' between two social formations. Such 'meetings' occur at numerous levels and in various permutations, given the differentiated character of each social formation. Given this dialectic, not only is it impossible to conceive of the colonised society without including the colonial presence, it is also inaccurate to depict the imperial society outside of its colonial connections. My research focusses on the impact of the colonised society on the metropolitan social formation. It sees colonised societies as dynamic actors and presences within 'our' – western – history, as much as the colonising powers have been in non-western histories.

I focus on women for several reasons. First, in the case of Britain and

India, both societies experienced parallel processes of development of a capitalist social formation, albeit refracted through their different positions within the colonial relationship. Part of this process included the construction of new gender orders and representations of women, providing a fruitful and comparative context within which to examine class and gender within processes of transition and transformation. Second, given the relational picture of colonialism summarised here, it is possible to draw out and emphasise the particular relations and roles between women as colonised and women as colonisers. Such an emphasis will permit contributions to the refinement of gender along both race and class cleavages.

My specific historical study focusses on British Christian missionary activities in what is now the state of Kerala, south-west India. Essentially, I suggest that missionaries acted as a 'transmission belt' between the two 'colonial' societies. As such, they were significant interpreters and expressors of the imperial experience and Indian realities within British society, especially in the latter half of the nineteenth and early twentieth centuries.

The missionaries operated within specific class dimensions in Kerala, with different emphases and relations among upper-class Keralans and the masses of low-caste workers. Moreover, there was a continuous and overt gender dimension to missionary interactions within the indigenous society. They were principal definers of one strand of the imperial mission – the resurrection of Indian civilisation from its nadir of heathen decadence and moral decay – exemplified in the status and condition of Indian women.

At the same time, missionaries were part of British society, in part produced by, and also active in, the major social upheavals of the nineteenth century, particularly the formation of the industrial working class. Involvement in the development of mass education and working-class cultures generally, especially their 'moral' and 'respectable' content, brought missionaries to the heart of the processes of class formation. Many missionaries were themselves from 'respectable' working-class backgrounds, whilst others were important in helping to articulate aspects of the interaction between working-class cultures and bourgeois ideologies.

This class dimension of missionary social characterisation was paralleled by specific gender features. Not only were missionaries differentiated as men and women, they were also significant participants in the debates over notions of gender and definition of femininity within British society. One of the purposes of the research is to trace the role and impact on these debates of missionaries' experiences in Kerala.

Kerala provides a particularly interesting and suggestive location within which to situate the historical research. This region has the reputation of having experienced a profound social transformation from what was reputedly a rigid and 'traditional' caste society to the most politically and socially progressive of Indian states. This perceived transformation spans precisely the period of colonial domination, offering a suitable context in which to situate the study of aspects of colonialism and social transformations. Moreover, the fact that significant sections of Keralan society were traditionally organised within matrilineal family organisations, coupled with the contemporary reputation of Keralan society as offering better life chances for women than in most of India (measured in terms of access to education and employment, female mortality, age of marriage), suggests that notions of gender and the position of women were important dimensions in this recent past. Also, historical evidence suggests that Keralan matrilineal organisation was the first time British colonialists had observed such a family and inheritance form. As such it had a significant impact on the British in Kerala and was translated back to Britain, challenging notions about the universality of patriliny.

These boundaries of change take on particular resonance given that Kerala was a focus of British missionary activities throughout the colonial era. A dynamic and highly varied series of interactions between missionaries and sections of the Keralan population ensued. In particular, there appear to have been close links between missionaries and indigenous groups involved in social protest and social uplift movements directly concerned with the nature of, and changes in, the conceptions of gender roles and definitions of women.

I intend to examine examples of such social protest movements in order to elucidate the various 'interpretations' of their gender components by the missionaries, Keralan participants (especially Christian converts), and officials of the colonial state. This will provide the Keralan context with which to trace the impact of colonial experiences and realities – through the missionaries – on aspects of British society. By tracing out the personal official biographies of missionaries, and their friendship and organisational networks in Britain, some understandings of the construction of 'representations' of Keralan and Indian gender relations and notions of womanhood, and how these representations fed into the development and consolidation of new gender orders more reflective of a European capitalist social formation, will be gleaned.

Two different kinds of material will provide the research data on which this study is based. The largest source is formed by historical documents, consisting of personal correspondence and unpublished memoirs of missionaries; the official archives of the missionary societies active in Kerala (the London Missionary Society and the Church Missionary Society in particular), which include official reports and records as well as volumes of correspondence between the missionaries in the field and the head offices of the societies which employed them; a sizeable published literature of society journals and pamphlets, missionary accounts, autobiographies and novels; in India, journals, memoirs and novels written by converts and others influenced by missionary teachings and actions. The second primary source is based on oral accounts of missionaries, converts and others. Such interviews will be, by and large, personal recollections by people of a past they themselves were not a part of. My intention is, in part, to use these oral recollections as a comparative measure alongside the historical documents.

Such a diverse range of primary material poses special problems as well as offering many opportunities for research and writing. It is the use of these materials that I find one of the most challenging aspects in trying to do feminist research.

Essentially, I view the 'items' listed above as representative of particular 'voices' or 'interpretations' – lived experience – of the relationships I am attempting to document. One part of my project is to tease out as many of these layers of interpretation as I can. It is only in the telling of the many experiences, remembrances and constructions of the colonial relationship (in this instance centred on the gendered experience) that a hint of its 'reality' might be gained. No one voice can be privileged without risking the slighting of another, a danger sufficiently echoed in the manufactured silence of women's voices in the telling of history.

An awareness of exclusion in both epistemological and ontological terms is the ever-more sophisticated core of feminist theory. Any attempt to produce a 'knowledge' cognisant of feminist consciousness therefore necessarily involves challenging the cognitive preconceptions of existing knowledges. I do not mean to suggest that feminist researchers gain some kind of privileged perspicacity by virtue of their conscious sociopolitical stance. However, out of their own sense of 'Otherness' they can start to recognise both the layers of exclusions operating within western knowledge and begin to grasp their own contradictory location within such knowledge. Unlike the working class (whose conceptual terrain is largely determined by outside, intellectual sympathisers), and until recently non-western peoples, second-wave feminists have – by the skin of their teeth – managed to participate within formal knowledge production. They have done so almost by virtue of their exclusion from such structures.

Thus to be a writer of feminist theory requires an independent intellectual base and awareness outside the academy. Such a base is often forged, in various ways, in dialogue with that inchoate 'women's movement' whose disparate and 'unorganised' impact men especially have difficulty in acknowledging. A similar kind of intellectual 'independence' seems to be developing among black people in white majority societies, and among Third World people. Certainly, the ways in which black and non-western women are establishing their own knowledge within feminist thought would indicate this (Carby 1982; Amos and Parmar 1984; Bandarage 1984; hooks 1984, 1986). I have tried to indicate how this qualitatively different intellectual practice has been reflected in my own preliminary research. I would go further and suggest that a qualitatively different research methodology and product is the end result of this intellectual journey.

Another 'voice' participating in this research project remains to be mentioned: my own. My voice obtains at least three qualities in this quilt of interpretation:

1 it is my reading of the primary accounts (or the hearing of the oral material) which will be presented as the historical dimension;
2 this reading will take further shape around my interest in the form in which I choose to write the text;
3 embracing both 1 and 2 are my thematic interests, which are already shaping the questions I ask, relevance I give, and reasons for my research and the material I am using.

At the most general level, it is I, as a woman of a specific background and experience in late twentieth-century Europe and Australia, who demands of the research material understandings of 'gender' and 'colonialism' – words with little, or different, meanings for the missionaries and converts in their own time. Doing feminist research demands that my participation and presence – my voice – within my research project must be explicitly admitted and included in the product of that research. My 'voice' is as much a part of the 'colonial' relationships I wish to describe as those from the nineteenth century I intend to sift and sort.

At this stage, accomplishing this polyphonic text is some distance away. The challenge will be, must be, met in the process of researching, and most particularly, in the writing of my thesis. Suffice at this stage to say that it is difficult to imagine the dominant conventions of objective expert scholarship being of much assistance in the search for a literary vehicle for my research.

Conclusion

In conclusion, my comments on the feminist research process are not intended to read as a paean to its superiority. I do not believe that feminism holds some ultimate 'truth' or 'correct' method. However, it seems to me that, at this particular juncture, the kind of research that feminists are forced to consider by virtue of their recognition of the exclusionary practices within western knowledge, and their self-conscious awareness of the public/private connection, involves them in more profound questioning of the bases of western knowledge than many other perspectives. In so doing, feminists challenge not only the dominant epistemological and methodological practices of western social science, but also the recognised form of the intellectual/academic product.

© 1990 Jane Haggis

References

Alavi, Hamza (1983) 'India: Transition to Colonial Capitalism', in Hamza Alavi, Peter Burns, Roger Knight and Peter Mayer, *Capitalism and Colonial Production*, London: Croom Helm, pp.23–75.

Amos, Valerie and Parmar, Pratibha (1984) 'Challenging Imperial Feminism', *Feminist Review* 17:3–19.

Bandarage, Asoka (1984) 'Women in Development: Liberalism, Marxism and Marxist-feminism', *Development and Change* 15:495–515.

Barrett, Michele (1980) *Women's Oppression Today: Problems in Marxist Feminist Analysis*, London: Verso.

Bourque, Susan and Warren, Kay (1981) *Women of the Andes: Patriarchy and Social Change in Two Peruvian Towns*, Ann Arbor: University of Michigan Press.

Bridenthal, Renate and Koonz, Claudia (eds) (1977) *Becoming Visible: Women in European History*, Boston: Houghton Mifflin.

Carby, Hazel (1982) 'White Women Listen! Black Feminism and the Boundaries of Sisterhood', in Centre for Contemporary Cultural Studies, *The Empire Strikes Back: Race and Racism in 70s Britain*, London: Hutchinson, pp. 212–35.

El Saadawi, Nawal (1980) *The Hidden Face of Eve*, London: Zed Press.

Etienne, Mona and Leacock, Eleanor (eds) (1980) *Women and Colonialization – Anthropological Perspectives*, New York: Praeger Publications.

Fox-Genovese, Elizabeth (1982) 'Placing Women's History in History', *New Left Review* 133:5–29.

Frank, André Gunter (1969) *Capitalism and Underdevelopment in Latin America*, Harmondsworth: Penguin.

Hartmann, Mary and Banner, Lois (eds) (1976) *Clio's Consciousness Raised: New Perspectives on the History of Women*, New York: Farrar, Straus & Giroux.

Higgot, Richard (1983) *Political Development Theory: the Contemporary Debate*, London: Croom Helm.

hooks, bell (1984) *Feminist Theory: From Margin to Centre*, Boston: South End Press.

——(1986) 'Sisterhood: Political Solidarity between Women', *Feminist Review* 23:125–38.

Jeffery, Patricia (1979) *Frogs in a Well: Indian Women in Purdah*, London: Zed Press.

Leacock, Eleanor (1979) 'Women, Development and Anthropological Facts and Fictions', in Latin American Perspectives (ed.), *Women in Latin America: an Anthology from Latin American Perspectives*, Latin American Perspectives, Cal., pp. 45–70.

——(1983) 'Interpreting the Origins of Gender Inequality: Conceptual and Historical Problems', *Dialectical Anthropology* 7:263–84.

Moller-Ohlin, Susan (1979) *Women in Western Political Thought*, Princeton, NJ: Princeton University Press.

Rogers, Barbara (1980) *The Domestication of Women: Discrimination in Developing Societies*, London: Tavistock.

Rowbotham, Sheila (1973) *Hidden from History: 300 Years of Women's Oppression and the Fight Against It*, Harmondsworth: Penguin.

Sacks, Karen (1979) *Sisters and Wives: the Past and Future of Sexual Equality*, Westport, Conn.: Greenwood.

Silveira, Jeanette (1980) 'Generic Masculinising Words and Thinking', *Women's Studies International Quarterly* 3:165–78.

Smith, Dorothy (1979) 'A Sociology for Women', in Julia Sherman and Evelyn Beck (eds), *The Prism of Sex: Essays in the Sociology of Knowledge*, Madison: University of Wisconsin Press, pp. 135–87.

Spender, Dale (ed.) (1981) *Men's Studies Modified: the Impact of Feminism on the Academic Disciplines*, Oxford: Pergamon Press.

Taylor, Barbara (1983) *Eve and the New Jerusalem: Socialism and Feminism in the Nineteenth Century*, London: Virago.

Chapter five

The history of a 'failed' research topic
The case of the childminders

Fiona Poland

Starting the evaluation

When I was working as a researcher for a Social Services Department (SSD) I was asked to evaluate the work of a local Support Project for childminders. It was receiving grants from the department as part of a policy to improve the services offered to childminders. There were also posts set up within the SSD in two local Area Offices to co-ordinate care to under-fives, including through childminders.

Until shortly before the research began, the Support Project had been the main local base for work with childminders. The childminders' contact with the SSD was usually limited to meeting social workers when they were first registered. The social workers carried out the SSD's legal duties to assess whether childminders' homes and family conditions met the minimum conditions for registering and also set the maximum numbers of children that could be minded per home. Childminders tended to be infrequently visited after registration. The Support Project provided:

- 'drop-ins' where minders could meet and children take part in a playgroup;
- support for the minders' professional association;
- a newsletter;
- transport to 'drop-ins' and outings;
- a toy library and a play advice worker to visit minders at home.

The SSD Day Care Co-ordinators also supported drop-ins, loaned out childcare and child safety equipment and provided training on childcare and childminding issues. I was originally asked by the SSD to assess just the Support Project, partly because of reservations among some SSD staff about it. As I did not want to become the means of sanctioning the Project, I extended my work to include a comparative assessment of the childminding support work done by the SSD's Co-ordinator staff.

Because of this I decided to base my evaluation on an analysis of a range of different sources of information about the work done. I talked to Project workers and co-ordinators, departmental play-scheme and nursery development staff, childminders at home and at drop-ins. Workers filled in time–budget forms for me and provided minutes, publicity literature and job descriptions. After all this, I found it impossible to complete my evaluation because of unresolved doubts and reservations about how to analyse and present the differences I uncovered. How and why this was so is the main theme of this chapter, which illustrates the political and other pitfalls that can prevent research from being finished.

As I made contact with the various people involved, I became very aware of the differences, tensions and ambivalences in their views of what the priorities for work with childminders should be. These were embedded in all kinds of unspoken assumptions about what women should do as parents and carers, about SSD powers to intervene in these processes in the home, and trying to work on the boundaries of the formal and informal networks of care. Many of these assumptions hinge on what women 'should' be doing with their time and what counts as legitimate work and leisure.

There were clear differences between the priorities of the Support Project's staff and those of the SSD. They would both have said that they wanted to promote 'good childcare in the minding situation', but differed in important ways about how to achieve this.

The Support Project's staff felt it was important to support and relate to the childminders' work, to give them a sense of being 'professional', to provide settings where they could talk together about minding issues: safety, organising play and other activities for children, meals, relations with parents, hours, payments and 'extras' (such as washing) provided, insurance. They also built relationships with minders in their homes, providing a toy library as a focus for discussing individual children's progress and needs. SSD staff were anxious to assess what was being provided to children at any one time by the minders and to ensure that minimum conditions were being met. However, establishing this was problematic, given that they had only limited formal links with childminders, who were not in any case employed by the department but directly by parents.

'Good childcare through effective supervision'

SSD staff stressed that their priority focus was on the 'welfare of the child' and the 'care that children received'. They felt it was important for the department to have some kind of supervision of what went on in childminders' homes. They were particularly concerned with 'over-minding' (minders taking in more children than their terms of registration allowed). However, their legal powers to intervene in the minding process (as opposed to gross child neglect or abuse) were limited to the processes of registration and, *in extremis* (but this was very rare), de-registration.

The SSD Day Care Co-ordinators wanted to refer parents to child-minders as part of a system of integrated childcare provision, along with providing nursery places and playgroups: the aim was day nurseries for children who needed them or the security of continuous home-care where this seemed more suitable. However, this was not the reality of how the allocation of council services worked. Childminders worked for themselves and were not employed by the SSD. Also there were long waiting lists for all forms of council provision, including nursery places, because of chronic underfunding. Thus places were likely to be allocated according to whether a child was perceived as being 'at risk' by SSD staff, and this is a very different basis for providing care from the idea of diverse styles of childcare allocated by individual need.

There was also something of a debate within the SSD about whether minders provided a 'second-class' childcare option in comparison to the monitoring and stimulation provided in SSD day nurseries. The day-nursery option was felt to be most reliably the best. Childminding was more 'suspect' because minders were not trained or employed by the SSD, used their homes rather than safer purpose-built accommodation, and were open to the temptation to overmind rather than concentrate on the care of children.

'Better childcare from better childminding practice'

The Support Project workers saw an important part of their work as bringing childminders together to give them the chance to see what they did as 'real work' with professional skills and obligations. This was seen as problematic for a whole range of reasons by staff from the SSD, who felt that, since they were funding the Project, it should extend the supervisory capacity of the SSD in preventing 'overminding'. Several SSD staff felt that by putting their emphasis on building relationships with minders the Project would become too tolerant of bad practice in the interim. There was also a suspicion, as the Project provided a number of drop-ins and other activities for minders, that some minders were distracted from actually minding: if minders were really an alter-native to nurseries, complementing them by providing continuous home-based care, they were not doing this if they were gadding about to drop-ins and outings.

Another problematic factor for SSD staff was that childminders were highly critical of them. They disliked the length of time it took for the registration process to be completed – often several months. Many minders started minding when asked by a particular neighbour or friend to look after a child, perhaps only for eighteen months until they started school. So if the registration took six months to be completed, it took a considerable proportion of that time and perhaps meant that the mother would change her mind.

The childminders also felt they were being supervised and criticised without much support (such as in obtaining unusual or expensive items of safety equipment) or guidance in handling some of the more problematic aspects of dealing with parents, like negotiating the terms of minding, the legal aspects and insurance. Also they felt that contact with SSD staff was infrequent and irregular.

However, there was little impetus within the SSD to provide these kinds of support. There were stringent financial cuts being imposed, and so little spare cash and few spare staff to go out on visits to people not employed by the department. Social workers were in any case rarely trained in the areas of most direct interest to the minders. The whole field was, besides, a source of frustration to some social workers, who would have preferred stronger sanctions to block unsuitable practices, more decision over who could be a minder, and greater capacity to persuade the unsuitable to stop minding. There were further ambivalences on the part of SSD staff because several women became minders after unsuccessfully applying to be foster parents, or were in the process of making such applications and expressing dissatisfaction with the process.

Minding and mothering

There were a number of paradoxes and tensions here which key into the question of what families 'ought' to be like and what mothers 'ought' to do or be which simply do not reflect everyday life. Certainly, when I talked to minders they stressed that they looked after children 'like my own': they provided this kind of care and felt they already knew what it was to provide it to the best of their ability. The paradox is that parents can have as many children as they like, regardless of space, time and skills, and without being specially trained or supervised. Producing and rearing children is something that people 'just do' and it is not seen as being special, economically valuable or especially skilled. Mothers can experience a terrible weight of guilt about what they should provide for their children and it can be a shock to find out just how demanding is this thing that 'everybody can do'.

Which are the areas of family life where the mother is a person separate from her work as a mother producing the child? There is no clear distinction. This gives scope to mothers to do whatever they see fit to make up their day, because any of it could be 'mothering'; but it also gives scope for whatever they do to be interpreted as 'not mothering'. In any case it is not paid for and does not come into the public domain of the market. However, this is precisely what happens with minding. Something that might be 'good enough for my own children' can become questionable if it is a service to be sold. What is the buyer getting for her money and how should this be regulated? This is a sensitive area for SSD staff to enquire into, because it is someone else's home and competence as a mother that is being scrutinised and called into question. And this is the one area of a woman's life where she might expect to have some control on her own terms.

In addition, minding is not well paid. In many cases a minder will barely break even by the time she has bought safety equipment, a double buggy, food, toys and has paid for lighting and heating. However, if she is looking after her own children as well she will be subsidising this. The low rates of pay are typical to most 'caring' work but are obviously more 'appropriate' when a woman is doing something for which she is normally not paid at all in the very place where this is most appropriately carried out – her own home.

The entire question of pay was a sensitive one for minders, many of whom found it difficult to discuss this with parents. If they were really caring for the children they looked after, how could they talk about money in this way? They found it difficult to chase non-paying parents, to discuss the question of whether they should be paid if children were sick and had to remain at home, or when parents were late in picking children up. It was also often a problem for them to decide how to stop minding, or stop minding a particular child, if they were truly 'caring'; and this sometimes resulted in parents being informed somewhat abruptly that a minding arrangement was coming to an end.

There were all kinds of ambivalences concerning minding as paid work: whether minders were likely to be doing a good job and caring well if they were paid for it; and whether it could really be taken seriously as *work*. The nature of the SSD visits they occasionally received could be seen as calling into question whether they were good carers. Yet the Support Project's attempts to support a sense of professionalism could be seen as encouraging them to be 'less caring'. Project staff certainly found it difficult to encourage minders to do this. They were unlikely to get them to attend any meetings without their children – because of other domestic commitments when they had finished their minding work, but also because many minders found it difficult to take seriously the notion that they were doing a *job*.

When I asked minders if there was any training they would have liked the SSD or the Support Project to provide, nothing was raised which would have brought out the more professional, job-like or commercial aspects of what they did. Some minders quite explicitly said they did minding to stay at home with their children and found it important to distinguish between what they were doing and 'mothers who went out to work'.

Both the SSD's and the Support Project's approaches raised problems for the minders, then. At that time, the SSD was often seen by the minders as something which made awkward demands on them, and imposed limits and formalities without understanding or supporting their situation. However, although many felt more comfortable with the Support Project staff, who, they felt, did help them talk about things that mattered to them, there still remained a great reluctance to talk about minding as a job.

Reaching belated conclusions?

There were all kinds of reasons why I found the road to concluding my evaluation of the childminding project impassable. These were partly tied to the way in which I chose as a researcher to respond to the political difficulties. Elsewhere (Poland 1986) I have discussed the difficulties in using *any* textbook methods to do research in such a practical setting. However, at the time I found it very difficult to untangle the many tensions which existed in this situation, why they were there and which of them to address. Consequently I found it difficult to set out a framework for a final analysis and report to be written up in the time limits available which would address the varied concerns which shaped my enquiries.

As I have tried to show, the settings and times within which 'childcare' is done, and interpretations of what it is, are not fixed or formal almost by definition. Also, attempts to make it so can open up many areas for sometimes painful negotiation. Looking back on the experience, many of the tensions I encountered related to dealing with:

(a) an area of activity chosen by one group of women to do because it was something they already knew how to do by virtue of being women and mothers;

(b) which allowed them to stay at home 'without a job' with all that that meant;

(c) but which was then transformed by parents, agencies and the SSD into 'a job'.

And the interpretation of this can threaten their presentation of what they do both as minders and as mothers: if they are devalued by being found wanting as minders, then in their eyes they themselves as 'naturally mothering' women are also found wanting.

The SSD and the Support Project experienced a multiplicity of problems in working with minders and each felt that the approach of the other could threaten their priorities in promoting 'good childcare'. But in many ways they were in agreement as to what constituted good childcare; for instance, concerning the importance of play and a child-centred approach and of providing settings which would be stimulating and encourage children to be active and outgoing.

My initial misgivings about carrying out the research arose from how it was presented to me and my concern not simply to collect information about the work of one group. Focussing on that group alone would have forced me to set a value on their work and to describe problems they might be having in isolation. I felt it was important to set their work in a context which included the activities of other services to childminders. However, I encountered new dilemmas as my information about what was going on increased, as I got to know the various workers in the Project and the department and, of course, the minders themselves.

Dilemma 1: resolvable with hindsight or experience?

One dilemma concerned how I was to act on my knowledge of the differences in approach between the SSD and the Project. With the benefit of hindsight and more experience as an applied social researcher, I can now see a number of courses of action which I could have taken.

I could have facilitated communication between the SSD and the Project about such differences, to clarify a number of misunderstandings which had arisen over their relative roles, and to encourage shared work in areas which they agreed were important. The discussion of differences in a 'final report' would thus have been set in a context of co-operative activity; and information about such differences in the report would have been neither 'news' nor open to easy assumptions about one approach being 'wrong'. However, I did not have the experience at that stage to think through all these issues.

Neither had I then enough confidence to conduct research which prioritised real-life situations rather than textbook methods and solutions. So I was unable to make the decisions I needed to from my own research practice to come up with an end product which would address these differences in a workable way. However, even if I had managed to deal with such differences in this way it still seems to me now that, within the time available and as a feminist, I could not have come to a resolution of other issues. In particular, if I dealt with the apparently less controversial issues surrounding assessment of the standards of childcare provided by minders – but which in feminist terms raised immense problematics – I could not have come to any 'resolution' at all.

Dilemma 2: no answers at all?

Although I found it problematic to uncover the tensions between department and Project, these were relatively 'public' and related to the 'work' presentations of the staff involved. However, in dealing with minders and childcare I necessarily raised issues concerning an area of women's lives ordinarily private and within their control. I sensed these issues at the time rather than thinking them through in a thorough-going way. However, I was definitely uneasy about using apparently universal ideas about 'good standards', the invocation of which carried an implied threat to minders' conceptions of themselves as women and as mothers, and about which there was definite unease on their parts.

Many of the working-class minders I came into contact with were already uncomfortable with the extent to which their caring competencies were measured and linked with other public and work-related features they found threatening to their self-conception. My assessment activities would have added to this. Furthermore, I could not at the time reconcile myself to the basic assumptions underlying much of the textbook discussion of what constituted good childcare. However, I was employed by an organisation which existed in part to regulate certain minimum standards of care. At the time I was unable to bring the two sets of practices together in a way that would not lead to the subordination of the minders' views and activities to those of the department *and* the Project.

Different audiences, different research?

This chapter is related to a paper I gave at a workshop for an audience of mainly social services researchers (Poland 1986). In it I concentrated almost entirely on the research issues I have labelled as 'Dilemma 1', those I might have been able with hindsight to deal with. I made almost no mention of 'Dilemma 2' issues.

My concern in that workshop was to encourage recognition that many of the maxims of research methodology are little informed by a discussion of the practical and contextually specific realities that researchers must deal with. I felt this research example would enable these other social services researchers to recognise their own experience in having to mediate different interests and tensions between groups. My aim was to suggest that by using ideas about research which reflected their own experiences and situations, and by redefining what was acceptable as appropriate research design and behaviour, SSD researchers would be able to produce research which more realistically reflected their active presence in the settings they researched. This, I argued, would be more likely to produce 'useful' and acceptable research from such settings than is often the case.

It did not seem to me that a discussion of Dilemma 2 issues in this context and with this audience would get very far. Doing so would raise more issues than I could deal with in a workshop setting. Relatedly, the tensions involved would have been readily recognisable to a feminist audience but not to this one. Consequently I chose to discuss my 'minder research' in relation to the more tangible and manageable world of my work and that of the SSD and the Project. Paradoxically, I left almost untouched the less manageable world of the care work done by the minders themselves. I raise this to make one final point. 'Research' is rarely a *single* product. Different and appropriate versions of it are produced for different kinds of audiences, in the above situation relative to what I thought workshop members could understand, given the everyday organisational practices they help constitute and which in turn are constitutive of their own work.

References

Poland, Fiona (1986) 'Matching Research to the Realities of Research and What Happens If We Don't: a Case Study', paper given to the Annual Conference of the Social Services Research Group on 'Services Under Pressure: the New Climate', Manchester.

Demolishing the 'Quantitative *v.* Qualitative' Divide

Chapter six

'Seeking Susan'
Producing statistical information on young people's leisure

Denise Farran

Introduction

This is not so much a chapter on feminist ideas about leisure (Wimbush and Talbot 1988), as one on how knowledge about leisure was constructed by me as a feminist researcher for the practical purpose of fulfilling a particular commissioned research brief. As the chapter title suggests, I see this research process as irretrievably practical: about down-to-earth, everyday and often mundane activities and actions. This is something with which textbooks on 'how to do research' never really come to grips. Although I recognise that of course 'reality' is much more complex than descriptions/analyses/theories of that reality can ever be, there is still room for change. More literature needs to be written by social scientists telling of their diverse and various *experience* of actually *producing* sociology, anthropology and so on. This is what I do here.

This chapter examines research produced for the British Sports Council (North West Region). It was a piece of 'traditional' research, the findings of which will no doubt be seen as 'objective facts' by many of its readers. In contrast, the emphasis in this chapter is that *any* piece of research is a product resulting from consequential practices and processes which influence what the nature of that research product is to be. In essence my argument is that an objective world of facts about leisure do not exist for the feminist sociologist to gather up; but, rather, knowledge about leisure is socially interpreted and created.

The 'point' of the chapter is to demonstrate that the research product is an account, but also to emphasise that so too is this chapter. All accounts are partial; they hide more than they provide. This is not therefore the 'complete ABC' of every relevant aspect of my research process, for how could it be? What I have chosen to explore is how 'data collection' is effectively 'data *construction*'; I discuss this mainly in relation to the statistical data I dealt with, although I could have argued a very similar case in relation to the participant observation work that was also a component of my research brief.

The research project

The research was undertaken during a five-month period and involved two months of data collection and three months of analysis and writing. My research brief from the Sports Council was as follows:

1 The first part of the research was concerned to detail the objectives of a 'Water Adventure Centre' (WAC).
2 The second part of the research was concerned to examine the extent to which these objectives were being achieved. In particular it focussed on:
    (a) the use of the centre by groups, and individuals within groups;
    (b) the use of the centre by individual local members;
    (c) the views of groups and individuals on the objectives and practice of the centre, especially in relation to outdoor activities;
    (d) the value of the centre as perceived by groups and individuals;
    (e) the other outdoor activities in which groups and individuals using the centre engage;
    (f) other outdoor activities in which groups and individuals using the centre would like to engage.

In the first part of the research information was supplied primarily by semi-structured interviews with key personnel at the centre: its founder, Chairperson of the Executive Committee, two members of the Executive Committee and the six workers. Written information, such as previous annual reports, Executive Meeting minutes and draft discussion papers, were also made available to me. In the second part of the research, the principal research method was participant observation. This was supplemented with semi-structured interviews with local users and questionnaires for group users.

The research took place when the centre's outdoor activities were prominent. It also looked at differences between the six weeks' summer holiday and the period immediately before this. Data collection began in mid-June and continued until the last week of August. Because of the seasonal pattern in the centre's operation, research during the winter would have focussed on a different aspect of the Water Adventure Centre's activities.

Seeking Susan

Here I am concerned with how a lived social experience – an interview – is transformed into statistical data. I have entitled this section 'Seeking Susan' because, paradoxically, once a statistical table is produced there is no way in which the ordinary reader can seek and find the individuals and their experiences which are what the table is supposedly 'about'. I use the example of Susan (all the names in this chapter bar my own are fictitious) because, like a great majority of the young people at the WAC, she was so interesting. However, making sense of this 'experience of and with her' for the purposes of research means stripping *her* from *it* in order to produce 'a number' as a generalising gloss. As this is different in *form*, not just *degree*, from 'the data' I started out with, it is useful to see how this happens. I begin with some background information concerning the interview with Susan.

In the interview transcript which follows, Susan's words were taken down as near verbatim as possible. In contrast, my words were constructed *post hoc*: I didn't write down my words in the actual interview situation because I wanted to keep the flow of conversation as near to an ordinary conversation as possible. For the same reason, the interviews did not consist of a series of pre-set questions which I read out; rather, I had a mental list of all the areas I wanted to cover in the interview, and asked them in a way appropriate to each particular interview experience.

The interview was done during the last week of my fieldwork at the WAC during a very busy session, with girls and boys all over the place. Susan and I sat on the stairs of the WAC building. This was a very sociable place as many boys and girls sat there talking to their friends. Some of Susan's friends had been interviewed, and they said to her why don't you tell Denise why you came and what you think of it. Her friends and other people were all around us as we sat and talked.

Readers may be thinking that those friends would influence what Susan says; and of course, as they too were part of this interview situation, they will have been important constituents in what happened. All I could do was note that as I sat talking to her she seemed to be all right and not disturbed by the others. However, as to how influential her friends were, all I can do is speculate. At the end of the day those were the responses she made to me: those were my data. Part of the actual interview is as follows:

DENISE:	How old are you?
SUSAN:	Ten.
DENISE:	How long have you been coming?
SUSAN:	About two weeks.
DENISE:	How did you find out about it?
SUSAN:	I was just walking past with Jenny me mate, and we saw all these kids in the canal having a right laugh, and then Mark, though we didn't know it was him at the time, paddled over to where we was and told us all about it. Then he got John to get us some membership cards and

we went off straight away and got our mums to sign it –
then we came back straight away with our stuff and had
our first go.

DENISE: And what did you think?

SUSAN: It was ACE, dead brilliant, you know? That first day, well,
it was really, really good; I enjoyed it, made new friends
and decided to come again.

DENISE: What d'ya like best?

SUSAN: The canoeing, definitely the canoeing, I couldn't believe
that I could actually do it...it's like well, yer get a great
feeling of power in a canoe, freedom and power when you
can feel your strength pulling against the water.

DENISE: How did you learn to canoe?

SUSAN: I learnt myself when I first got in, I got offers of help, but
you pick it up by yourself, don't ya? Getting in the canoe
was the scariest part, but you soon manage to handle it.

DENISE: And what d'ya think of the other water activities, like the
raft and the rubber rings?

SUSAN: At first I didn't like those rings, they looked dead
unstable, you know, just look at her there, she's soaking
and she can't get back on it properly; well I didn't fancy it
at all 'cos you do get drenched. But when I capsized one
day, last Tuesday it was, I was already wet through so I
thought I might as well have a go; Jill and them were
messin' around in them at the time so I thought I'd be OK.
And I was, it was dead good we had a real laugh and I
wished I'd got in 'em sooner.

DENISE: And the raft?

SUSAN: It's OK, but the lads are always on it. I really hate them.

DENISE: Why?

SUSAN: 'Cos look at them, they're always in our way, there's so
many of them and they're always splashing you, they
think it's a joke, some joke.

DENISE: Do ya go to girls' afternoon?

SUSAN: Yeah.

DENISE: What d'ya think?

SUSAN: It's good, they're not in the way then and you can get on
with it.

DENISE: What d'ya do when they start messin' around you?

SUSAN: I give 'em what for.

DENISE: What d'ya mean?

SUSAN: I splash 'em back and that but when they're on the raft we
all start to shout at them, but there's usually more of them

and we just get 'em shouting and splashing, we splash but
we can never move 'em.

DENISE: Do you understand why there is a girls' afternoon?

SUSAN: Yeah, 'cos some girls want time to be on their own
without the lads messin' so they can have a laugh and play
on the rafts and that.

DENISE: And you like it?

SUSAN: Yeah.

DENISE: Have you made a lot of friends here?

SUSAN: Yeah, that's one of the dead good things about this place,
everyone's dead friendly, that's one of the reasons I keep
coming. I like the canoeing, that's dead good but well it
makes all the difference dunnit? Like, if you came and
everyone was a bit funny with you, you wouldn't keep
coming back would you? See them all there?

DENISE: Yeah.

SUSAN: Well, I'm dead friendly with 'em, they call for me to come
here, and yet two weeks ago I didn't even know 'em! It's
a really good place, it's the type of place where you could
come down on your own and you'd be OK. It's sort of like
a big family.

DENISE: D'ya see any of these friends outside the WAC?

SUSAN: Well only when they come to call for me....

Out of this rich interview, Susan's responses were turned into constituents of statistical tables, like the following:

Table 6.1 Sources of information about the WAC

	Girls	Boys	Total
Friends	10	9	19
Walking past and saw it:			
(a) Saw – asked themselves	6	6	12
(b) Saw – approached by workers	5	3	8
By coming with a group	3	4	7
Sisters or brothers	1	1	2
Saw Zoë in the precinct	1	0	1
Found a membership card in the hills, previously thought it was private	0	1	1
Parents walking past saw it	0	1	1
Not asked	1	0	1
	27	25	52

How does Susan fit into this? How is the transformation accomplished?

The first step happened at the time of the interview itself. As we sat there I also scribbled away in one of my notebooks. After we had finished, Susan went back to playing in the canal in a boat and I was left with the pages full of writing. This was now divorced from the context of which it had been a part and wherein it had been produced.

During the fieldwork part of the research I had no time for any rigorous analysis of the interview, I just gave them a quick skim through at night, adding any further words that came to mind that I hadn't managed to scribble down. Although I wasn't consciously analysing these materials, I was in a way doing so because each interview I did or read led to rough comparisons in my head with what had gone on in other interviews. This prior experience will have influenced my talk with Susan, and what kinds of questions and probes I asked of her. For example, I ask at one point: 'D'ya see any of these friends outside the WAC?' This was due to responses from previous interviewees who had said, when I asked them about making friends at WAC, that they'd also gone out with these new friends to other clubs and took part in other activities together.

After the fieldwork had finished I put all the interview schedules into a pile, in a rough sequential order. I started reading quickly through the ones that were on the top. I read about fifteen of them in this quick manner. I didn't make any notes at this stage, I just wanted a feel of the information I'd got on certain questions: had enough kids said something about the 'same' subject? Roughly how many 'subjects' had been covered? What counted as a 'subject' and what was interlinked? And what was irrelevant?

In reading through at this stage, I was looking ahead, not just to the next stage but also to the end of the process – 'the statistics' – and this doubtless informed my opinion of what was the 'same', what was 'important' and 'irrelevant' and so on. It was also very much dependent on my knowledge-so-far, from what I'd experienced during the participant observation and from the experience of the interviews themselves.

The next stage was to think of ways of chopping the interviews up, of making them more manageable, to separate out discrete parcels of information on the 'same' thing. My practical purpose wasn't to understand 'Susan' as a whole, but to examine how bits of 'her' compared to bits of other people. This is, I think, the crux of the quantitative methods approach, certainly as I experience it.

To try and put these things into action I decided to go through a process of transferring the information from the interviews to a larger piece of paper, so that the information could be compared to other people and I could see this at a glance. There were fifty-two interviews. Textbooks generally advise you to read through a good number of interviews and construct a codebook, and/or write down in full the response of a number of interviews and then construct your codebook. In contrast I decided that I wanted the 'gist' of a whole, all its inter-connections and richness; and from this I would produce a codebook. However, the process wasn't as straightforward as it might sound. The only piece of paper I could find which was the right length was wall-paper: I could just keep unrolling it. I put down the side of the paper a list of the interviewees' names; then across the top I put a list of headings which correspond to the questions and subject areas I had asked about. For example:

	Age	How long been coming	How found out about WAC
Susan			
Pete			
John			
Pat			
Steve			
Gaynor			

In the previous stage, when I had skimmed through the interviews, I was keen to see what were discrete bodies of information. I wanted to know how much space to leave for this information – that is, how big the columns needed to be under these headings – for if there was a large range of responses the columns would have to be wide.

In creating the headings across the page, I took the first interview and read the first few lines and created the first few columns. Say, for the sake of illustration, the first interview I picked up was Susan's; I went through and put across the top as headings:

	Age	How long been coming	How found out about WAC
Susan	10	about two weeks	I was just walking past. . .

I continued with this process until the end of the first interview, creating the headings and putting the information in. Because of my knowledge from skimming through the interviews, I also left room for columns to be inserted, because I knew there were some questions that 'had come up' in other interviews but not with Susan and vice versa.

I also decided to put the information down word for word, as I wanted to keep it in full at this stage. However, after transferring the first few interviews this became extremely tedious so I went into note form, still taking copious notes but losing the words which I thought didn't add much to their meaning for this practical purpose. For example:

Me Dad was walking past and saw it. He thought it looked dead good and he thought it 'ud be somewhere I could go, so he came in and asked Jane who was standing around on the bank and she told him all about it...

became in note form:

Dad was walking past, saw it, thought it looked good, asked Jane.

This process was carried out for the next twenty interviews. I then read through the whole lot, just quickly surveying the pattern which was emerging. Then I did the other thirty interviews, and here my notes became shorter and shorter. By this time I had gained a grasp of the typical responses. In doing this certain processes and outcomes were involved:

1 Some of the columns weren't wide enough for all the information, others were too wide.
2 Some columns had a quantity of information which in turn could be broken down into further sub-sections of 'separate' pieces of information.
3 Because some information could go into one or two columns, and other information didn't have a column, and yet other information didn't have a column on its own – an extremely large miscellaneous column developed; sometimes there were problems about which column to put information in; my rule of thumb here was, when in doubt, duplicate.
4 I was already reducing the richness of the response given by cutting down. Material was being lost and made unrecoverable.
5 The whole of what Susan said was now separated and a new whole was created; that is, a whole list of information on, for example, how young people found out about the WAC.
6 Relatedly, the order in which Susan had said things was rearranged in this new format. In all the interviews, although I attempted to cover the same ground, the order in which I transcribed especially the first interview led to the order in which the column headings were written. This then became the order in which the information was put.
7 Also, in looking at this master sheet, physically it looked very

uneven. Some kids had said many things on a certain subject, others hadn't said very much, and so on. But at the end of the day, whatever the volume of response to any one subject, these all had to be equalled out and made to count as 'the same'.

8   This process was extremely tedious.

My decisions on relevancy (and inclusion) or irrelevancy (and exclusion) depended on the frequency of response and also what the main themes of my report were going to be. At this stage, these were still being worked out. In a way it would depend upon what the statistics would tell me, but, as I hadn't produced the statistics yet, this depended on my knowledge-thus-far. The other prime and interlinked consideration was the research brief and the questions this was addressing – I say 'interlinked' because this influenced the kinds of things I was interested in during my WAC experience (which might not have been the same had this been 'pure' rather than commissioned research).

The next stage was to look at each column, examining the frequency and type of responses and what seemed to be the most important. From this I produced a small list of the most frequent responses: my codes. Codes are essentially summarising devices, under which 'what-counts-as-the-same-knowledge-for-this-practical-purpose' is marshalled. This was the part of the process I really hated, as although in most columns there was a certain amount (which varied) of responses which could be seen as the same, there were always some that couldn't.

I produced quite a long list of codes; again I was trying to keep as close to the data as possible. It was at this stage that I felt most constrained by the use of quantitative methods because, even though I had made quite a few decisions to ensure rich, in-depth material and produce it, what did I now have to do with it? If I wanted to produce statistics, then I had to follow the conventions as to what counts as a competent statistic and have only a small number of eventual codes.

The table at the beginning of this section shows the results of my coding of responses concerning how the young people found out about the WAC. Why did I code thus? The most important thing which guided me, following the actual responses themselves, was my knowledge and experience of the setting. For example, I separated out into two codes the young people who came to WAC (1) because they were approached by the workers and (2) who came of their own accord and then asked someone about it. I did this because, during the fieldwork, I had seen a lot of kids walking past, and the workers would go to them and tell them all about WAC. This I thought was a really good thing as it made the young people feel welcome in this 'new' place and it also made sure they knew it was open to them and wasn't private.

Another category I used was 'approached by Zoë'. I could have coded this in with 'approached by the workers'. I gave it a separate code even though there was only one response, because it was an important part of the work Zoë had started doing, going to local shopping precincts and other gathering places to tell girls about the centre.

My knowledge of the setting was helpful in more fundamental ways. This includes knowing things like who 'Zoë' is, but also provides me with contextual specifics such that I can count as 'the same', 'I came with a group' and 'I came with the Guides' because I know that the Guides is a regular user group, rather than a one-off group of girls who were also Guides.

The basic point here is that there is no such thing as objective coding; rather, contextual information is required to make sense of these responses (as other commentators have noted, coders who have only the interview schedules to go on use their knowledge of these as a set to provide this contextual knowledge). During the coding process a socio-logical vanishing trick has occurred wherein the uniqueness of what Susan has said has disappeared in the final format. All the things which were interesting about *her* have been removed; her experience has been sieved through my classificatory schema. The product is composed of 'mere numbers' which, by definition, exclude the specific experience. The statistic so formed *constructs* the reality within the numbers yet appears as if it were simply just *commentating* on it. It also constructs for us 'types of behaviour' and 'types of people' who do this behaviour.

Some implications

The place of the researcher in the research process

The title I have given this chapter implicitly conjures up the image of the researcher doing things on and to respondents/participants. In a sense power is involved; but just what is 'power'? Certainly I made the decision to use questionnaires, interviews and so on; I decided what questions to ask, it was my frame of reference imposed on what the respondents said, my frame of reference imposed on the coding of the results, and I wrote up the 'findings' in the research report.

But it was more complex than this makes it sound. For example: 'I made the decision to use questionnaires.' Well, yes I did. But this decision didn't occur in a vacuum: it was made after long talks with the workers at the WAC in particular, and also with the supervisors of the research. Also, 'I imposed my frame of reference on what the respondents said'. In talking to the young people during interviews, yes I did ask the questions (or most of them) but they always had the right to reply, and sometimes this reply knocked me for six. The way in which I imposed my frame of reference varied – it depended on the interactional specifics of what I said there and then, and what the young person said in reply. However, this is not to deny that they neither did nor could write the research report or this chapter, both of which present to a wider and anonymous audience aspects of their lives and experiences.

What are statistics?

Statistics are conventionally seen as a *representation* of social reality, one which has a strict *correspondence* with the reality so presented. My argument, in contrast, has been that statistics are a *construction* of reality. They have their own social organisation, and this is inextricably linked to the social organisation of reality, but in a rather different way from that suggested by the conventional view.

Once produced, statistics have a life of their own. They appear as if they exist in their own right. In part this is due to cultural convention – this is the way we 'see' things. However, in larger part it is because they pass out of the researcher's control: the report comments on them, but also they are 'there' for the reader to make what they will of them. The researcher's interpretation is highly linked, as I emphasised earlier, to knowledge of the particular research context. However, statistics are then divorced from the context of their construction and thus lose the meanings they had for the people involved; moreover, readers bring to them their own 'reading context' (Lury 1982).

I have argued that *ad hoc* reasoning, contextually located knowledge, interpretation and so on are at the heart of supposedly more 'interpretive' approaches. These approaches are not poles apart in the way traditionally conceived, for the same interpretive procedures necessarily underpin *both*. It is often said that ethnography/participant observation embodies one person's subjectivism, one person's power and control. But in my experience, this 'subjectivism' is just as central to more traditional methods as it is to interpretive ones (Farran 1985). And although traditionally it is questionnaires which are seen as partial and cutting down the richness of data, I found that although my participant observation got me beautiful, rich, complex data, I also had to cut these down into 'crude' data because they were *too* rich. I simply hadn't time or space to do them justice.

© 1990 Denise Farran

References

Farran, Denise (1985) 'Practices in the Compilation of Fieldwork Notes',

Department of Sociology, University of Manchester, Occasional Paper No.18.

Lury, Celia (1982) 'An Ethnography of an Ethnography: Reading Sociology', Department of Sociology, University of Manchester, Occasional Paper No.9.

Wimbush, Erica and Talbot, Margaret (eds) (1988) *Relative Freedoms: Women and Leisure*, Milton Keynes: Open University Press.

Chapter seven

My statistics and feminism –
a true story

Anne Pugh

Introduction

This chapter discusses some work I have done on statistics and which is reported more fully in *Counting Homelessness: Statistics in Shades* (Pugh 1986a). First, I say something about this statistics work itself, then I show how my feminism affects the research process and, indeed, in what ways I regard this particular research process as feminist. I also assess the research product in terms of a feminist perspective.

These statistics concern young homeless people's usage of a small youth advice and counselling agency, Shades. Shades, a voluntary organisation, has four paid workers, of which I am the research worker, and is based in Manchester's city centre, in the north west of England. My statistics work was in two parts: the first was a statistical summary of some aspects of Shades usage (Pugh 1986a); the second was a critique of this first statistics study (Pugh 1986b).

Part 1: the statistics study

As an organisation, Shades had a number of reasons for an interest in statistics. One was the need for accountability to our funders, the local Social Services Department. In the time-honoured tradition we assumed that this meant quantifying usage (how many people came into Shades and in what circumstances), to supply facts to demonstrate what we did and that the service was essential and working well. This was comparatively easy to do, not too time-consuming, and it allowed us to get on with the work that we were really doing. Yet why were we bothering with an exercise that we knew did not adequately reflect or summarise our work on Shades usage?

As an agency we supported a philosophy of quality not quantity in our youth work, and always stated that we did not believe in 'playing the numbers game'. Yet we did: we did rough and ready head counts and tabulations in all our reports. We were, it seemed, fascinated by numbers and allocated to them a power and legitimacy about which, though, we always felt ambiguous. So it was decided that I should do a study on Shades usage, thus compiling some statistics on youth homelessness; and relatedly I should consider our stance on statistics: the role of counting and numbers in our youth work organisation.

I set to work on the task of translating the variety of the comings and goings at Shades into a form amenable to quantitative analysis. Here was my first stumbling block: different people use Shades in ways as different as their lives. Newcomers are almost invariably homeless (and penniless), but the circumstances of their homelessness are as many and varied as the people themselves. Their needs change and their reasons for visiting Shades vary as their relationship with the agency changes and develops.

In a summary of Shades usage I was looking for the reasons why people visited Shades: was it to use the phones, sort out their Social Security benefit, socialise, have a cup of tea, talk confidentially with a worker, volunteer or friend, ask about courses, or find out about contraception? Often it was all of these things – and more. The nature of the agency itself, with its emphasis on developing relationships which facilitate the young people's personal development, is at odds with an approach which relies on hard-and-fast categorising. Yet I also felt that the difficulties that I faced were not peculiar to Shades. After all, other statistics-makers face a similarly complex social world, yet they arrive at what they presumably regard as satisfactory decisions.

So I pressed on, refining and defining my area of study until it became of manageable proportions. Practical considerations, agency ways of working and constraints entailed using existing records as the data. These were constituted by Shades' 'Day Book', a log of comings and goings written by workers, volunteers and the young people, and some forms. The latter were devised by me as summaries of the Day Book entries and they were completed at the end of each week by the other workers. Using the Day Book, the other workers would translate its entries on to the forms.

Later, I had to further refine these forms: categories were thrown out as unviable or irrelevant until I was left with the following variables as my basic data for the study:

Name
Date
Age
Sex
Ethnicity
Referrer
Where they are from

Homeless or not
Sexuality

I took a six-month period of forms, April to September, and transformed these into a shape ready for mainframe computer analysis, using the software package SPSS. There were 268 cases (people) in the data set and this represented the number of Shades users in the profiles being completed by me. I chased up any gaps by referring back to the Day Book or by asking my colleagues at Shades. Completing the profiles needed a fair amount of detective work on my part, piecing together bits of information until I had something that made sense and had filled all the blank cells in my matrix, albeit sometimes with a 'don't know'.

My intention to construct a visits' profile for each person was not fulfilled. The visits' profiles were beyond the scope of the study because the forms had established the individual person as the basic unit of analysis, not each visit. I either had to abandon the intention of constructing a visits' profile or abandon the forms. Since the forms appeared to provide more than enough to be going on with, I decided in favour of abandoning the visits' profile, reserving it for future studies.

Once on the computer, I developed my data into some statistics. Using these I was able to explore some hypotheses, which had indeed been the aim of the study. I was able to comment on such issues as how many people used Shades, were they increasing or decreasing, whether they were local to Manchester or came from further afield, their age range, their ethnicity, whether young women's experience of homelessness was different from men's, all of which were important to Shades in its policy formation. The data and its analysis could also be useful for other organisations or groups with an interest in youth homelessness in Britain.

Part 2: the critique of the first study

Mission accomplished then? I had, after all, produced some statistics and was able to use them to provide some comment on young homeless people's situation. Unfortunately, I was less than happy with the process of producing the statistics. I knew what tricks I had had to perform to create them and then make them speak to me: all of which, I might add, are conventional and ethical procedures in research terms. Further, my misgivings were compounded by my failure to recognise any of the homeless young people that I knew in my statistics. What was this all about? I wondered, and consequently started the second study.

This second study amounts to a critique of the first. It unwraps the processes of creating the statistics, examines what they represent and looks at their connections to the life at Shades which they are intended to summarise but seem to obliterate. I trace the careers of some of the statistics, selecting the ones that I know most about from my own experience as a worker in Shades when I met these young people and recorded their visits in the Day Book. I took all my entries in the Day Book in the six-month period of April to September and examined what place that entry had in the statistics study. In doing this I investigated the correspondence, if any, between the Day Book entry, the people involved, and the statistics study.

In this second study, by examining entries in the Day Book – which are the source of the statistics – I discovered that my statistics are a very particular and partial representation of Shades usage. For example, many of these entries do not figure in the statistics at all. Some are excluded by virtue of not being visits by young people (for example, they are entries about phone calls or passing on arrangements for rendezvous, aspects of Shades usage which had to be excluded from the study on practical grounds). And this, I discovered, was one of the main problems of the statistics: they represented a very partial and dilute look at Shades usage, certainly a mini-demography of some homeless young people, but one where it was easy to forget the context of the statistics production and ignore their humble origins, so that other people – outsiders to their production process – would construe them as general statements about youth homelessness.

Importantly, even the recordings that are included in the statistics study, the ones which represent visits by young people, often leave a lot to be desired. For example, Dick (entry 100 in the study) is not counted as homeless, even though his housing circumstances are similar to Geoff's (entry 13), who *is* counted as homeless. This is because of the agency's perception of Dick as an older hand who can handle living in the arduous circumstances of bed-and-breakfast-land, whereas the novice Geoff is younger and this is not thought of as appropriate accommodation for him. In the study's definition somebody was homeless if they did not have 'suitable accommodation' available to them. Geoff was homeless then, quite clearly; but Dick slipped through as 'not homeless'. Deciding whether somebody is homeless or not is certainly not without its problems; and, as in this example, any replies will vary with people's perceptions and priorities. The statistics here tell you more about Shades as the rate-producing agency than about the housing situation of these two people.

In the course of the second study I uncovered some of the difficulties entailed in the process of constructing Shades statistics. Some of these difficulties could be termed doubts about the study's internal reliability, established through detective work. This was sometimes straightforward, but often, as in the example above, it was not. How do you decide: if somebody really is homeless; whether you have got their age recorded correctly; where they really come from; where they have been staying for the past year? There were even difficulties in deciding apparently simple factual things like whether somebody had used the emergency one-night stay, night-stop facility: Kathy (entry 11) had gone to the night-stop house, I had left her there, but she went out later that night and did not return. My Shades colleagues had filled the form in as Yes/No in the night-stop column. Finally I opted for yes; she had after all been there.

These difficulties are intrinsic to the topic and I would argue intrinsic to statistics research in most social settings. Improvements could of course be made – for example, by using more sophisticated techniques or by being more thorough. Yet these improvements would not resolve the central difficulties. That is, at some stage a code would still have to be assigned applying a definition of, say, homelessness or usage of the night-stop house, which would be more valid to some conditions than to others. I am suggesting that the internal reliability of such studies is always going to be a problem, for life will always be more complex and ambiguous than any possible usable system of coding and classification.

In themselves, these reservations do not negate the value of my or any other statistics studies. My argument is a different one: that such reservations are not spelt out, publicised or seen as an essential means of understanding statistics and without which they do not make realistic sense. In writing, and often in teaching, these and other difficulties are made light of and removed from existence. Instead statistics assume a monopoly of utility and knowledge. They become very powerful and are credited with being scientific measurements, 'the facts', and are the definitive and authoritative statement of 'what is'.

In the analysis of my statistics, by way of contrast, I can point not only to the statistics' partial and sometimes inadequate summary of their intended social reality, but also to other means of researching that social reality. There are other equally legitimate ways of researching a topic, and depending upon your concerns and what you are trying to find out or demonstrate, these might be more useful or appropriate. Instead, though, the statistics type of approach gains the political upper hand as being real research, as providing 'the facts'.

For instance, I recognise that many different types of homelessness are lumped together in the statistics study as if they were the same thing. It might be useful to analyse some of these different experiences, for example by comparing Dick's homelessness to Geoff's, which is different from Karen's, and use the statistics in the service of this study rather than the other way round. It is only a close inspection which reveals the damage done to the data, the juggling and the transformations that have had to be undertaken in order to get people to fit into their statistical boxes. In the critique of the statistics' study I discover alternative ways of researching my entries in the Day Book, different ways of summarising them – for example, so as to investigate the concept of care in the community for the institutionalised group or how the process of labelling influences the interactions between Shades and the young homeless people.

The statistics, then, by no means constitute the 'objective facts' of what is going on, a status which is ordinarily and commonly assumed for them. In the introduction I mentioned that I could not recognise any of the homeless young people that I knew in the statistics which purported to be summaries about them: the statistics have a problematic connection with the life they claim to represent. For example, one of the findings of the statistical research is that 16- and 17-year-old women are particularly vulnerable to homelessness and prey to circumstances, thus needing special treatment and to be looked after. For young males, however, my findings suggest that the statistics counteract the dominant image of the wandering drifter with multiple problems, replacing it with ordinary young men in housing need. The statistics contribute to the formation of a new ideology or stereotyping about homeless people.

However, most (or to put it more strongly, more than three-quarters) of the women in the study are far removed from this image of the victim. They are lively, competent and shrewd. They know what to do and how to go about it, if only they had the opportunity to get themselves decently housed. Some of the young men, on the other hand, actually do approach the homeless stereotype of readily apparent social problems; others of them are nearer the counter-image that Shades is trying to project; and still others fall in between.

Similarly, very different phenomena are lumped together in the statistics study as if they were the same thing: Sue's homelessness, entry 5 (a 16-year-old pregnant incest survivor from a middle-class family), is taken as the same thing as Grant's homelessness, entry 109 (a 26-year-old institutionalised aggressive male who has a drink problem). Their homelessness and other details are compared and contrasted, put together in various permutations, as if this was relevant to anything. The only thing they have in common is that, by a variety of routes, they have arrived at Shades. But what Sue and Grant show is that the dynamic of some people's contact with Shades is their homelessness, whereas for others their homelessness is merely a symptom of something else and not the real issue. Yet in the statistics' study there is only one criterion: homeless or not. And this, it is assumed, actually gives you the facts about homelessness.

Part 3: are this woman's statistics feminist?

In my original study on statistics I followed accepted and conventional procedures for compiling statistics, procedures which are common and legitimate amongst social researchers. But I was not happy with the process or the results. Something was wrong with these statistics and now I would conclude that the piece of work runs contrary to some of my usual ways of working as a feminist. The critique of these statistics that I describe in the above section attempts to remedy this and as such draws on a feminist perspective as its inspiration. In this final section I illustrate how feminism is and is not present in my work.

A feminist approach makes you aware of relationships of power, of who gets what and why. As members of a 'minority' group, some women have become finely tuned to the nuances and discrepancies of power, such as why relationships are structured in a certain way, who benefits from these arrangements, and the injustice of them. As a feminist I am accustomed to questioning relationships of power to see what lies behind them – why is the status quo like it is and are 'the facts' indeed the facts? Considerations like these are close to the inspiration of feminism.

Feminism provides a way of looking at the world and a set of values which will influence how you approach a topic (and indeed, at least in theory, how you live your life). Feminist concerns include understanding social relationships, pointing out inequalities, injustices and discrimination, how resources are allocated and, for example, why and how women's lives have been marginalised and disregarded as domestic or 'only' servicing others. As a feminist I understand just how important servicing relationships are, how central the personal aspects are in everyday life. Much of women's experience has traditionally been hidden from view. As a feminist, then, I am accustomed to questioning the apparent surface realities and the accepted ways of doing things. This is how I approached my critique of my statistics.

I was suspicious of the easy power my statistics commanded, for I felt that this was at the expense of other equally legitimate or more credible alternatives. In the critique I unmask the statistics, showing how they were compiled, what their constituent relationships are, and I question their worthiness in the role of being 'IT' in research terms. I try to knock them down to size, suggesting that they do have a place in research, which is alongside other ways of summarising social settings but not necessarily in a paramount or superior position *vis-à-vis* these other ways.

Statistics, I would suggest, need chaperoning. Users do all sorts of things to even good statistics if these are let out into the world on their own: they use them in inappropriately generalising ways, taking them away from the context of production and generalising them to entirely different contexts. To be of any use, statistics need to be closely supervised and kept within their originating context – otherwise all sorts of claims are made on their behalf. In fact, in 'cutting statistics down to size', I suggest that they should be used in the service of their localised contexts. In this way statistics can remain meaningful and relevant to people, they can recognise the summaries that the statistics are presenting and flesh out these numerical generalisations with contextual detail. My critique of Shades' statistical study encourages a diversity of research investigations, recognising that there is hardly ever only one right answer or approach to an issue. These concerns of context, relevance and the experience of the servicing relationships and a suspicion of monopolistic claims on the part of statistics are inspired, at least in my case, by my feminism.

There is more to feminist research than work done by and about women. For instance, in my statistics paper (Pugh 1986a) I consider women as separate from men, something which is indeed a progressive step; however, it is still tokenist, for in the way the study is structured women get a separate mention which, it can be argued, maintains their marginal position. It would be much better if the study was organised along lines suggested in my critique, which would consider the variety of interests at the outset. My statistical study had women as a topic, yet I do not regard it as feminist.

Instead, I regard my statistics as being crude, on the macho side, simplistically commanding. Numbers have an appeal, and indeed they are powerful. Their power needs to be used circumspectly: we need to recognise that numbers can be used in the same way as we use words – as a way of putting forward a case, a point of view, an alternative to other possibilities, and without suggesting that they deserve awed obedience because they are apparently 'hard' measurements. They are not. They are only numbers: they are constructed, as words are in an ethnography; and they reflect their construction *even if outsiders do not know enough about the context of production to recognise this*. Equally it is important not to be frightened by statistics, to let them intimidate you, or naïvely to believe that 'statistics = bad'. Counting is an everyday action basic to many activities. Statistics need to be demystified. Yet their power remains: '75 per cent' sounds stronger, more assertive than saying 'most' or even 'three-quarters'. Numbers have an impact, but they are no more scientific or objective or correct than anything else. Their actual status depends on their context and the frames of reference of those who construct them.

The process of creating the statistics is crucial to their outcome: the relationships of their creation need to be evident, put alongside the statistics, in order for the statistics to remain sensible. How the statistics were made will tell you a lot about them, and then they can be connected back to what they are in fact measuring. Too often they are divorced from the life they are supposed to represent, as was the case with the Shades statistics.

My original statistics, upon further investigation, are more a measure of Shades' organisational priorities and practices, things which in themselves are legitimate areas of study, than they are a measure of objective rates of homelessness. For in deciding who was and who was not homeless, I was presenting an agency view and perception, rather than measuring youth homelessness, as the statistics appear to suggest.

My statistics were divorced from their context, and consequently people's lives and experiences are lost in the study. The statistics do not reflect the lives of the young homeless: I do not recognise the young people in the images that the statistics encourage. Yet as a feminist researcher I aspire to respect and portray people's experiences, something which is hard to achieve in my conventionally done statistical study.

My critique of the statistical study is, I have argued, more in line with feminist principles. Here I recognised my own central role as researcher and sought to use that positively in the research process. I decided to unwrap the statistics that I had created so as to see how they had been put together and what they did and did not represent. I did this drawing on my experience in, first, making the statistics, and, second, by relating these statistics to my own entries in the Day Book. I was my primary source of data: using my work as a fieldworker in Shades, I selected my entries because these were the ones I knew most about. I knew what was written down and what was left out and the meanings behind the entries because I had written them. Thus I was in the best position that any researcher could be in to make assessments of the connections between the Day Book entries, the young people and the statistics. Other approaches may avoid using the researcher's own experience on the grounds that this may introduce 'bias'; in complete contrast I use my 'subjectivity', my socially enacted and analytically recoverable practices as a Shades worker, as a strength which can help uncover what is going on. My own experience is central to the critique and is used as the constructive element instead of something to be controlled or avoided.

Conclusions

My feminist appraisal of my statistics work leads me to conclude that, with due attention to the research process of producing them, there is a place for statistics in feminist as well as other research. Specific statistics can be created that serve a wider research aim. For example, in the case of homeless people, statistics are usually cited to say that there are X homeless people. On its own this statistic tells you very little about homelessness and encourages the sort of deadlock which currently characterised the homelessness debates: we say there are X thousand forced to sleep on the streets every night and it's getting worse; policy-makers absorb this 'pressure'. Whereas if those of us involved in agencies dealing with the young homeless were able to produce statistics which were servicing a more realistic (in experiential terms) portrayal of youth homelessness, these studies might command more serious attention than is currently experienced. These sorts of statistics, I have argued here, are possible within a feminist framework which considers the researcher as central in the research process and which challenges the monopoly by statistics of correct practice and correct research products.

© 1990 Anne Pugh

References

Pugh, Anne (1986a) *Counting Homelessness: Statistics in Shades*, Working Paper No. 8, Applied Social Research, Sociology Department, University of Manchester.
——(1986b) 'Deconstructing Shades Statistics: the Day Book Entries', unpublished M.A. dissertation, Sociology Department, University of Manchester.

Chapter eight

'A referral was made'

Behind the scenes during the creation of a Social
Services Department 'elderly' statistic

Liz Stanley

A feminist preamble

This chapter deals with tragedy in the lives of two elderly people, much
of which could have been easily avoided. Its two 'parts' are, first, a
paper that I gave at a conference of the Social Services Research Group
(SSRG) and later published (Stanley 1988); and, second, a feminist
postscript to this which adds material played down or omitted in the
paper.

The 'official' paper is concerned with research methods and the
necessity for more Social Services research to be done by 'insiders':
people writing from and about their own experience as research
workers, as social workers, as care assistants and so on, rather than yet
more 'scientific' research on Social Services. However, as the postscript
makes apparent, there are two sub-texts within it.

One is concerned with the 'official paper's' role in working out, more
or less between the written lines, my own emotional and intellectual
engagement in and with the 'case study of the Westons'. The other is
why this was not dealt with overtly: because it involved themes and
issues I was either unwilling to discuss with a non-feminist audience or
which I felt I could not deal with if I did so in the form I would want to
(that is, in a feminist form).

Introduction

The Social Care and Research Seminar (SCARS) had an active life from
just after the publication of the Barclay Report on the role and tasks of
British social workers in 1982, until 1986. The SCARS seminar was
based in the Sociology Department at Manchester University and
composed partly by feminist social and community workers, partly by
feminist academics and researchers. SCARS seminars discussed many
substantive topics, but in doing so focussed on 'carers' and 'caring'
from various analytic viewpoints (for example, EOC 1980, 1982; Finch
1984; Finch and Groves 1983). Its discussions are reflected in a

collection of papers, which covers a wide range of topics and themes on 'care', including the process of feminist research and evaluation itself (SCARS 1986). This present discussion is of a case study of a particular 'elderly referral' made to the local Area office of a southern Social Services Department (referred to hereafter as 'Southern SSD'). This case study was originally discussed in a number of SCARS sessions. It sheds interesting light on the role – both actual and potential – of SSD researchers in the production of 'knowledge', in the form of statistics. In doing so it also demonstrates that such knowledge represents only the visible tip – '*official* institutional knowledge' – of a large iceberg of events, some of which involved practitioners but most of which did not.

The case study is of an elderly married couple, referred to hereafter as 'the Westons', and is one in which I was at times involved as a carer; this is how I came to gain the 'unofficial' knowledge at my disposal. Specific features of the case, and in particular the interaction between a social worker and one of the main participants, debarred the SSD from most of the official knowledge that *could* have been collected, in case notes and similar official means of recording information, but was not. Initially this was because the social worker failed to elicit this information, later it was deliberately withheld from him, and later still it was because 'the case' was closed although its actual events continued unabated.

The case study illustrates salient features of the relationship between 'official' knowledge of one form or another but especially local SSD statistics and how these relate to other, central government, statistical knowledge. It also illustrates something of the usually unrecorded (and therefore non-existent in institutional terms) experiences of receivers of professional interventions, including by Social Services workers.

Official and unofficial knowledge

The case study of the Westons will have been recorded as three kinds of statistics: (1) a SSD referral, case allocation and case closure; (2) a compulsory admission to an Elderly Senile and Mentally Infirm (ESMI) Unit under Section 2 of the 1983 Mental Health Act; and (3) the registration of a death by the Registrar for Births, Marriages and Deaths. My concern here is with the dynamics of the first local SSD statistic.

Mr and Mr Weston were a married couple in their late sixties. Both of their children lived long distances away (their daughter in the North of England, their son abroad), while most of their extended family had died and younger family members had moved from the area. The Westons were very family-oriented, and this loss of relations also represented a loss of friends for them. They thus relied almost entirely on each other for company, backed up by brief but frequent visits from a nephew and less frequent, longer visits from their daughter, who was also in telephone contact several times a week.

Mr Weston suffered a long series of strokes from age 63 on. Initially he recovered well from their physical effects but became more and more withdrawn, angry and resentful, not only at the effects of the strokes but also those of ageing itself. One particular stroke at age 69 left Mr Weston doubly incontinent and in a confused mental state which meant that he could not be left. Mrs Weston at first managed well; however, later her ability to cope was over-stretched. Particular problems were constant soiling of bed linen and mattress and the drying of these; and also the fact that no essential food shopping could be done.

At this point requests for basic help were made without result to the family general practitioner (GP). A short time after, at her mother's request Mrs Weston's daughter made a referral to the local SSD. The situation that engendered the referral included not only the above problems, important though these were, but the fact that Mr Weston's behaviour now included unpredictable physical attacks. These were on Mrs Weston alone at first, but later included first his daughter and then an elderly female neighbour.

The case of the Westons will have been recorded as the three statistics, but these tell us very little. Much like an iceberg, they represent only the officially visible tip, while the most relevant aspects, which explain this tip, are hidden beneath the surface. I outline four important invisibilities.

Invisibility 1

There is no way of relating these three statistics to each other. Relating them is something done here. I can do so because I was involved in the details of the case study; however, even were they able to do so, most SSD researchers do not see the importance of collecting and using this kind of detailed experiential knowledge as 'research'.

As far as existing 'official knowledge' goes, these statistics are unrelatable because no regular means presently exist for matching up what are actually, in human terms, closely related facts about particular officially noted transition points in people's lives and deaths. Of course various statistical techniques can enable statements to be made about *statistical* relationships between groups of *aggregated numbers*. However, this is not the same thing at all as being able to trace out *sequential* patterns of actual movements *of persons* between these statistical headings. In fact there could be ways of actually relating such movements, if statistical returns to government departments were made available at a local level to local government researchers, including SSD researchers.

The second two national statistics arise from returns made to a central government department. If these statistics were provided back at a specifically local level, then researchers could begin the task of seeking out the actual connections that exist between the various statistical data that are collected but in a presently 'unrelatable' form. This would enable researchers to tease out the relationships between 'national' statistics and those that SSDs collect, disseminate and (it is hoped) use within a given SSD local area. However, what would still be required is recognition that using statistics in such a fashion is possible, useful and also 'respectable'.

In fact SSD researchers could already do this teasing out of actual relationships, using the specifically local information collected within SSDs; and yet they do not. The dominant notion of 'good, useful' research rejects connecting human relationships and movements to numerical research products, for it derives from naïve scientist ideas as well as the pressure of years of institutional practice.

Invisibility 2

The social relations underlying statistical data are complex, and a detailed knowledge of them is necessary if we are to read more usefully the actual statistics themselves. There is a lot more to 'statistics' than usually meets the eye that reads them. Most researchers determinedly strip from numbers, not only the processes by which these are collected, category headings for analysis constructed and data assigned to them, but also the actual institutional practices of the organisations which give rise to the numbers which are later used to represent symbolically organisational outputs. The resulting statistics, then, need to do a great deal of work, some of which they can appropriately do, and for some of which they are most inappropriate in their present form.

My interest is in a different and less static kind of statistics which can take cognisance of movements of actual persons/cases between particular statistical slots of 'official knowledge'. This is because my basic concern is with the relationship between different forms of official institutional knowledge, and also between official and unofficial knowledge. A relevant example is as follows.

SSD statistics exist concerning admissions to elderly person's homes. However, these statistics do not provide information about whether and to what extent different 'elderly careers' give rise to admission and what patterns there are concerning the point at which 'care in the community' broke down (Nisbet 1986). This information would chart and relate the different points at which elderly people's 'careers' brought them into contact with professionals and caring organisations and thus the points at which their lives become part of 'official knowledge'. Here, as in the case of the Westons, knowing the movement of persons between statistical headings/kinds of official knowledge enables statistics to say something much more useful: they are enabled to represent mobility and thus change; and clusters or groupings of particular 'careers' can then be analysed. However, this kind of statistical approach would be one in which 'numbers' would *not* be divorceable from more detailed information about particular cases and the processes involved in these.

Invisibility 3

The prime reason why the pattern of caring for Mr Weston broke down had surprisingly little to do with the direct nature of his incapacities, even though these included partial paralysis, transitory blindness, badly affected speech and double incontinence. It was rather that dealing with these by the principal carer, Mrs Weston, was adversely affected by the interrelationship of other factors. For example, because of the failure to provide simple support services, such as a soil-proof mattress covering, from the GP, one was obtained from a Northern SSD and taken on a 300-mile journey to the Westons' home. Before this Mrs Weston had spent hours each day washing and drying undersheets and mattress. The effects of Mr Weston's incapacities were made many times worse by his overt violence towards particular people. And both of these factors were exacerbated by the way in which this violence was treated, or rather not treated, originally by the GP and then by the social worker (SW) involved.

Both the GP and the SW recognised that 'something' was going on in the Weston household, but explicitly expressed this as Mr Weston exerting a necessary and proper control over 'bossy' women in a situation (surrounded by 'bossy' women) in which both of these men explicitly said (separately, for they never met each other, to the Westons' knowledge) that they too might feel the need to exert 'control'.

Because of their open expression of such attitudes, what neither found out from Mrs Weston, who resented deeply their 'man's man' attitudes, as she expressed it, was exactly what this 'something' was. It was not perhaps what they envisaged, but attacks with screwdrivers, attempted strangulation, attacks in the night while Mrs Weston was asleep and other extreme forms of overt physical violence, which were escaped largely because of Mr Weston's physical inability to run after his intended victims.

Both professionals certainly knew about Mrs Weston's inability to leave Mr Weston for more than a few seconds for fear that harm would come to him while she was absent. The GP 'failed to hear' about this when told, while the SW made it apparent that if Mrs Weston left her husband's side even for a moment she was 'shirking'. What neither man seemed to know about, let alone realise the gravity of, was that this meant that no food shopping could be done. But for two circumstances (a freezer; and a daughter who did a fortnightly 'shop' and brought it to them) the Westons would have gone very hungry.

However, what finally led to the 'breakdown of caring' in the Westons' case was nothing mentioned so far, although, obviously, these factors contributed to it. The GP and the SW failed to find out important pieces of information, which Mrs Weston kept from them because she did not trust men who made it clear to her that there were 'sides' to be taken and they had taken that of Mr Weston and against her. One was that she had effectively stopped sleeping except in short snatches in an armchair while Mr Weston was watching TV, for fear that harm would come to her while she was vulnerable. The other was that some weeks of not sleeping, coupled with attacks and resultant fears for her life, badly affected Mrs Weston's ability to care for her husband. In particular she began to answer anger with anger, so increasing the extremity of his moods and worries, rather than calming them as she had previously done.

Because of these things Mrs Weston herself verged on the knife-edge of a breakdown. At this stage the immediate problem was 'resolved' by Mr Weston's violent behaviour being extended to an elderly female neighbour. Anxious phone calls to the family general practice from nephew, daughter and son, and the absence on holiday of the original GP, resulted in his partner making a referral to a consultant psycho-geriatrician. She arranged three days per week attendance at an ESMI Unit for Mr Weston. In doing so she was immensely reassuring and helpful to both of the Westons, by recognising that there was indeed a serious situation and defusing it by accepting the legitimate worries of both spouses.

The day on which visits were to start, Mr Weston violently reacted not only to Mrs Weston and her nephew, but then the ambulance drivers who came to collect him. At this point his behaviour moved directly into institutional space, where it became immediately consequential for him. Following a subsequent attack on staff at the ESMI Unit, he was compulsorily sectioned under Section 2 of the 1983 Mental Health Act.

Invisibility 4

The professionals'-eye view of their interactions with the Westons and why they responded, or failed to respond, in the way that they did is also invisible. Looking at these events through the eyes of the carers/women involved, it seems clear that the GP and the SW identified with Mr Weston not just as a patient/client but also as a man; they resented on their own behalf as well as his Mr Weston's loss of control over 'his' women; and they actively legitimated and enabled the continuance of his violence by treating it as not 'real violence' at all, just as many professionals have done and continue to do with the violence of younger men.

What both men said to Mrs Weston about her 'proper' role and to Mr Weston about his 'rights', including with a variety of third parties present, makes the sexism incontrovertible. But it helps us surprisingly little in understanding what went on in this case if we simply gloss their responses as 'sexism'. Applying this summation to it tells us little about exactly *what* went on, *how* it was accomplished and *why* it happened that way. It seems to me that sexism is both constitutive, and also an outcome, of a particular (and peculiar) framework for thinking about the world, men and women, the family and marriage, sex and power, morality and authority. The sexism of the two men was *potent* because of its *institutional* basis: its use so as to refuse to carry out institutional practices that would 'do power over' a fellow man.

These male professionals probably had good professional and institutional commonsense reasons for acting as they did. And 'good' here means not that these were morally or professionally 'correct', but rather that they made sense to them and seemed to be the best thing to do at the time. These 'good reasons' arise out of the specific relationship between 'the client' and the male professionals. The GP and the SW treated Mr Weston and Mrs Weston as two people whose needs were in necessary opposition. The problem is that actually 'the client' was not this one person, Mr Weston, but 'the Westons'; and that a realistic professional view of 'Mr Weston' (like the female consultant psycho-geriatrician's) needed to incorporate Mrs Weston's view of him, as well as his of her, not exclude this as somehow illegitimate. 'Situations', and including all social work situations, are composed neither by purely formal and public interactions with GPs, SWs and the like; and nor are they, usually, composed by just one person – '*the* client'. What the participating carers in this group could have said, had either the GP or the SW been in the least interested in hearing, was that 'in public' Mr Weston had well-developed ways of relating to 'authority' from his work experience and his time in the Navy; but that 'in private', and with women in particular, he was a very different man indeed.

In research terms – and in relation to *each* of the three statistics and not just the first – a great deal more about 'the statistics' themselves can be discovered if we 'unpack' the underlying events.

A feminist postscript

What appears above is for reasons of space a shortened version of both my original conference paper and the published version of it. It is also substantially different from the paper I would have given and written had I produced it for a feminist audience. Why I tailored it for a non-feminist audience, the ways in which I did so and the consequences of this for the view of 'the case' and its relationship to 'the statistics' that result, I now briefly explore.

I tailored the paper, cut its cloth according to my measure of the audience present, not because they were predominantly male (though they were), but because I felt that almost by definition, as institutionally located researchers, they would be antithetical to feminist ways of looking at things. I don't mean that I expected there to be any fuss about either women or activities such as caring being treated as 'respectable' in research terms. It was more 'feminist ways of looking' and researching with which I expected there to be problems. Here, of course, when I say 'feminist' ways, I mean '*my* feminist ways' of doing these things, and so I very briefly outline what these are.

For me, feminism constitutes a way of seeing, living and indeed researching which is premised on the essential unity (however they might get written) of research processes and products. We wouldn't perceive a tin of baked beans or a television programme as somehow divorced from either production or consumption; and I can see no good reason why we should treat research, equally situated within a market place and equally a produced product, as different in kind from other products.

I see 'objectivity' and 'subjectivity' as false dichotomies. 'Objectivity' is a set of conversion rules applied to rather different practices, mainly through various conventions regarding the production of the written word. 'Subjectivity' is constructed as the failure to do objectivity, to *be* objective as a kind of person, not scientific in status. Both are artifacts within the sexual political system, and need deconstructing by looking closely and analytically at the constitutive social and institutional practices concerned, in the settings by which these are generated.

Consequently I am in favour of anything which helps to demystify 'research' and which legitimates 'the personal' as a respectable aspect of research, indeed as central to this as it is to every other human activity. By this I mean the centrality and analytic investigation of what I have elsewhere discussed as 'intellectual autobiography' (Stanley 1984): that is, much less a narrative format (I am this kind of person, first I did this, then I did that, the result was) and much more the teasing out of *how* research processes are understood so as to produce any particular product. This is for me the major way in which the power differential between the researcher/writer and the consumer/reader can begin to be broken down. After all, if readers know how I understand what I understand, you have a realistic chance of being able to make up your own mind rather than having to take things on trust because I only let you in on 'the findings'.

It was in the context of such convictions and feelings, then, that the feminist version of my paper is present in only a ghostly form. I finish by presenting something of what I deliberately played down or even completely removed.

'The Westons' are my mother and father and me (with my brother and cousin hovering sometimes in the wings, sometimes centrally present). The tragedy played out was ours. I have mixed feelings about each of these three major participants; however, whatever their faults I had no intention of making any of them vulnerable in a non-feminist context. For one thing, I felt that presenting 'the case study' as my own still-recent experience of caring would disqualify both me and it from 'research' and 'papers' in the eyes of those present. Whatever method-ological reservations other feminists might have, the actual experience we had gone through would be treated as a legitimate topic for discus-sion and analysis; I had no such certainty about the reactions of that audience and was unwilling to take the risk.

The active and deliberate collusion of the men, the GP and the SW, in the case with regard to my father's 'rights' to treat my mother and me as he wanted, and that they openly articulated this, still staggers me. Above I said it was a case of sexism: it was indeed, and this is much more central to my overall feelings about the 'help' we received than appears there. However, the consultant geriatrician was very different indeed. She (no coincidence this, I am sure) was wonderful with and about my father. But no sides for her, for she also took great pains to spell out first to my mother and then to me that she was sure that there was indeed something real to be frightened of. But for her involvement I cannot think (nor dare imagine) what would have become of my mother and what role my father would have played in this.

For many years, my feminist years, I lamented my mother's oppres-sion, that she was so much under my father's thumb and had no separate existence. I learned, the hard way, the ridiculous inadequacy of such a style of feminist interpretation of the lives and behaviours of 'non-feminist' women. When her existence (and I don't mean just physical life) really was threatened, my 'totally oppressed' mother totally transformed her entire mode of interaction with my father, to become a twenty-four hour-a-day embodiment of resistance and struggle. She has not only survived the most appallingly tragic decline and death of a deeply loved partner of forty-eight years, she has done so in much better shape than I, completely ambivalent and 300 miles removed from him. And, what's more, my mother can *smell* sexism. As she said about the SW, 'Do you know what a man's man is, Lizbeth? (No, I said, agog.)

Well, I can smell it on him, he thinks women are a *nothing.*'

Related to this is my increased awareness of just how much of parents' lives are and remain invisible to their children. My parents seem to have had a sophisticated 'under-life' which went on at the same time as they were with us, but in which they were immensely sensitive to information and signals which we, my brother and I, completely failed to pick up. Like the inhabitants of an invaded country under occupation, my parents lived lives which their small army of occupation got to know almost nothing about. And how similar this is to the ways in which women, like other oppressed people, develop multiple vision rather than the tunnel vision of oppressors. Food for thought here for all of us former children who have lived with parents.

The very last point. Many of my own generation of feminists are going through the experience of being carers; in the not so distant future those of us lucky enough to live that long may experience being elderly people being cared for by others. We must explore such experiences from the inside, as carers and cared for, not just as 'researchers' leeching on the experiences of others but unwilling to use our experiences as we do those of other people.

© 1990 Liz Stanley

References and bibliography

Barclay Report, The (1982) *Social Workers, Their Role and Tasks*, National Institute for Social Work, London.

Equal Opportunities Commission (1980) *The Experience of Caring for Elderly and Handicapped Dependants*, EOC, Manchester.

——(1982) *Who Cares for the Carers?* EOC, Manchester.

Finch, Janet (1984) 'Community Care: Developing Non-sexist Alternatives', *Critical Social Policy* 9:6–18.

Finch, Janet and Groves, Dulcie (eds) (1983) *A Labour of Love: Women, Work and Caring*, London: Routledge & Kegan Paul.

Nisbet, Gillian (1986) 'Official Selection Accounts Concerning Admission to a Home for Aged Persons', Working Papers in Applied Social Research No. 9, Sociology Department, University of Manchester.

SCARS (eds) (1986) *On Researching the Topic of Care*, Studies in Sexual Politics No. 11, Sociology Department, University of Manchester.

Stanley, Liz (1984) 'How the Social Science Research Process Discriminates against Women', in Sandra Acker and David Warren-Piper (eds), *Is Higher Education Fair to Women?* London: Nelson, pp. 189–209.

——(1988) 'Behind the Scenes during the Creation of a Social Services "Elderly" Statistic', *Policy, Planning, Research* 6:47–59.

Recognising the Role of Auto/Biography

Chapter nine

On the conflicts of doing feminist research into masculinity

Joyce Layland

Introduction

When I first decided to write about the processes by which gay men construct the social phenomenon of masculinity, I wasn't sure whether this could be seen as feminist research. The idea of spending time looking in depth at a topic which at first glance is related only to men seemed not to fit many ideas of what feminist research should be about. 'Doing research as a feminist means focusing in detail on some specific aspect of women's oppression', says Liz Kelly (1984:84), echoing what many women have said about what constitutes feminist research: that by definition its content must concern aspects of women's lives and the factors which affect them. With these ideas in mind, plus misgivings about 'putting energy into men', I experienced my interest in my chosen topic as paradoxical. Not for the first time, I questioned whether I was a feminist at all.

Awareness of feminist perspectives has changed my perception of the world I live in. And this is the problem: in the process of learning to see things differently it is all too easy to get caught up in a general ontological confusion of the kind Sandra Bartky (1977) identifies in her concept of 'double ontological shock'. Thus one finds, in Garfinkel's (1967) terms, several possible 'underlying patterns' of which any given 'indexical particulars' might be indicative. Hence my confusion, not only whether having a door opened for me is a kindness or a 'put-down', but also whether being interested in a piece of research is feminist or not.

While trying to synthesise my own kind of feminism from an eclectic hotchpotch of radical, liberal, Marxist, socialist and sociological analyses, I am also trying to select criteria on which to base my choice of what to spend time on, academically and personally. And the pivotal point, I feel, is not only what we spend time and energy on, but also how and why we spend it that way and that we do it from, as Elizabeth Sarah (1982:151) puts it, 'an independent perspective', 'outside the male framework'.

It is this independent perspective which I find challenging and exciting, but also difficult to define and achieve. How is it possible to develop a truly independent perspective? I don't think it is entirely to do with selecting one or any of the traditional analyses mentioned above, nor is it necessary to develop a completely separatist lifestyle. Even if your personal network includes no men, in Britain anyway the electricity meter-reader, television repair man, postman, are mostly men (Stanley 1982). And they are in our lives, for however short a time and however marginally. Perhaps this last word – 'marginal' – holds the key.

Seeing men as marginal

Elizabeth Sarah suggests that while heterosexual men see women's concerns as subordinate, gay men see them as marginal. The idea of reversing power relations and subordinating men requires a large investment of time and energy to achieve. The ability to see them as marginal perhaps holds possibilities, but could turn out to be as difficult in practical terms as the achievement of complete separatism. Gay men have the power, in common with other men, to define women according to their own views and needs, and if they choose to see us as marginal, they have the ability to put this definition to work in their everyday lives. In contrast, we mostly cannot impose our definitions in the face of male resistance. Whatever choices we make regarding our relationship with men, the social dominance of their interests and values still impinges on our lives as feminists. Therefore any independent perspective I achieve will be subject to all sorts of revisions and adjustments over time, as my life-experience progresses and amasses more complexities.

Part of this complexity consists in being the mother of a gay son. This has had far-reaching effects, not only on the day-to-day content of my lifestyle, but also on my view of 'what is going on', individually, socially and sociologically. Having become involved, as an interested parent, in the running of a youth group at a gay centre, I found myself spending a great deal of time at the centre and on the 'gay scene' in general. All of this deeply influenced the way I construct my version of feminism. For one thing, it brought me, as a heterosexual woman, into contact with many more lesbians, some of whom are staunchly separatist, than I would otherwise have had the opportunity of meeting. Thus I became aware of a wider dimension of feminism: the feminism of women who appeared to me to have constructed lifestyles which were much less in conflict with their feminist ideals than I felt mine to be.

I also came into close contact with a great many gay men, many of whom became close friends, but (paradox again) amongst whom I experienced a kind of misogyny which seemed more virulent than any which heterosexual men can muster. To begin with, my perception of the men I met was that they were pleasanter company, more ready to listen and to treat women as equals than non-gay men. This, I thought, is how it ought to be! However, it soon became apparent that this 'equal treatment' only operated on male terms – a familiar scenario – and did not extend to areas felt by the men to be inappropriate. Thus, one example, lesbians have less chance of being admitted to certain gay clubs than heterosexual women. A possible explanation is that the latter are usually accompanied by gay men, whilst lesbians, unattached to men, are somehow seen as problematic, just as elsewhere in society women unattached to men are seen as social problems.

It was within this setting that I found myself working with the gay centre youth group, where the gender patterns seemed to mirror those of organisations at large, with young women being under-represented, less vocal and less visible. The paradoxes and conflicts which I began to experience between my developing feminist consciousness, and my desire to work with gay and lesbian young people of all backgrounds and situations, have still not been resolved; and I continue to experience them, at different levels.

They stem, in great measure, from the situation I find myself in as the mother of a gay son. As such, I have been in a position to see the great social and psychological stress which society exerts on gay and lesbian children and young people. At school, at play, in jobs, and youth clubs, not to mention their own families, this stress can be relentless and unremitting, stemming, as it does, from the ubiquitous prejudice against and misinformation about homosexuality. And with so few facilities for support and encouragement for these youngsters, there is a huge amount of work to be done, not only with the young people themselves, but also with parents, teachers, social workers – in fact with anyone who is involved with the welfare of young people in general. Having decided to try to contribute to filling this gap, I began to be confronted by the contradictions of my situation.

Young women came, and still come, to the youth group sporadically. Their presence contributes positively to the ethos of the group. And while the young men seem to share this feeling, this does not prompt them to provide an atmosphere which would encourage the young women to stay. These young men, mostly teenagers, come to the youth group bringing with them a complete baggage of commonsense attitudes and ideas about men and women which they have assembled from the 'knowledge' available in a heterosexual and sexist society. This is then filtered through a new set of values and attitudes which they meet as they become part of the gay male community. The result is a densely androcentric assemblage of meanings from which is created a world-view which often includes the unique brand of misogyny mentioned earlier. And despite attempts to prevent sexist and anti-lesbian language and behaviour, the young women still often experience their involvement with the youth group negatively. Thus at the centre of the conflict I experience as a feminist in this situation is my desire to support the young and vulnerable of both sexes whilst trying not to put myself in an intolerable situation from a feminist point of view.

I experienced these questions as particularly problematic in the light of my initial feelings about gay men as being 'different from' non-gay men. Now I ask: *are* they different? and if so, *how* are they different? In short, I am asking, 'What is going on here?' both socially and sociologically. In addition to this, contact with heterosexual fathers provided opportunities to observe reaffirmation of heterosexual male values, often in head-on collision with those of the gay son. One example of this is that of a son with a 'gender-bender' self-presentation: a mixture of 'male' and 'female' clothing, startling make-up, and shaved hair, clinging aggressively to all this despite his father's anger and beatings at school. His father was just as aggressive in clinging to 'traditional' masculine presentation including memories of 'picking up girls' and 'fights with me mates' which had added spice to his nights out as a youngster.

The research topic of masculinity

It was as a result of finding myself as a mediator between these positions that the research topic of the construction of masculinity suggested itself to me. The production of the various roles and meanings involved in 'doing' masculinity affect me and all women, both in their production and their employment, as these seem to centre on power differentials between men and men and men and women. Even when this 'masculine' power is not done directly to women, or done when we are not present, the fact that it is a central construct in how men live their lives means that it is a factor we have to take into consideration in deciding how we live ours. Men may be absent as I walk home alone at night, but their absence does not allow me to dismiss the potential for their presence, and my perception of my social and physical surroundings is affected by this potential presence.

Many of the day-to-day decisions I make in my life are shaped by considerations of having to coexist with this masculine power: whether to walk down a darkened street, whether to use a certain shop, whether to take a certain job, whether I will get the job if a man applies. These are obvious considerations, but there are more subtle ones. The almost imperceptible differences in my own and other women's interactive patterns in the presence of men are the result of how we perceive what is going on, and these perceptions in turn are the result of the expectations both we and the men bring to the situation. I know my expectations are still partly shaped by ideas of 'femininity', of being soft, kind, compliant. And it still gives me pause for thought when certain (gay) men tell me that I 'come over as a strong woman'. Is this an all-right thing to be, or is it a contradiction in terms?

Many women have written about their experiences of these effects, but often the men and the processes involved seem to disappear in our accounts almost as completely as we have been made to do in mainstream history, sociology and anthropology, but with different results. The latent effect of seeing feminist research as exclusively about women's lives is that it allows things male to go uninvestigated, almost as though the idea of the male-as-norm were not being questioned any more. However, we must demystify power and its components, one of which is the production of 'masculinity' and 'masculine' behaviour. Having the opportunity of seeing the social interaction of gay men has allowed me to see the possible variations in the construction of these phenomena.

There are many shades of difference and similarity between the ways in which gay and non-gay men 'do masculinity'. The aggression and competitive spirit which is part of masculinity is just as much present in gay male interaction as in non-gay. The difference here seems to be that the aggression and competition is channelled into sexual pursuit and conquest, rather than the 'fights with me mates' which characterised the 'fun' of the heterosexual father mentioned earlier. Therefore my experience of gay men, socially, is in many ways more positive because of this. Since they neither fight with me, nor over me, nor prey upon me sexually, there is an absence of the social pressure I feel in the presence of non-gay men. And I have had the opportunity, with gay men, to begin to see and experience men in general differently. I feel a degree of demystification about men and how to interact with them, which gives me more confidence in handling interaction with them, particularly in situations which contain elements of sexuality and/or threat. This is a result of listening to and observing gay male friends in various situations; not necessarily blandly absorbing their ideas and attitudes, but having the opportunity of seeing different possibilities of how to make sense of what is going on – my own sense, not theirs! Thus it occurs to me that the production of 'masculinity' or 'femininity' is, in part, the result of individuals being presented with different sets of possibilities of how to make sense of a given social situation.

Another motive for wanting to look at masculinity as produced by gay men goes back to my feelings as the mother of one such young man. My way of motherhood has meant that I have identified closely with both my sons, and the fact that one of them is gay has led to a great deal of anger and dissatisfaction on my part with the misinformation and mythology about homosexuality which exists throughout our society.

This makes me interested, as a sociologist, in saying something about gay men as ordinary members of that society rather than some kind of exotic community in our midst, starting from the position that gay men come from all classes, occupations, races, ages, and are a cross-section of the male sex distinguished only by a same-sex sexual preference. The men I am focussing on are members of the gay community, and as such have helped to construct, and continue to maintain, the category 'gay men'. In so doing they question much of the social knowledge constructed by heterosexual society, but not the knowledge of the existence of the 'facts' about men and women that are premised on the two sex/gender model of society. These facts are incorporated into mechanisms for constructing a personal identity and as part of a prescriptive framework for the behaviour involved in being a gay man; and this locates them firmly within the male gender, with its perceived requirements of masculinising behaviour and self-image.

These basic assumptions about sex and gender, along with the procedural knowledge involved in 'doing sex' and its component masculinity, are shared in common with the rest of society. The 'differences' which I perceived are the result of these commonly held assumptions being filtered through specific sets of perceptions based on the particular social context in which gay men find themselves.

The result is that we are not looking at one monolithic construct of 'masculinity', but a multitude of variously constructed 'masculinities'. But whatever the differences of each, I still experience their effects on me as 'doing masculinity'. There are 'clones' with check shirts, denims, moustaches, and short-back-and-sides haircuts; there are the 'leather-men' in leather jackets, trousers and 'biker boots'. Both have strong 'macho' images. These two categories are made up of individuals, who, when I've talked to them about it, report feelings of 'superior' masculinity to that of the 'screaming queen', whom they view as an embarrassment with their seeming 'effeminacy'. However, I experience just as great a degree of masculine qualities in my dealings with 'screaming queens' as I do with the apparently more macho self-presentation. Each 'category' of gay male is equally assertive, even aggressive, in its claims to the right to dress and behave as it chooses, with no concessions – much like the situation between the heterosexual father and gay son mentioned earlier.

Despite their lack of conventional 'macho', the 'queens' seem to me to be seriously misnamed as 'effeminate'. There is little in their behaviour and self-presentation which is woman-like. I do not relate to them or their behaviour, nor recognise it as the same thing that I am doing as a woman. Both 'clone' and 'queen' claim more social space than I do and assert their presence more demandingly than I or most women do. Indeed, at times the queens seem to produce these 'masculine' characteristics *more* loudly and aggressively. Perhaps it was no accident of history that the Stonewall Riot, which gave such a boost to gay liberation, was started by 'drag queens'.

All this is some indication of the complexity of the phenomenon. Even 'drag' itself is not a simple, unified construct. It is often seen as simply being about misogyny, with no other motivation. But quite often it seems to be a camp caricature of the whole heterosexual value system. And it is suggested by some gay men that it is often poking fun at – by 'sending up' – gay men themselves. It is interesting, however, that it is not the dress and characteristics of heterosexual men which are usually used in this way. One British drag artist said in interview on television that he feels he is in drag if he wears a conventional three-piece suit and tie as much as when he appears in an evening gown. This suggests that for him at least drag is about deflating all conventional social images, especially those concerned with gender expectations. According to this view, John Wayne was always in drag!

The fact remains, however, that it is female dress and presentation that is used in this way; and its effects on me are complex and differ depending on the situation, the performer and performance. Sometimes it seems to have nothing to do with me, and I can detachedly speculate on the effects of the dynamics of the situation on the men involved. Are they buying into heterosexual society's view of them as failed men, second-class citizens, like women? Or are they trying to distance themselves from women by sending us up, thus proving that they are really men? Or are they justifying their rejection of women in gross, obscene portrayals of them, as Peter Ackroyd (1979) suggests?

I think there is a complex relationship between the use of drag to flout prevailing social codes and its use, more individually, as a reality-altering device, much as drugs and alcohol are used. Certainly this version seems to have nothing to do with real women's lives, and much more to do with a male fantasy of what women's lives are about – all make-up and slipper-satin lingerie! The 'problems' of being a man can be avoided for a while by changing reality and becoming what he imagines a woman to be – carefree and cosseted. Quentin Crisp saw this reality-altering function when he said that exhibitionism is a drug and that he took it in doses big enough to kill a beginner (Crisp 1981).

Thus the effects of this on me vary with my perceptions of 'what is going on'. On one level, I see it as nothing to do with me: it is a problem some men have with being men. On another level it is very much to do with me, as it reinforces societal views of women as empty-headed, decorative and essentially pathetic creatures, whose only function is to float around looking aesthetically pleasing and being victims – a view of us which gay men in particular cling to. Drag, then, is about how men see not just women but the whole world. It is an androcentric

131

phenomenon which, while using images of women as central, manages to make us peripheral at the same time – a very masculine thing to do indeed.

So looking at masculinity on the 'gay scene' involves not looking at a unitary phenomenon, fixed over time and space, but a multi-faceted set of constructs, changing consistently, not only over time and space but also between men and groups of men. The meanings attached to it are constantly negotiated and re-negotiated in processes of interpretation and communication. I am not sure how much these processes are open to investigation by a woman. My presence qualitatively alters any social situation existing between gay men. Although this must be true to some degree of any researcher in whatever situation, I am aware of it to a greater degree as a heterosexual woman researching the lives and behaviour of gay men.

Part of the production and use of masculinity involves power processes. In what way am I changing these processes by 'doing' the researcher role? My motive is not so much to exercise power over men as to help myself demystify and thus defuse the effects of what they are doing, as noted earlier. I wonder, however, whether I am already 'doing power', not so much as a researcher but because 'I am the mother of a gay son, therefore I have the right, as "your Mum", to do this!'. Indeed, most of the gay men I know collude with me in this by accepting that I have the right to be in their lives in some way or other.

These problems of 'the researcher' and 'the researched' are not resolved in my mind. Perhaps the course of my research will help me to do so. And perhaps it will help to explain what I experience as the central paradox of being a feminist involved with gay men. This is that the very feminist awareness which makes me aware of their misogyny and phallocentricity also allows me, through my understanding of the processes of oppression, to identify with them on several levels. Many of the oppressive mechanisms within society which affect women so drastically also affect gay men, even while they are busy adding to and reinforcing them. This is a paradox embedded deeply in their social and political being as much as it is in mine. It unites and it divides them, and it unites and divides them and me. I do not fully understand it. I hope my research will be another step towards my doing so.

© 1990 Joyce Layland

References

Ackroyd, Peter (1979) *Dressing Up: Transvestism and Drag: the History of an Obsession*, London: Thames & Hudson.
Bartky, Sandra (1977) 'Towards a Phenomenology of Feminist Consciousness',

in Mary Vetterling-Braggin, Frederick Elliston and Jane English (eds), *Philosophy and Feminism*, Totowa, NJ: Littlefield, Adams & Co., pp. 22–37.

Crisp, Quentin (1981) *How to Become a Virgin*, London: Duckworth.

Garfinkel, Harold (1967) *Studies in Ethnomethodology*, Englewood Cliffs, NJ: Prentice-Hall.

Kelly, Liz (1984) 'Some Thoughts on Feminist Experience in Research on Male Sexual Violence', in Olivia Butler (ed.), *Feminist Experience in Feminist Research*, Studies in Sexual Politics No.2, pp. 61–88.

Sarah, Elizabeth (1982) 'Female Performers on a Male Stage: the First Women's Liberation Movement and the Authority of Men, 1890–1930', in Scarlet Friedman and Elizabeth Sarah (eds), *On the Problem of Men: Two Feminist Conferences*, London: The Women's Press, pp. 135–73.

Stanley, Liz (1982) '"Male Needs": the Problems of Working with Gay Men', in Scarlet Friedman and Elizabeth Sarah (eds), *On the Problem of Men: Two Feminist Conferences*, London: The Women's Press, pp. 190–213.

Chapter ten

From butch god to teddy bear?

Some thoughts on my relationship with Elvis Presley[1]

Sue Wise

Who is Elvis, what is he ...?

'Whose are all those ELVIS records? aargh!' is a commonly heard question in my home, and has been ever since it has been regularly frequented by feminists. I usually reply, sheepishly, 'Well, actually, er um, they're mine ... but I never listen to them anymore.' 'But how could you ever have *been* an Elvis fan?' is the predictable next question. 'I was very young,' I excuse myself, and this is usually enough to get me off the hook. Yet I know that if the truth was known – that I am still fond of Elvis's memory, that I love the records, that I still own a very large scrapbook of clippings, photos and mementoes that I cannot bring myself to part with – then my feminist credibility would be open to question, my credentials re-examined and my right-on-ness wondered about in the light of this new information. And so it is not without some trepidation that I come out here publicly as – AN ELVIS FAN.

Elvis Presley may not rank highly in most feminists' list of interesting and important subjects, and, indeed, many have probably never given him a second thought. However, I hope it will become quickly apparent that this chapter is not 'about Elvis', nor even about biographies of Elvis. Rather, I have taken my own involvement, past and present, with Elvis as the topic for analysis, working from the starting point that to be a feminist and an Elvis fan is problematic given the current view of each that exists, and that this relationship opens up interesting features of 'feminist biography' for discussion.

Tracing the strands of this relationship has raised ideas and problems for me which I take to be crucial for my own feminist understanding of the world. These include the relationship between subjective and supposedly objective accounts of reality and the existence of a powerful feminist orthodoxy which, paradoxically, accepts objective and 'male' accounts of the rock-'n'-roll phenomenon at the expense of women's personal and subjective experience of it; and, equally paradoxically, focusses the genre of feminist biography on a new pantheon of stars –

but this time specifically feminist stars, the Simone de Beauvoirs, Alexandra Kollontais and Emma Goldmans of the feminist world rather than the Elvis Presleys, Marilyn Monroes, Maria Callases of other people's (*other* people's? not feminists'?) world.

Elvis the butch god

That Elvis is portrayed as a macho folk hero is easily apparent from any number of written accounts:

> The teddy boys were waiting for Elvis Presley. Everyone under twenty all over the world was waiting. He was the super salesman of mass distribution hip ... he was a public butch god with the insolence of a Genet murderer.... Most of all he was unvarnished sex taken and set way out in the open.... The Presley riots were the first spontaneous gatherings of the community of the new sensibilities.
>
> (Nuttall 1969: 29-30)

This quotation beautifully encapsulates the elements which supposedly explain Elvis's impact on popular culture. First, it suggests that Elvis's impact had world-wide cultural significance. Second, it assumes that his appeal was to young people, inciting them in rebellion against the 'old order' of adults, thus creating or expressing a 'generation gap'. And, third, it also assumes that the central component of this extraordinary impact was his expression of rampant male sexuality.

The cultural significance of the emergence of Elvis in the 1950s is never doubted by those who write about him (for example, Cohn 1969). In such accounts the 1950s are depicted as a time of stagnation, with a post-war generation disillusioned by the war and looking for a symbol of rejection of the past and hope for the future. That change, that revolution, which youth throughout the world was waiting for was, they suggest, epitomised in the expression of Elvis's sexuality. Consider this:

> Always, he came back to sex. In the earlier generations, singers might carry great sex appeal but they'd have to cloak it under the trappings of romanticism, they'd never spell anything out. By contrast Elvis was blatant. When those axis hips got moving, there was no more pretence about moonlight and hand-holding; it was hard physical fact.
>
> (Cohn 1969:25)

There are any number of accounts like this, which purport to describe the atmosphere of the 1950s and the consequent impact of Elvis on a world which was 'waiting' for a modern, positive, exciting challenge to

135

the old order. That this 'challenge' should turn out to be an uncontrolled and rampant male sexuality is invariably accepted as unproblematic by the male writers who wax lyrical about Elvis's hips and 'revolutionary' impact:

> Presley's breakthrough was that he was the first male white singer to propose that fucking was a desirable activity in itself and that, given sufficient sex appeal, it was possible for a man to lay girls without any of the traditional gestures or promises.... He was the master of the sexual simile, treating his guitar as both phallus and girl, punctuating his lyrics with the animal grunts and groans of the male approaching orgasm. He made it quite clear that he felt he was doing any woman he accepted a favour. He dressed to emphasise both his masculinity and basic narcissism, and rumour had it that into his skin-tight jeans was sewn a lead bar to suggest a weapon of heroic proportions.
>
> (Melly 1970:36-7)

'The revolution' seems to be war under the name of sex, with the phallus (of course a heroic one!) as the main weapon – so guess who is the enemy?

Elvis's appeal is traditionally depicted as an appeal to young girls who, overwhelmed by his animal male magnetism, were able to lose their sexual inhibitions and, albeit in the safety of a concert hall, 'respond' to being turned on by the male sexual hero, a response in which they displayed mass (sexual) hysteria. But some of the preceding quotations suggest very clearly the rarely mentioned and never analysed impact that Elvis had on boys. It was teddy boys who were 'waiting' for Elvis, it was young men who identified with him and his supposed ability to 'lay girls' with ease and without consequence. It is no coincidence that the male archivists of popular culture were only interested in Elvis while he represented their sexual fantasies. Although he had a career of over twenty years, male writers dwell upon only the first couple of these, when they can identify with the super-butch sexual hero that they themselves have promoted and lauded. And when their folk hero loses his 'potency', as they see Elvis doing, they look to explanations outside of his control in order to explain his (sexual) 'downfall', just as they do for other 'failed' rock stars:

> his appeal in the first place was to young males.... Each successive pop music explosion has come roaring out of the clubs in which it was born like an angry young bull.... Commercial exploitation advances towards it holding out a bucketful of recording contracts, television appearances and world-wide fame. Then, once the muzzle is safely buried in the golden mash, the cunning butcher

nips deftly along the flanks and castrates the animal.... The trick is to shift the emphasis so that the pop rebellion is transformed into a masturbation fantasy-object for adolescent girls.

(Melly 1970: 39-40)

Perhaps this is where I come in.

Elvis the teddy bear

I've always been an Elvis fan. My mother loves to embarrass me by telling how I used to jig around in my pram when his records came on the radio (perhaps a mum's poetic licence, as I was born in 1953 and at least a toddler before Elvis arrived on the scene). This story demonstrates how, within my family, I was identified as an Elvis fan and this was seen as an important part of my life.

I must have been about 11 or 12 when Elvis became for me a full-time hobby. By this age I was able actively to seek out all things Elvis. I saved pocket money to buy his records, see his films, buy fan magazines and stick posters on my bedroom walls. My closest childhood friend was also an Elvis fan and we would spend hours discussing him, listening to records and swapping pictures and stories. But mostly my interest in Elvis took the form of a solitary hobby, a private thing between 'him' and me. If I spent large amounts of time in my (shared) bedroom alone fixing pictures in my scrapbook, this was OK because I was absorbed in my hobby. So it was also a way of spending a considerable time alone in an overcrowded household which was accepted as legitimate by my family.

I remained actively interested in Elvis throughout my teens, until the age of 20 or 21, when I 'got feminism'. The 'getting of feminism' was, for me, a fairly lengthy process. No shattering bolt of lightning, but instead a slow and gradual re-shaping of my view of the world brought about by things I read, talked about and heard over a couple of years, as this was sifted through my own biographical history, experience and consciousness. During this period of course I began to reconstrue present and past events in a new light.

The overwhelming feature of this period in my life is that of rejection. So many things were reconstrued and rejected at this time, when I had a clear-out of twenty years of accumulated sexist junk. And of course feminism touched every inch and every aspect of my existence, from relationships to the way I looked, to my goals and ambitions in life, to the things that were dear to my heart. And so at the same time that I threw out the frocks and the make-up, changed my career and stopped feeling obliged to be interested in men, I also rejected Elvis.

This rejection of Elvis along with the rest is interesting to me in retrospect. I had never analysed my fondness for or interest in him as I grew up – he had always been important to me and I had never questioned how or why or the exact nature of the 'him' I was interested in. Similarly, when the time came to leave him behind I did it without question or analysis. All I knew was that he did not fit into my new-found beliefs and was frowned upon by my newly acquired peers.

I don't remember reading or hearing any specific feminist analysis which said 'Elvis can seriously damage your health'. Occasional feminist references to rock music in general invariably pointed the finger at the Rolling Stones and Elvis as epitomising the male-dominated, woman-hating bias of rock music. But the main pressure always came from incredulous friends, who were always quick to point out the ideological impurity of Elvis – they never explained why, and I never asked. I guess we all thought we knew what the problem was without having to spell it out: Elvis was the very worst kind of male super-hero, no further explanation was necessary. Somehow (quite how I don't know) Elvis was a central part of the patriarchal plot, for 'Elvis' consisted of a social phenomenon and personal image which down-graded women by elevating the male macho hero to unprecedented heights. And of course being 'a fan' of any description was highly suspect, unless the 'star' was a certified, right-on woman like Dory Previn or Joan Armatrading for women of my age or Annie Lennox or Yazz for those a bit younger, for 'being a fan' was to collude in one's own oppression.

This took place during what I call my 'zealot' period, when I rejected many things from my past because they did not fit into my new way of life. My feminist consciousness acted as an all-purpose purgative; having expurgated myself of all unwholesome things past I had achieved the desired effect: I felt pure, new-born, I fitted in with my feminist friends, my life was an integrated whole.

Integrity is vital to sanity, as any woman knows only too well. But as the years went by echoes of my past (in the voice of Elvis?) have from time to time surfaced, demanding to be analysed and explained. Such a thing occurred in 1977 when Elvis died. I was surprised at how much his death touched me. I hadn't thought about him for years; as far as I was concerned he was a relic of a past 'false consciousness'. And yet his death was significant to me and it made me very sad. Of course it said something about my own mortality, about the fact that I was growing older. Elvis had always been around and his death was a reminder of time moving along and death coming closer to us all. But it was also more than that.

I felt I had lost something that was very special and dear to me, something that had played an important part in my life. As a now-mature feminist, something simply didn't fit – I had to try and understand why

I was sad. Why was I grieving for a 'butch god' when he represented everything that I loathed and fought against? Was it just nostalgia, a yearning for my youth, or was it more than this?

In order to answer these questions I turned to the proliferation of books and articles about Elvis. And yes, there it was in black and white: Elvis the butch god, Elvis the phallus, Elvis the macho folk-hero. And then I turned to my own mementoes of Elvis; I listened to the records and I dragged out the scrapbooks (significantly, I had never been able to discard these and they had been relegated to dusty shelves and cup-boards). As I listened to records and delved into clippings, cuttings and photos, they evoked memories and feelings from my youth. And the memories that were evoked had nothing to do with sex, nothing even to do with romance. The overwhelming feelings and memories were of warmth and affection for a very dear friend.

As an adolescent I had been a lonely person, never fitting in any-where, never 'connecting' with another human being. In later years I understood this in terms of my early awareness of being gay; at the time it was just confusing. Elvis filled a yawning gap in my life in many different ways. He was an interesting hobby when life was boring and meaningless. He was a way of being acceptably 'different' because it simply wasn't fashionable to be an Elvis fan when I was one. Most of all, he was another human being to whom I could relate and with whom I could be identified. When I felt lonely and totally alone in the world, there was always Elvis. He was a private, special friend who was always there, no matter what, and I didn't have to share him with anybody. He was someone to care about, to be interested in and to defend against criticism. In my own private Elvis world I could forget I was miserable and lonely by listening to his records and going to see his films. Some people who feel alone in an alien world turn to religion or to heroin or to football teams to give their lives purpose. I turned to Elvis; and he was always there and he never let me down.

This experience of Elvis is one I find difficult to explain, but I know it is one which was shared by many other people. Flipping through the pages of *Elvis Monthlys* and remembering conversations with other fans reminds me time and time again that very many female and male fans experienced Elvis in this way. For us Elvis the macho super-hero might just as well have been another and totally different person, for he certainly wasn't *our* Elvis.

Will the real Elvis Presley...?

The two accounts of Elvis, as butch god and as teddy bear, are so dissimilar that one could be forgiven for thinking that they describe two different people. But of course they are describing the same person from two quite different perspectives, and neither can be said to be the 'true' or 'real' picture of what Elvis 'meant' in terms of popular culture. Some people will have experienced Elvis as I did, to some he will have been a butch god (see, for example, Welburn 1982 for another woman's 'Elvis'), and to others he will have meant very little or nothing at all. Yet archivists do not present such a relativist view. On the contrary – for the overwhelming feature of their accounts is their similarity, their complete accord that Elvis was first and last about rampant male sexuality. But once we accept that some people did not experience him in this way, as I didn't, it becomes interesting to ponder the question of how such a one-sided view came into being, why it gained the currency that it did, and why it has remained largely unquestioned for so long.

I have already suggested that most writers about Elvis, then and now, are men; and it remains true that women have written very little about him (interestingly, those who do invariably focus on 'Elvis the person' rather than 'Elvis the cultural hero', like Yancy (1977) and Beaulieu Presley (1985)). The first component in this artful construction of Elvis is therefore the simple and familiar one to feminists: that of men interpreting and encoding knowledge, in their own interests and after their own image, and then calling this an objective account of the world as it truly is.

The second component is the careful selection of particular bits of Elvis's career to support their theories. Elvis had a show-business career spanning more than twenty years, and yet these writers invariably focus on only the first couple of years as the significant part of it. This period is seen as representing the elemental Elvis, the sexual hero who is subsequently 'castrated' by the American army/commercial exploitation/his manager/his mother (take your pick), leaving just a eunuch/teddy bear/pap for adolescent female teenage consumption. This is what they mean when they talk about Elvis's appeal having first been to men and why they feel so betrayed by all the rest – the 'real' Elvis, their Elvis, got taken away from them.

Elvis's rise to fame was inextricably linked with the moral panic surrounding the behaviour of women and girls at his live performances. They screamed and cried and lost control in large numbers and must have presented a quite stupendous spectacle in their own right, just as with the female response to the Beatles later. The media found it disturbing on one level, but they also loved it and fuelled and fostered it. Since this kind of mass crowd expression of power from women and girls was supposedly both unprecedented and unthinkable (in fact, longer memories will recall 'bobby-soxers' behaving in the same way over Frank Sinatra, or the mass hysteria at Rudolph Valentino's funeral), explanations for it were sought. What better way to explain the frightening spectacle of hordes of uncontrollable females than by

'discovering' that they were only responding to being sexually stimu-
lated and manipulated by a man – literally, man-ipulated.

How suitable! how unthreatening! and how ego-stroking for the men
who looked on approvingly. By turning Elvis from what in effect he was
– an *object* of his fans – into a subject, the girls' behaviour was made
unthreatening by being controlled. It was but a small 'logical' step from
here to say that if Elvis could do this then what he represented must be
the phallus – after all, it must have been something rather wonderful to
produce this reaction in girls, and what is more wonderful than the
phallus? Lead bar in his trousers or no, when these male writers saw him
on stage they saw a 'weapon' of 'heroic' proportions, for how else could
he have this effect on women?

Paradoxically, there was nothing new about this at all. Elvis was
merely invested with all the properties and preoccupations that had
previously been reserved as a stereotype for black men (Wallace 1979).
So not only did this view of Elvis explain away threatening women, it
also transformed folk devil into folk hero in a way that was extremely
ego-enhancing to white men.

All of the above is about men. It was men who claimed Elvis as their
butch god, men who bathed in his reflected glory, men who felt betrayed
when the girls stopped screaming, men who depicted this phallic hero as
having world-wide cultural significance. What women thought then and
now is largely unknown because, quite simply, no one bothered to ask
us or thought that our views were worth anything. After all, what is the
point in talking to someone, let alone taking what they say seriously,
who merely reacts to male cues?

This version of Elvis is so widely accepted that it is difficult to
question it without first-hand knowledge of a different experience. For
all practical purposes it is the only extended version of 'Elvis' that
exists. And it demonstrates how people who are involved in the
production of 'knowledge' find exactly what they set out to look for –
by looking in selected places, asking only some questions and ignoring,
or failing to see, information that is uncomfortable or doesn't fit. And
this is something which feminists must recognise. We should never take
anything on trust, we should ask our own questions, seek out our own
knowledge and always look gift horses, in the form of other people's
knowledge, firmly in the mouth.

Perhaps feminists have adopted the butch-god version of Elvis
because there hasn't been another version available to those who didn't
go through the kinds of experiences I did. Yet it still seems paradoxical
that feminists, myself included, have taken over these male ideas about
rock music without ever bothering to ask how women experienced this
phenomenon. Feminism was supposed to be about questioning all male
constructions of reality, about re-working male commonsense under-

standings of the world. In the case of Elvis, male writers have taken their subjective sexual fantasies and turned them into 'objective fact'. And feminists have gone along with this.

At least one contributory factor has been the implicit assumption that subjects such as Elvis and rock music are not the 'proper' concerns of feminist writers. More than this, even if it were (grudgingly) acknowledged that a feminist analysis of Elvis was legitimate, I think it unlikely that this would spill over into acknowledgement of the need for feminist biography of him.

As I have tried to show in relation to my experience, Elvis was for me a source of liberation and not oppression. He was largely the product – the object – of girls and women who jettisoned him when it suited; and the sexist man turned out to have been also a mommy's boy who was totally bereft when left by his wife. However, this doesn't mean I'm not interested in the dominant view of Elvis nor that I haven't been influenced by it; rather the contrary, as I've shown. Rather than trying to replace one apparent 'truth', the dominant view of Elvis, with another 'truth', my experiential version of him, I have instead tried to show how closely – and how complexly – these two facets are intertwined within my own relationship with 'Elvis'. Feminist biography for me, then, is much less about who is the chosen subject, and much more about why they are chosen and how we go about looking at them. I finish by briefly considering what a feminist biography of Elvis Presley might look like.

A feminist biography of Elvis?

Alternatives to the 'straight' approach to writing biography are hard to come by. Notable exceptions are those biographies which utilise fiction as a means of illuminating the subject (like Weldon 1985; Barnes 1984; Lively 1987). Liz Stanley (1985) suggests the need to eschew easy distinctions between fiction and non-fiction and, in addition, proposes a multi-dimensional approach which includes focussing on the means of production; that is, the biographer herself. In terms of my own thinking about producing a biography of Elvis, the following seem feasible.

One way to produce a feminist biography of Elvis would be to do a fairly standard biographical study, but this time with a sexual political analysis shot through it. This would probably yield similar information to that produced in conventional biographies of Elvis but obviously would analyse this information differently. For example, those aspects of Elvis's image so exalted by male biographers would no doubt be criticised by a feminist one. The emphasis here would be on 'getting the story right' by including the experiences of those who are usually left out – the female fans – and by interpreting what is usually included in a 'proper' (namely, feminist) way. The result would be a biography different from any other on Elvis, but similar in the sense that it would work within the given parameters of 'here is Elvis the star as you've never seen him before'.

A second kind of feminist biography of Elvis would provide a feminist critique of existing biographies in order to expose the sexist bias of male writers. My analysis of Elvis shows, I think, that this is a useful exercise and exposes how certain white male journalists have constructed an 'objective' dominant ideology out of their own sub-jective experiences. Not 'this is what he meant to me' or 'this is the effect he had on me', but instead 'this is the effect he had world-wide (he must have had, because of his effect on me)'.

The third way to produce a feminist biography of Elvis would be a mingling of the biography of Elvis and the autobiography of the writer. It should be clear from what has gone before that this latter approach is one I most favour, not least because carrying out the other two approaches necessitates their location within this latter: without this experiential analysis (whether it appeared as, or in, a published biography or not), what would the critique/re-analysis be based on? Perhaps it might be based on yet more 'objective fact'; but, as I hope I have shown, an experiential analysis provides an incomparably stronger and more interesting basis for radical critique and new analysis. For me, then, a feminist biography of Elvis would include all three approaches, worked out around the analysis of the point at which autobiography and biography meet: the relationship between biographer and subject. And of course this, the relationship between researcher and researched, is the heart and mind of all feminist research processes.

© 1990 Sue Wise

Note

1   An earlier version of this chapter appeared under the title 'Sexing Elvis' in *Women's Studies International Forum* 1984, 7(1):13-17, and is reproduced here with the kind permission of the editor.

References

Barnes, Julian (1984) *Flaubert's Parrot*, London: Picador.
Beaulieu Presley, Priscilla (1985) *Elvis and Me*, London: Arrow Books.
Cohn, Nick (1969) *A WopBopaLooBop A LopBamBoom*, London: Paladin.
Elvis Monthly (various).
Lively, Penelope (1987) *Moon Tiger*, Harmondsworth: Penguin.
Melly, George (1970) *Revolt into Style*, Harmondsworth: Penguin.
Nuttall, Jeff (1969) *Bomb Culture*, London: Paladin.
Stanley, Liz (1985) *Feminism and Friendship*, Studies in Sexual Politics No.8,

Sociology Department, University of Manchester.

Wallace, Michelle (1979) *Black Macho and the Myth of the Superwoman*, London: John Calder.

Welburn, Vivienne (1982) 'Elvis: the Way It Was', *Forum* 15(7):46–51.

Weldon, Fay (1985) *Rebecca West*, Harmondsworth: Penguin.

Yancy, Becky (1977) *My Life with Elvis*, St Albans: Granada.

Chapter eleven

The professional and the personal
A study of women quantity surveyors

Clara Greed

Introduction

This chapter is based on my experiences as a feminist surveyor of doing research on the position of women in surveying. Women chartered surveyors form a very small minority (4.8 per cent) of the membership of one of the main professional bodies concerned with land-use and development. Unlike many works of feminist biography, I am dealing with women who are not famous, indeed somewhat 'hidden', not particularly feminist themselves, and not dead but very much alive. Therefore when the research is done I cannot just close the books and put the women back on the library shelves. Rather, it is quite likely that I will meet them again both at a professional and personal level; and frankly it might prove embarrassing. I cannot indulge in the safety and detachment of a 'hit-and-run' mentality towards research. Rather, I hope to continue to live and work amongst surveyors when I have finished. I actually like the world of surveying, and feel this is where I am meant to be.

So I am studying a world of which I myself am part, with all the emotional involvement and accusations of subjectivity that this creates. I do not attempt to keep my surveyors at arm's length and do research 'on' them as my subjects whilst maintaining a dominant position, as is common in much traditional 'objective' research. I see my research as a two-way process of interaction and sharing between myself and the other women. In particular, in trying to encompass both the professional and personal elements of their lives in my research, I need to be willing to give as well as take. If I expect women to tell me what their lives are really like at a personal level, they expect that in return I will share with them information about my personal life and feelings. If I pretend that I have authority to do research because I myself have superior understanding, and have no problems in my life, I would get nowhere because the empathy based on similar life experiences between researcher and researched would no longer exist. Therefore I am not attempting to 'control' my 'subjects' by keeping off topics that might affect me personally and which might reduce my credibility in the eyes of my 'subjects'. Rather, I am, albeit reluctantly, willing to take the risk of making myself vulnerable in the process of doing research; to getting hurt and admitting I have never been in control of my own life.

The aim of my research is not to look at women surveyors 'just' because it is another contribution to the growing number of studies of women in male-dominated professions (Podmore and Spencer 1987) or as part of the drive to get more women interested in science and technology (Whyte 1986). Rather, I am interested in the possible effects of the increase in the numbers of women entering the profession on urban policy-making. Also I am interested in the broader issue of how the predominantly male surveying profession perceives and treats women, both as fellow professionals and as members of urban society with their own particular land-use and development needs (WGSG 1984).

Surveyors are involved in all aspects of property and development, being particularly prominent within the private sector (Thompson 1968). Surveying is a very broad profession comprising within it everything from the technological areas of building and quantity surveying, where there are few women, through to the more 'Sloanie' areas of property investment, development and management, where the majority of women are found. In recent years there has been a marked increase in the numbers of women entering the land-use professions as a whole, and a greater interest from feminists in issues related to the built environment in general (Matrix 1985). This is reflected in the fact that nearly 20 per cent of surveying students are now women.

At the time of writing this chapter, I have been working on my research for about two and a half years on a part-time basis out of a five-year programme for a higher research degree. I am also a full-time lecturer in town planning in a Polytechnic Department of Surveying. I am actually not a mainstream surveyor but a town planner. However, to confuse matters, I am entitled to call myself a town planning surveyor by dint of membership of certain professional bodies; and I certainly feel I am myself 'a woman in surveying'. I experienced a similar professional education, and in practice encountered many of the problems that affect women in the land-use professions as a whole. In doing my research, I have been using three ethnographic methods (Atkinson 1979), all of which have led inevitably and naturally (although I was at first almost unwilling, because I felt it was all getting too 'personal' and subjective) to my putting emphasis on the study of the personal life experiences of individual women surveyors – that is, a group biography of sorts. Briefly, my three main approaches are as follows: (1) selective ethnographic observation of the educational setting of my own department; (2) retrospective ethnography, sometimes called 'personal anthropology' (Pocock 1973); and (3) dispersed ethnography – that is, going out and about to wherever the surveying sub-culture is found, and holding informal group interviews with women surveyors. This latter approach is common in studies of professions where people are dotted about in a range of professional practices. I am triangulating between the three methods (Hammersley and Atkinson 1983:198) in order to compare and contrast the observations from each source and, I hope, to develop 'sensitising concepts'.

Using my research approaches

My first approach, that of educational ethnography, is to help me build up a better picture of the male backcloth of the surveying sub-culture. In education the values and attitudes of the sub-culture are more likely to be openly stated as they are passed on to the next generation, than out in practice where they are taken as so natural that they are seldom commented upon. It is very difficult to find out what surveyors think about women, as there are no people, let alone women, in the surveying discourse, as a perusal of the journals and other professional literature shows (Joseph 1978, 1980). The world is populated by buildings and land values, and property rights. I suppose that the needs of the average man are so obvious that there is no need to state them. But men and their needs and motivations are there, taken as 'given', somewhere in the background. As Barthes says, man is everywhere and nowhere like the sky (1973). Occasionally 'the developer', 'the client' or even the non-gendered 'consumer' who drives 'his' car in 'his' leisure time to spend 'his' disposable income at the new out-of-town retail centre appears as a phantom – or, more likely, as a line drawing of a young male executive.

My other two methods put more emphasis on finding out about the experiences of individual women both at the personal and professional level. First, through retrospective ethnography I draw on my own experience, almost as if I were making an autobiography. Relatively speaking, I have already lived what I am researching (Wright Mills 1978). The idea is that I look back on events from my past life and observe and analyse them giving them the same research treatment as the events that happen today, almost like an 'action replay'. Since I am both the researcher and one of the researched, I cannot help but 'leave the researcher in' (Lury 1987), as 'in this process I too am subject' (Mulford 1986). My past experience enables me to develop 'sensitising concepts' more readily, because I already have an awareness and empathy with the issues that an outsider would not be able to develop so effectively in the time available. However, I am very aware of accusations that I am desensitised by over-familiarity. Therefore I struggle constantly to 'make the familiar strange' (Delamont 1985). Retrospective ethnography is not a straightforward and impersonal research approach. Indeed, it is the aspect of my research that upsets me most. When I look back over my life and compare it with the experiences of other women whom I have contacted in the course of my research I am overwhelmed by my own ignorance then, and how stupid and unaware I was; and how obvious it all is now in retrospect. Perhaps this is an occupational hazard of doing research in my late thirties. When I was a student in the late 1960s and early 1970s there were very few women in the areas of technology and male professions in general, and relatively speaking it was still the pre-feminist era (well, it was for me). When I see young women students who seem to know, without any apparent effort, all the things it took me twenty years to fathom out, it hurts, although I should rejoice for them.

My third approach, of dispersed ethnography, of going out and meeting women surveyors, has developed almost by default into what I call 'telephone ethnography'. I found that if I wrote to surveyors to see if they would be willing for me to come and visit them, they had to check with their boss, and whilst everyone hummed and haahed, very little was achieved. When I subsequently phoned to check progress, one thing led to another and I found myself there and then conducting an informal telephone interview which developed quite spontaneously. I now interview women directly on the phone as one of my main approaches (Frey 1983) either by prior arrangement or on the off-chance. The latter method is often the most rewarding and yields the longest conversations. Once women sense that I am giving out the right sub-cultural signals, the conversation develops and deepens most rewardingly. The telephone has the advantage of giving anonymity and invisibility, which, surprisingly, makes the women more open. However, in many cases the women in question already know of me through the grapevine, or I will subsequently meet the women in a social or professional context.

When talking on the phone, I have in mind certain questions which I always aim to cover. However, as we talk the women usually answer most of these without my having formally to 'ask' them. It is as if almost telepathically we share a knowledge of what we think is obviously important and of relevance. Indeed, asking formal questions can break the spell and restrict the flow. I only have to say at the beginning of the conversation, 'Why did you go into surveying?' and they are under starter's orders and off; and one thing leads to another – for over an hour in many instances. Women surveyors are always very busy and tend to be very economical and to the point in the use of the time (especially if it is also the firm's time). This is not to say that I have not also spent much longer with other women in more intensive, face-to-face discussion. However, it never ceases to amaze me that in a relatively short conversation many women are willing to bare their souls.

Sometimes I feel quite overwhelmed afterwards because of the intensity of it all. Therefore to some extent I try to be hardened and look at my watch and go on to the next person on my list and not let it get to me. But there have been certain interviews when I have been very upset afterwards and felt quite unable to sit down and objectively classify my findings. This tends to happen when: first, a woman is so successful, and so aware of every male trick in the book, that I feel that my whole life was worthless and that I am utterly stupid in comparison and I actually feel jealousy and envy towards her; or, second, when someone has obviously had a bitter experience themselves and we both get very upset. The woman in question may try to shift some of the weight on to me, and ask me what she should do. I feel utterly inadequate and useless. My only solution is to give her the name of some other woman surveyor in her area who I know would be a help to her. Many such women have hardened themselves to the blows of this world and are often actually quite lonely and without any feminist network. In a predominantly male profession one has to be seen to be tough and not admit to any weakness, and 'keep your head below the parapet', so many women are unwilling to let go and admit they have had problems (SBP 1987) – to admit you are a feminist is definitely a sign of weakness. I feel a great responsibility that my interviews may have in fact brought to the surface a mass of insoluble issues in their lives that they could not cope with, and I have opened a Pandora's box. I may have to admit that I too have never really faced the issues we have been discussing in my life either. This is not to suggest that every conversation is devastating, as the majority are far less traumatic and more routine. However, I am constantly embarrassed at the thought that after they have trusted me with their innermost thoughts and treated me as a friend, I am going to spend the evening 'objectifying them'.

I did at first try to be 'balanced' and talk to men surveyors as well as women. However, if I try to discuss with men the relationship between professional and domestic roles, they don't understand what I am getting at. If I try to talk to them as I do to the women, I find that they will either try to move the conversation back to the impersonal or alternatively confuse my motives as social rather than sociological: 'we must continue this conversation over a glass of wine'. In any case, I consider that the men's world-view is already fully represented in the professional journals and literature of the sub-culture and one is instinctively always making comparisons with the known male norms. After all, the men are all around me, and if I don't know by now in my life what makes them tick I never will. In contrast, women surveyors will volunteer feelings and observations on personal and domestic matters without my even asking, quite spontaneously and entirely mixed up with their comments on professional issues. Many women surveyors see everything in such a different light and can hold on to two realities at once, the professional and the personal.

Indeed, it may never have crossed their minds consciously that there is meant to be a major division in their lives between the two realms, although of course they will daily experience the inconveniences created by the fact that men subscribe to such a division. Many such women would never see themselves as feminists ('I'm not a feminist, of course') and appear not to have read any feminist books. They will use their own language and concepts, and may never even have heard of the word 'patriarchy', but are bound to describe its effects. Nevertheless they will demonstrate a great sensitivity to what are in fact 'feminist' issues in very refreshing and personal ways. Even when discussing impersonal issues such as land-uses they immediately relate the discussion to their own personal experience: 'after all, the men can't know, they don't use the shopping centres and the buses themselves, they just sit in their offices playing with retail figures'. In particular, women who have been 'housewives' as well as surveyors see things very differently from the young women straight out of college, many of whom still side with the men and can't see what all the fuss is about.

The research process is very much a two-way exchange of ideas and feelings; and I have learnt so much from other women that the traditional research model of subject and object is totally inappropriate. Very few have refused to talk to me. One woman, who had been 'used' as a token woman in the late 1970s and knew it, was quite rude but still talked to me. There was so much pain in her voice as she sought to convince me that my research was worthless, that I could hardly hear what she was saying, as part of her seemed to be communicating quite the opposite to me as a background vibration as we spoke. I have also had one incident of a group of women surveyors writing me a paper which stated that I was 'a danger to the profession', presumably because I was drawing attention to the very gender differences they had spent all their careers trying to minimise in order to gain acceptance into the world of men.

I am also dependent on women surveyors I know, to give me contacts that will lead me on to others. I am trying to contact a range of women of different ages, specialisms, levels of seniority and diverse life experiences. It is very helpful and pleasing when I have talked to a particular woman, if the next time I see her at a surveyors' meeting she rushes up to me with another woman in tow, saying, 'Look I've found you a woman who dropped out of surveying and then went back into it, you wanted one of these didn't you?' It can be embarrassing as the stranger and I stare at each other wondering what to say next, both being

150

totally unprepared for the encounter. However, I do get many of my contacts this way. Incidentally, I have overheard women surveyors enquiring of each other regards my research interviews, 'I've been done. Have you been done yet?', which makes me feel as if I'm administering some medical injection! I cannot claim a statistically correct sample, rather, a serendipitous selection, but I am trying to get a representative spread of women. So far I have spoken to at least 150 women. This method is called 'snowball sampling' and has been described as being used 'where populations are clandestine or deviant' (Rose 1982:50)!

Biography, ethnography or academic research?

Quite 'what' I am 'really doing' and what its true value is, and whether it counts as biography or ethnography or academic research, I leave the reader to decide. I simply have an urge to make more sense of both my own personal life and the urban environment in which I live, and also a concomitant curiosity about how others manage. This involves me in much ferreting about in books, observation of the urban world around me, and much chatting to people I meet along my way. To be honest, I was doing all this instinctively before it became official research, and in view of my more quantitative background I was quite surprised at first that my work counted as 'real research'. It is a pursuit that involves and affects my personal and emotional self totally, and which I can never limit to purely the academic or professional compartments of my life. Indeed, my research will not just end tidily with a completed thesis, but rather is likely to lead on my being aware of even more and deeper questions for further development later on in my life. My research interacts with my life, and both it and I myself change and go through different stages of development in parallel as the work progresses. Needless to say, such methods do not increase the status of my research in the eyes of men. Doing qualitative research from a feminist perspective within a predominantly male professional area, on a topic of which I am part and which has the word 'women' in it, means I am scrutinised twice as much by the men around me. They see it as their business and responsibility to judge on behalf of society as to whether my research is biased or not. Indeed, I get the distinct impression that they feel threatened by me.

Surveyors' professional decisions are not determined by neutral impartial 'asexual' factors, but rather they reflect their own personal interests and world-view. 'Everyone has a car nowadays', and 'Everyone wants to play rugby' are common statements within the world of surveying, and if any persons are not covered by either of these descriptions it may be 'because it is their own fault, as they have not tried and got on in life' or because 'they are not one of us, they are not the right type'. Therefore the personal element, far from being trivial and biased, is central in understanding how the sub-culture of surveying is maintained by making some individuals feel welcome whilst others are made to feel awkward, thus effecting professional closure (Parkin 1979). Undesirable elements are excluded before they can exert any alternative influence on the nature of the profession. This in turn affects the range of perspectives the profession has to draw upon in urban decision-making, and this ultimately shapes the nature of the built environment.

Therefore, a major tenet of my research is that, *at the personal level all the little nastinesses and nicenesses of daily life, far from being trivial or irrelevant, are in fact the very building blocks of the main-tenance of the sub-culture, making some feel welcome and others unwanted and ill at ease.* Women will never reach decision-making positions in the profession, and thus influence 'what is built', if they are subtly shunted sideways into unimportant areas, or more blatantly excluded, or not taken seriously, or even totally ignored within the daily life of the surveying tribe. This is my justification for use of the personal and the biographical in what is essentially urban spatial research, concerned with buildings and land. To substantiate this in terms of conceptual argument, I studied the ideas of Bourdieu (Bourdieu and Passeron 1977), Bernstein (1975), Delamont (1976), Atkinson (1985) and also Olin Wright (1985), all of whom in their various ways combine a wider structural perspective of society with an awareness of the role of the individual and the sub-culture in the reproduction of social relations and thus spatial relations.

However, real life is not simple and one cannot always 'see' manifestations of the workings out of various theories, as one may have to wait for certain occurrences to show their true fruit in the course of time. Men surveyors do not walk around with a blue-print of capitalism or patriarchy in their pockets to which they constantly refer to decide what to do next. Rather, they do what comes 'naturally' almost without thinking. Likewise, the women who recount their experiences to me do not usually compartmentalise them as being caused by 'capitalism' or 'patriarchy'. The majority of the men and the women in surveying are unlikely to have studied sociological theory themselves, and as stated earlier the women have very little awareness of feminist theory. Rather, they are likely to see the individual that caused them trouble, or more sadly to blame themselves as if they were entirely responsible for all that has happened in their lives. This is only 'natural' if they subscribe to values in which success or failure is a sign of personal effort and worth and not of higher economic and social forces. 'You've got to paddle your own canoe' is one of the most frequent phrases I hear from women surveyors. This does put a tremendous burden on some of them, and diverts the blame away from 'society' and 'men'. This attitude is particularly noticeable from women who have been relatively isolated from other women and alternative feminist ways of thinking: 'You just don't think about it, you just get on with the job.'

I have been struck by how complex women surveyors are. Internally, they seem to possess many different, contradictory levels of being; externally, their life experience spans a range of areas, both personal and professional. They certainly don't fit into mono-dimensional 'class' and sociopolitical categories that are usually created by the sort of people (chiefly men) who want to categorise others as being right or wrong, politically sound or incorrect. Whatever the area of surveying that women enter, they are likely to be motivated by a desire to achieve and be equal at a personal level, than by a sense of injustice, or anger, or a desire to change everything. However, many women surveyors may later experience an inner conflict and 'turn' when they discover they are not treated on equal terms in spite of all their efforts (Kanter 1977). Nevertheless, initially many are inspired by the role model of the successful businesswoman sometimes called the 'bourgeois feminist' (Hertz 1986). This model seems to give such women enough incentive to overcome any initial misgivings created by the technological image of surveying and stories of abusive workmen, heavy equipment and difficult maths, and to have faith to believe they will actually succeed in their chosen career. Indeed, many will accept the world of men and business without question, and would describe themselves as 'a surveyor first and a woman second'.

There are class as well as gender factors to be taken into account, and many of the women may cultivate the image of being 'above' or 'different' from other women. Although, at a personal level, they may see the inequity of their situation, it is another matter again for them to see the needs of other women in society. As one very open and honest woman surveyor admitted, 'I really have no idea how the average housewife lives, no more than the average man, I suppose.'

Most women surveyors are a complex and conflicting mixture of many different 'selves', each self having a different role and sense of reality. In addition, many seem to be able to hold on to an alternative, more liberal, internal perspective on life, although externally they may appear to be boring bourgeois businesswomen (Marshall 1984). In my research interviews a certain amount of encouragement, even a bit of nerve to make comments against the grain of the conversation, is needed to reach these various 'other' levels of being, beneath the surface of the public image of the mono-dimensional woman surveyor. Many will respond almost with relief when I do this, as they may be suppressing many dilemmas within their being.

Women often use a different accent and demeanour in recounting very personal accounts – of, for example, harassment – from their 'normal' manner and presentation of themselves as a professional woman. Indeed it is almost as if I am expected to go through a ritual warming-up session asking all the 'proper' questions about their careers and professional practice, during which time they will affirm there are no problems and everything is as it should be. Then at a certain point the conversation seems to change gear and they will then proceed to say many other things that may actually contradict what they said earlier. It is almost as if women are so used to having to keep face both with men and other official women, and acting out the role of the equal woman, that they cannot easily let go of this image. Once they have sized me up then they can trust me to say what they really want to say. I suspect that researchers (especially men) using conventional interview methods may never break through to this second stage.

Many women seem to have almost a burden to bear witness of their experiences: 'You must write this down but don't say I said it' is a common statement. For example, one woman told me how in a certain provincial practice a woman announced she was going to get married. It happened to be the time when the firm's headed notepaper was being reprinted. She was astounded to find her name was left off the list of associate partners at the top of the page: 'Oh, we thought you were going to leave, women always do when they get married.' Some appear very upset when they recount such events, and several have said if they bottle it up it does come back to them later and wears them down: 'It's not so much outright discrimination, it's all the little things that get to you after a while.' Some are very conscious of their own life history. For example, one of the first women building surveyors rather dispassionately said she kept a scrapbook like a film star of all the times she got the 'first woman' treatment in the professional press, and treated it all as rather amusing and separate from the 'real her': 'I just wanted to be left alone to get on with my job.' There is indeed a great richness and diversity in the experiences of women surveyors.

© 1990 Clara Greed

References

Acker, Sandra and Warren Piper, David (1984) *Is Higher Education Fair to Women?* Guildford: SRHE and NFER-Nelson.

Atkinson, Paul (1979) 'Research Design in Ethnography', in Block 3B, *Research Design, DE304, Research Methods in Education and the Social Sciences,* Milton Keynes: Open University.

—— (1985) *Language, Structure and Reproduction,* London: Methuen.

Barthes, Roland (1973) *Mythologies,* London: Paladin.

Bernstein, Basil (1975) *Class, Codes and Control*, London: Routledge & Kegan Paul.

Bourdieu, Pierre and Passeron, Jean-Claude (1977) *Reproduction of Education, Society and Culture*, London: Sage.

Delamont, Sarah (1976) 'The Girls Most Likely to: Cultural Reproduction and Scottish Elites', *Scottish Journal of Sociology* 1:29–43.

—— (1985) 'Fighting Familiarity', Paper from ESRC Summer School, *Strategies of Qualitative Research in Education*, Warwick.

Frey, James (1983) *Survey Research by Telephone*, London: Sage.

Hammersley, Michael and Atkinson, Paul (1983) *Ethnography, Principles in Practice*, London: Tavistock.

Hertz, Leah (1986) *The Business Amazons*, London: André Deutsch.

Joseph, Martin (1978) 'Professional Values, a Case Study of Professional Students in a Polytechnic', *Research in Education* (May): 49–65.

—— (1980) 'Professional Socialisation: a Case Study of Estate Management Students', D.Phil., Oxford University.

Kanter, Rosabeth Moss (1977) *Men and Women of the Corporation*, New York: Basic Books.

Lury, Celia (1987) *The Difference of Women's Writing: Essays on the Use of Personal Experience*, Studies in Sexual Politics No. 15, University of Manchester.

Marshall, Judith (1984) *Women Managers – Travellers in a Male World*, London: Wiley.

Matrix (Women Architects) (1985) *Making Space, Women and the Man-made Environment*, London: Pluto.

Mulford, Wendy (1986) 'In This Process, I Too Am Subject', in Denise Farran, Sue Scott and Liz Stanley (eds), *Writing Feminist Biography*, Studies in Sexual Politics No. 13/14, University of Manchester, pp. 53–72.

Olin Wright, Erik (1985) *Classes*, London: Verso.

Parkin, Frank (1979) *Marxism and Class Theory: a Bourgeois Critique*, London: Tavistock.

Pocock, David (1973) 'The Idea of a Personal Anthropology', Paper, ASA Conference.

Podmore, David and Spencer, Anne (1987) *In a Man's World: Essays on Women in Male-dominated Professions*, London: Tavistock.

Rose, Gerry (1982) *Deciphering Sociological Research*, London: Macmillan.

SBP (South Bank Polytechnic) (1987) *Women and their Built Environment*, Conference Proceedings, London.

Thompson, F.L.M. (1968) *Chartered Surveyors, the Growth of a Profession*, London: Routledge & Kegan Paul.

Whyte, June (1986) *Girls into Science and Technology*, London: Routledge & Kegan Paul.

WGSG (Women and Geography Study Group) (1984) Institute of British Geographers, *Geography and Gender*, London: Hutchinson.

Wright Mills, Charles (1978) *The Sociological Imagination*, Harmondsworth: Penguin.

Analytically Using Experience

Chapter twelve

Breaking the rules
Assessing the assessment of a girls' project

Fiona Poland

Introduction

Much feminist research deals with the problems involved in processing
data by producing a number of 'guarantees of good faith': by having a
woman researcher; by studying women subjects; and sometimes by
researching in small-scale, more 'natural' contexts and reproducing
lengthy quotes from research subjects. Yet none of this removes the fact
that it is the researcher who decides how to collect 'data', what to
include, and how to process these data so as to produce 'findings'.
Indeed, such practicalities are only rarely touched on. My argument is
that the selection and presentation of data is crucial to an understanding
of the resulting texts, and that feminist research should explain these
aspects of its production process.

This chapter focusses on the researcher as central to research, as the
means by which topics are selected, data are collected and interpreted,
and conclusions reached and presented to the reader. My conviction is
that the only important differences between an 'objective' account and
one including 'the researcher' as central are that in an 'objective
account': (1) aspects of the researcher's experience which constitute
'what was collected' are highly glossed as 'fact', unattributed to the
researcher and her doings; and (2) the researcher's actual participation
in the social activity within which the data were collected is not
described. I therefore propose to make these two aspects central to my
account of a substantive research project in which I was involved.

This chapter deals with these questions in relation to a feminist
'action research' project (Kelly 1985). I begin with an outline of the
history of the project and my role within it, then examine these questions
as they arise in connection with a tape-recorded meeting of the action
project's management committee.

A feminist action research project and its data

For over three years I was a management member of a feminist action research project which was looking at a neighbourhood's youth provision for girls, who typically 'missed out' in a number of ways. One aspect of it was to produce a research study of local youth provision. Originally there was one paid 'action research' worker managed by women actively involved with girls' work. I was asked to join to support the research activities. More recently the project entered a new phase. It took on another full-time paid worker, several part-time paid workers and volunteers, new management members, and new areas of activity. Its research on youth provision was carried out by management members as well as by the paid worker.

The management committee decided to assess the previous years' work, mostly developed by the original worker. She and I were 'designated researchers', so it seemed appropriate that we should be responsible for the assessment. With full agreement, my M.A. dissertation concerned my part in the assessment process.

Initially we had no clear idea about how to produce an assessment useful and acceptable to project members and a 'wider public' which would also be consistent with the 'feminist principles' on which the project operated. We decided to interview each management member individually (including one another) to examine, first, our ideas and practice in assessing work; second, what uses and focus were wanted for the assessment; third, what each member had done over the year; that is, to 'place' them and to see how effectively skills and experience as 'project resources' were being used.

I also had ideas about how I thought the assessment should be done. I wanted to ensure control of its progress by all group members, rather than their feeling they were 'research objects' or treating me as a 'research expert'. I also felt the assessment could be a learning experience in conceptualising and analysing how we worked. Therefore I wanted to make visible how I worked and reached my conclusions so that people could decide whether or not they agreed.

Copies of the interview questions and all completed interviews were sent to each management member – in order to give them an idea of the work involved; to see what their views looked like in this form; and to decide whether my 'topic headings' summarising their views seemed appropriate. A meeting was organised to talk about the assessment, committee members having seen the interviews. This meeting was recorded to help me collect material for my dissertation while playing a full part in the discussion. As only five out of twelve management members turned up, it was also used so that those absent could hear what the others had said. Both paid workers, two out of three regular volunteer workers, and two 'purely management' members were unable to attend. The participants were two founder members and managers (C.

and B.), a relatively recent member of management (F.), one of the regular volunteer workers (A.) and myself (R.).

All those parts of the meeting in which I spoke were transcribed and appear in full in Poland 1985. However, here I discuss Transcript 5 only. Because it is one of the shortest and I intervene in it only once, it is suitable to use in order to outline what I think are six possible ways in which to use the transcripts in research terms.

Having collected information – whether notes of someone talking or responses to a questionnaire or anything else – there remains the problem of 'what to do next'. In many established research approaches this appears completely straightforward, with a process specified for turning collected material into 'findings'.

In the interview stage I followed an 'established' approach, grouping each person's interview statements into 'project management' topics. I emphasised that project members were free to alter or add to my summarising categories, but I took the decision that this was the next step and presented the interviews in the form of 'management topics' rather than anything else.

Following the recording and transcription of this meeting, I then also had a set of transcripts but was left with the problem of deciding what to do with them. Simply: what sort of data did they constitute? There are no indisputably 'right' criteria for putting order into such material. I produced the following list of six things the transcripts could be seen as representing: (1) examples of 'doing research'; (2) examples of 'doing feminist research'; (3) examples of 'conversation'; (4) examples of 'my own intentionality'; (5) examples of the 'planning research/research experience' disjuncture; and (6) examples of 'how policy-makers (that is, project management members) see assessment and use it'. These ways of seeing and using the transcripts are now examined in relation to Transcript 5. I also discuss whether relating the categories to the data make it tell us the *same* thing in six different ways, or whether it tells us *different* things.

In the transcript which follows I have used brackets enclosing two or more speakers' words to indicate that they were spoken together; and stops (.) to indicate one second's pause in the speaker's utterance per stop. I have used initials to denote speakers' names – these are not their own initials – and 'R'. (researcher) to refer to me.

Using Transcript 5, an outline of the possibilities

Transcript 5

1 B: I haven't had, I don't feel like I've had a new idea about (girl's work)

A: (But I feel)
   (But I feel) like that
5 B: (for *ages*)
  A: B
  B: Do you?
  A: Especially since I've been doing like the activities and staff
    for the, uh, summer. And it's like you've done it all before
10   and you think 'Jesus'. And it, it just feels flat. You know
  B: It, it might not though, 'cause you might have a really good
  A: Well, I mean
  B: (have a really good summer)
  A: (you know, the trips and stuff), like, the roller skating and
15   things that we've
    (done)
  C: (Yeah)
  A: We took seventeen on the bus and staff. But I kind of think
    "Well, there's got to be more than the roller skating or
20   something, you know."
  B: Maybe it's just how you're feeling about it.
    ((laughs))
  A: ((laughs)) No I'm not feeling tired or anything
  B: But maybe just a bit negative,
25   (maybe about it)
  A: (Yeah, yeah.) Mm it's difficult. It's like we're just
    doing.things we've we've
    (done before)
  C: (I think you) see I think you have to *build* from what you're
30 doing
  A: (Mm)
  C: (I really do)
    (um)
  A: (Mm)
35 C: But then I just think that comes from, through closer
    relationships...
  A: It's like, you know it, it's not the quality of what
    you're doing. It's like you were saying it's like the quantity,
    it's like you've *got* to be taking fifteen or
40   seventeen girls. Or you *think* that, or it's not much
    good or something
  B: Whereas you might go and just wander round someplace with a
    few girls and have a really good
    (chat with them)
45 C: (Yeah)

B: and that would be
   (worth more)
A: (Yeah)
B: (wouldn't it?)
50 A: (Well that's what) I *feel* about, you know,
   (I mean)
B: (But you)'ve *got* to fill the minibus every time
A: And. and in a lot of ways I don't want to, I don't want to
   do that. I'd rather take eight or whatever and do something
55 that, that is really good. But, you know. Or, or not that's
   really good but that I, I get a good feeling out of, perhaps
   . than, than all the time pushing, like numbers and that.
   The L.G. syndrome isn't it?
C: Mm, yes...
60 R: Although it was interesting that in, I mean like in, in your
   interview you said, um, you know how, how would you
   assess the uh. the only thing you were able to think of was the
   numbers thing, because that was the only thing that ever came
   up sort of
65 (thing)
A: (Yeah.) Yeah, perhaps it's just the way I look at things.
   Perhaps I've got a guilt (laugh) complex about me working
   with them, you know
   (when)
70 B: (You see) if we're trying to look at how effective we are as
   managers or whatever and individuals I think what I, I
   was feeling was, um....that I don't feel....you know when
   I said I don't feel in control I don't feel I'm inspiring
   anybody any more. 'Cause quite often that's how you have to
75 feel when you're in a position, you know like you're really
   sort of like. encouraging people to. to do the work and things.
   I don't feel I'm doing that any more. And yet, in spite of
   that, the Project's going *wonderfully* well *without* me doing
   that, and in a way that's a relief. I suppose I do feel I'm
80 being more effective with G. You know, working more closely
   with her, um. but I think there's quite a lot there that I'm *not*
   doing as well

1 Transcript 5 as an example of 'doing research'

If I take T5 as an example of 'doing research', I need to know what
'doing research' in general is like. If I look at a methods textbook,
research is seen to consist of activities such as 'data collection' in which

the researcher carries out activities like 'building rapport' and 'maintaining neutrality' as well as 'recording data'. Yet it is difficult to see what these activities (and, therefore, 'doing research') actually look like 'on the ground', to distinguish them from social activities and conversations.

In T5 there is not, apparently, a lot of 'doing research' to be seen except for the fact that I taped and transcribed it and in doing so intended it as research. So how *do* I identify it as 'research'? The means of identification lie primarily outside the transcript, in intentionality.

First, one of my intentions in organising the meeting was to discuss project assessment; but for most of its duration this was not discussed. However, the transcript does contain one conventionally obvious 'doing research' remark which refers explicitly to assessment (T5: 60–5); interestingly, it was not taken up or discussed further. Second, the transcript can be read as an example of some project members (particularly A.) deciding to discuss their feeling that an important criterion of assessment is the quality of experience of a trip or activity rather than the number of girls doing it. Here A. said (T5: 54–8), 'I'd rather take eight or whatever and do something that, that is really good. But, you know. Or, or not that's really good but that I, I get a good feeling out of, perhaps . than, than all the time pushing, like numbers and that.' However, that this relates to 'assessment criteria' is only clear when a reader shares my knowledge and therefore my ability to 'read' it in such a way. And, additionally, the connection between this and 'doing research' similarly requires a great deal of knowledge and work to trace out.

I intervened (T5: 60) to point out to A. that previously in her interviews 'the only thing you were able to think of was the numbers thing' (T5: 62–3) – in the interview she had described 'numbers of girls' rather than 'quality of feeling' as a criterion. This intervention might well be seen as 'bad research technique': my biasing her response by putting words into her mouth. It could equally well be seen as 'good member's behaviour' by taking up a pause in the conversation and filling it in, or indeed as 'bad member's behaviour' in making apparent a contradiction, an inconsistency, and so making for awkwardness in the conversation.

Seen in the context of A.'s response (T5: 66–9), my remark seems out of place because not governed by the flow of the conversation: it is rather 'a piece of research' cutting across the things the others are talking about and the way they are talking about them. A. gives only a vague reply (T5: 66–9) and is 'rescued' from further 'accusation' from me by B.'s lengthy discussion of what effectiveness might be for her (T5: 70–82); and this also prevents 'more research' from occurring. But an alternative reading exists here because of my particular role within the project. The others may well have expected me-as-researcher to say 'that kind of thing'; and it could, therefore, have been legitimate for me to say such a thing in that conversation, requiring a different explanation of A.'s reply and B.'s intervention.

Reading this transcript as 'doing research' may offer only one, limited example (T5: 60–2) of 'research' being done. However, my knowledge of the context, especially that the meeting was 'about assessment', makes other remarks 'research-significant', like A.'s and B.'s comments about success criteria. Furthermore, part of my knowledge of the situation is that other project members may also think it legitimate for me to say such things as T5: 60–5 even though they are voicing other concerns at the time.

2 *Transcript 5 as an example of 'doing feminist research'*

I have to look outside the actual data to tell me what defines T5 as an example of 'doing feminist research'. Likely criteria include the importance of a participatory approach, respecting other people's experience, and 'feeling' as a legitimate source of data. Certainly the participants are women who see themselves as feminist; and in various instances they stress the importance of relying on feelings and relationships (for example, T5: 35–6). However, I still cannot tell from this that it is a piece of feminist research.

Perhaps what makes it 'feminist research' lies in the arrangements leading up to the meeting (and whether I did these in a feminist way), and then how the material was dealt with afterwards. It might be located in the very fact that the meeting as it occurred was not explicitly and formally 'about' the research/assessment and my role as researcher was very low key. This is still unsatisfactory, but it exemplifies how using the transcript as an example of 'feminist research' requires knowledge of 'something wider' than what occurred in the meeting itself.

There are non-feminist studies of girls and women and non-feminist 'participatory' action research. There are also controversies about research carried out by a feminist where others disagree that it constitutes feminist research (see, for example, Nava 1982; but also Birmingham Lesbian Offensive Group 1983; Camden Girls Project 1983). My difficulties in using the transcript as 'feminist research' therefore derive in part from difficulties in the development of feminist research concepts. However, some aspects could be seen as self-evidently demonstrating feminist concerns.

The key example is that the transcript (perhaps particularly at T5: 37–59) is of a group of women discussing the use of feelings and experience ('the subjective') as a basis for deciding how well some activity went, rather than the numbers involved ('the objective'). This reading might, however, be contradicted by my intervention (T5: 60–5),

165

which could be seen as a rebuke for doing so. The others are agreeing that 'pushing numbers' (T5: 57) is unsatisfactory, yet I point out that A., who had just said this, said the opposite in her interview. Do I imply that she isn't really a feminist? is inconsistent or illogical? However, A.'s reluctance to take this any further (T5: 66–9) and B.'s subsequent 'rescuing' intervention (T5: 70–82) demonstrate that 'research criteria' do not control the flow of discussion.

It is difficult to say how this is an example of doing research in a feminist way. It may in fact be an example of feminist research because of what is *not* happening, in terms of control and structuring of the situation; mostly those present talk about things as a group and my formal research role does not entitle me to lead or control this.

3 *Transcript 5 as an example of 'a conversation'*

To examine the extract as 'a conversation', I feel I need to know something about formal ways of describing and analysing conversations. I do not have the knowledge of a conversational analyst; but I took part with a 'member's competence' and have some ideas of what the conversation is 'about'. At a formal level, I can see from the transcript that there is little overt disagreement or contradiction. Where there are overlaps or interruptions these tend to consist of 'agreeing' sounds or remarks. But I am unlikely to get much further than this with my use of T5 as conversation unless I set out a detailed description of what is said in it.

It begins with B. saying (T5: 1) that she had not had a new ideal about 'girls' work' for ages. A. reinforced this point: she felt like this as well (T5: 3–4). This particularly applied to her feelings about the activities organised for the summer (T5: 8–10). She was explaining that 'it's like you've done it all before' when B. (T5: 11) cut in to say that the summer activities might turn out all right. A., however, continued to make the same point (T5: 12, 14–16) and mentioned some activities which on the face of it are successful, in terms of numbers ('seventeen on the bus' (T5: 18)). She added that 'there's got to be more than the roller skating' (T5: 19). Just 'doing activities' did not seem to be 'achieving'.

B. intervened again (T5: 21) to say that this is not really the case; it could be just how A. was feeling about it. A. could be seen as implying that her taking part in activities might be seen as a good thing by some project members but was not satisfactory to her. This is confirmed by A.'s continuing (T5: 23) to deny B.'s interpretation. B. then qualified her point by repeating it in a slightly different form: 'But maybe just a bit negative, maybe about it' (T5: 24–5). This is more tentative than her previous remarks, with more 'maybes' and hesitations; and A. also qualified her reply: 'Yeah, yeah .. Mm it's difficult' (T5: 26). However, she continued to make the point that it was like 'doing things we've done before'.

C. then intervened (T5: 29–30) to put a different angle on the situation. The activities were just a foundation for something else to be built up through closer relationships (T5: 35–6). While she talked A. made neutral agreeing noises (T5: 32–5). However, when C. finished there was a long pause (five seconds) which indicated that other people were either unsure about what she said, did not know how to take it up, or simply wanted to talk about something else.

A. then continued (T5: 37–41) about 'having to take fifteen or seventeen girls'. She could be agreeing with C's point – taking so many girls might preclude 'closer relationships'. Equally she could be developing her explanation of the doubts she raised earlier, but now shifting attention from activities to the stress laid on the number of girls involved. Her observation between T5: 37 and T5: 41 is that concern is with quantity and not quality, so that unless there were 'fifteen or seventeen girls' an activity might be judged to be 'not much good' (T5: 40–1).

Potential for disagreement seems to have been successfully avoided with B. joining in (T5: 42). She enlarged on A.'s feeling by saying that it might be 'worth more' (T5: 42) to 'wander around' and have a 'really good chat' with some girls (T5: 42–5). As she talked A. agreed with her (T5: 45, 48, 50); she began to speak in T5: 50 but B. then reformulated the feeling that the main criterion for success is that 'you've got to fill the minibus every time' (T5: 52).

A. stated emphatically that she did not want to do so (T5: 53–4). She would rather take 'eight' (that is, a smaller number) and do something 'really good', that she got 'a good feeling out of' (T5: 56). She contrasted this with 'all the time pushing ... numbers' (T5: 57). She defined this as a 'Local Government' syndrome. C. vaguely agreed with this (T5: 59) and there was a long pause (five seconds).

At this point I observed (T5: 60–5) that in A's interview she had only mentioned 'numbers' (T5: 63) as a means of assessment, and added that the 'numbers criterion' was the only one ever mentioned. This remark was delivered very hesitantly and vaguely: a lot of pauses, repetitions and unfinished sentences. A. agreed with me briefly, with 'perhaps it's just the way I look at things, perhaps I've got a guilt (laughs) complex' (T5: 67–8). This could mean that she preferred to use one way of assessing activities while feeling obliged to use another. She did not have much option except to reply as she did. The choice was between making an issue of saying different things at different times or of being non-committal. For all she knew, I might have been trying to show her up or to make some point at her expense.

She might have continued (T5: 69) but B. broke in to talk about what 'effectiveness' might mean for her. This can be read as her developing the theme of gauging effectiveness by feelings. B's remarks here could relate to her earlier apparent reluctance to accept the point A. was making about finding 'activities' less than satisfactory. She stated a different source of dissatisfaction for herself: 'I don't feel I'm inspiring anybody any more' (T5: 73–4). She said that 'you have to feel when you're in a position, you know like you're really sort of like. encouraging people to . to do the work and things' (T5: 74–6). Her stated source of dissatisfaction and A.'s can be seen as clearly at odds, but this intervention was at a sufficient 'distance' from the earlier near-disagreement to make it more acceptable.

However, another reading of B.'s intervention is that it 'rescues' A. at T5: 70 from being further put on the spot by me. B. said that she did not feel she was 'encouraging people' any more (T5: 76) and was therefore ineffective; nevertheless she also thought that 'the project's going *wonderfully* well without me doing that' (T5: 78–9) as assessed by other criteria. She continued that she felt she was 'more effective' with G. (whom she supervises) but there was a lot she was not doing with her as well (T5: 80). The transcript ends just before the discussion drifted off on to some of the administrative details of B.'s job.

Much of this transcript is 'about' how project members assess whether what they are doing is effective and what criteria they use in doing so. However, this was talked about in a largely elliptical way. The transcript is also about how people can say what they want about effectiveness in a way that is acceptable to the others so as to preserve the climate of agreement. It is still not obvious what constitutes 'research in progress' here, although there are many signs of what constitutes 'agreement in progress' (and these come from the others rather than from me).

I think the extract can best be read as 'doing a conversation' first and foremost. My examination of T5 in these terms led me swiftly from looking at features of it relating to 'conversations' in general, to examining the particular details of what the events as represented by the transcript were about (that is, as a topic in its own right, rather than as a resource used to tell me about something external to the events in hand). In doing so I gained information necessary to my later examination of the transcript as an example of the 'planning research/research experience' disjuncture and of 'ways policy-makers see and use assessment', not to mention 'doing research' and 'doing feminist research'. Looking back at the previous two sections, it will be noted that I actually had to start this examination of the transcript as 'topic' there, even if only patchily. Indeed, it would have been more fruitful to have looked at what the transcript was 'about' in detail before beginning any attempt to use it as resource. However, I have preserved my actual order of working to show my learning process.

4 Transcript 5 as an example of 'my own intentionality'

One element of the situation excluded so far, because I have been treating all parties to the conversation in an even-handed way, is my own intentionality in responding and speaking as I did. My knowledge of myself and my experience of this conversation can highlight what *I* thought it was about. This cannot be unpacked from the transcript by 'any reader', but of course I am a 'privileged reader' of it.

I brought my own concerns to the meeting. I wanted people to use it to review their work and also to be more reflective about the means they used to draw conclusions; I wanted them to see research as a process of sharpening their awareness of what is involved in collecting and producing 'useful information'.

When A. emphasised (T5: 53–8) that she did not want to use numbers as a criterion for assessing 'successful activity', I realised she had said something different in her interview. I had to decide whether to break into the conversation. The hesitancy of the remark I finally delivered (T5: 60–5) is obvious. I think now it could be best explained in terms of my taking a part in the conversation rather than as a research or a feminist research contribution (although such considerations might have played a part). That is, I had not yet spoken, and soon my lack of involvement would have become open to negative interpretations.

My intervention cuts right across the general business of agreement taking place. Therefore I had good reason to be hesitant. At that moment, the conversation for me was about 'assessment', part of a wider process of collecting information and comparing different guidelines for my carrying out this activity. So my hesitation can be explained by my awareness of the difficulties involved in introducing these other concerns.

5 Transcript 5 as an example of the 'planning research/research experience' disjuncture

Much of the transcript is concerned with how project members assess whether what they do is effective and by what criteria. However, this is done in an elliptical way. An attempt by me to make this theme more explicit and to tie it in to a wider set of concerns led to me acting more 'like a researcher' than as a 'member of the group', and this was clearly disruptive. The particular intervention I made had the effect of setting me apart from the others by doing something which could easily be seen as non-empathetic, possibly even 'not feminist' because it pointed out someone's contradictions. However, were I to make *any* contribution 'as a researcher' this would have necessitated my cutting across the existing talk. Is taking part in my known research role an example of good or bad group membership, good or bad research behaviour? Whichever, it also shows how the 'planned research' aspects of the situation were made subordinate to the experiential and contextually specific concerns of other project members.

The disjuncture arose because I decided to carry out the research as much as possible in conjunction with the group. Researchers rarely take part in processing research which has interpersonal consequences; however, my research context was at one and the same time a social event with social consequences. Thus my intervention was no abstract exercise but, rather, socially and interpersonally charged. Moreover, in neither research nor social terms was there an obvious way for me to decide which of the two views expressed by A. was her 'real' view. Does one statement have to be right? Or is each the right thing to say in some situations but not others? Perhaps one thing to take into account here is that researchers often talk in one way to plan research, another to report results, and another when taking part in 'social life'; and considerable personal disruption would follow if they did not do so.

6 Transcript 5 as an example of 'how policy-makers see assessment' and use it

Examining T5 to see how policy-makers (that is, us as members of the project management committee) see and use assessment, it is clear that rather different concerns are voiced. The major theme is the identification of 'effectiveness'. A. talked about her dissatisfaction with 'just' doing activities (T5: 3–28). As C. and B. work more on the managerial side of the project's organisation (as I do), this may be relevant to B.'s interpretation of A.'s observation as 'just feelings' (T5: 21–2, 24–5). C.'s observation that one approach to the work might be 'through closer relationships' (T5: 34–6) was barely taken up. A. then expressed dissatisfaction with using 'numbers' as a criterion of success. She had not really taken up my intervention in T5: 60–5 before B. introduced her discussion of effectiveness.

One interesting aspect of T5 is the way in which participants work at 'agreeing' with one another. Different views are expressed without the differences being obviously put. A key means of doing this is 'spacing out' expressions of disagreement (as between A. and B., and A. and R.). The meeting offered people the chance to discuss sources of satisfaction and dissatisfaction and to come to an agreement about the usefulness of working to a 'quality, not quantity' criterion. However, these differences had to be managed around the felt need to be supportive and to find areas of agreement. One conclusion here seems to be that some sorts of assessment activities are more appropriate and acceptable in this context than others. Another is that 'as researcher' I have interactional problems in a discussion set up as part of a co-operative research exercise but in which other people do not share my ideas about what are 'research matters'.

Some conclusions about the possibilities for using the data

I have looked at the data comprised by Transcript 5 from six somewhat different starting points. In an earlier draft there were more, but problems of classification became apparent when 'working' some of them and they were dropped. The order in which these starting points are discussed may not seem entirely logical, given what I have said about the usefulness and importance of using the conversation 'as a topic' in its own right in order to be able to use it as a resource. However, my six starting points are presented in the order in which I originally worked through them, to provide the reader with some indication of my learning process, and also to enable them to contrast the kinds of analysis thus allowed.

These six ways of using the data are clearly not mutually exclusive, but neither are they completely overlapping. Overall the transcript seems to make most sense when seen as a conversation in which individual concerns are voiced and carefully managed within the whole. Seeing it as 'research' or as 'feminist research' is not very helpful, though perhaps relevant to the importance of being careful about how I interacted. The examination of the 'planning research/research experience' disjuncture is useful in pointing up 'research' as only one concern among several which appeared to govern the way discussion went in the conversation.

© 1990 Fiona Poland

References

Birmingham Lesbian Offensive Group (1983) 'Letter about Mica Nava's article', *Feminist Review* 13:103.
Camden Girls Project (1983) 'Letter about Mica Nava's article', *Feminist Review* 13:103–4.
Kelly, Alison (1985) 'Action Research: What Is It and What Can It Do?' in Robert Burgess (ed.), *Issues in Educational Research*, Brighton: Falmer Press, pp. 129–51.
Nava, Mica (1982) 'Everybody's Views were Just Broadened: a Girls' Project and Some Responses to Lesbianism', *Feminist Review* 10:37–58.
Poland, F. (1985) 'Breaking the rules: assessing the assessment of a girls' project', *Studies in Sexual Politics* 4.

Chapter thirteen

The mastectomy experience

Ann Tait

Introduction

This chapter comprises a sociological analysis of a transcript from a
tape-recorded interview made in 1976 with a woman I shall call R. The
interview was a part of a medical research project which took place
mainly in a hospital, although some interviews occurred in patients'
homes.

Research in England had shown that many women with breast cancer
who underwent mastectomy (removal of the breast) suffered 'psychiatric morbidity' in the form of depressive illnesses or anxiety states. A
research project was set up to test the hypothesis that counselling by a
specialist nurse might prevent or lessen this 'mor- bidity'. Patients who
agreed to take part in it were randomly allocated to one of two groups.
Those in the experimental group were given routine care plus visits by
the specialist nurse. Those in the control group were given routine care
alone. My involvement, following the departure of the original
specialist nurse, was to undertake this role.

There were some hopeful findings from this project, for it seemed
that my ability to assess and pick up emotional problems had led me to
make adequate referrals for many of the women to other agencies.
Consequently, when the women were assessed one year after they had
undergone mastectomy, there was a reduction in the psychiatric
morbidity experienced by those in the experimental group compared
with those in the control group (Maguire *et al.* 1980; see also Maguire
1976; Maguire *et al.* 1982, 1983; Tait *et al.* 1980; Wilkinson *et al.*
1983).

The relative success of the project led to the role of the specialist
nurse becoming institutionalised and funded by the local district health
authority. In addition, a further research project was supported by the
then Department of Health and Social Security, also a controlled clinical
trial.

A second 1983 interview took place with R. when this second research project was nearly finished, but not as an integral part of the research. By 1983 R. had suffered a recurrence of her cancer and I was still in contact with her; and this second interview took place for various complex reasons. The discussion in this chapter is of the 1976 interview only; a detailed discussion of the 1983 interview and a fuller one of the 1976 interview is contained in Tait (1986).

R.'s career as a breast cancer patient

The transcript derives from a recording made, with permission, on my first visit to R.'s home a few weeks following her discharge from hospital. I had met R. briefly in the out-patient clinic and had heard about her in conversation with other staff. I had also read my predecessor's notes about her. When I decided to use the transcript for my personal research I asked R., the research director and the professor of surgery for permission; and they all agreed. R. particularly was pleased that her transcripts would be 'useful'.

My point of departure, in research terms, is that though I was the 'A.' who listens and speaks with R. in the transcript, I am necessarily always at least at one remove. By being able to write this now, I am separated, already abstracted from the there and then, and ready with my concepts and analysis. In one sense I have, to use Garfinkel's (1967) phrase, 'a docile text' and I could simply use the transcript as a description; however, I prefer to take into account the situation in which the transcript was produced by R. and myself.

Using the 1976 transcript as my raw data, I take as my first topic 'R.'s career as a breast cancer patient'. The notion of 'career' is familiar to sociologists and seems a peculiarly apt vehicle to convey the meaning that having breast cancer held, not only for R. but for also many other women I interviewed. R.'s experience was unique to her and yet it contained numerous facets common to others. Within this framework I can encapsulate some of these general characteristics of a 'moral career': its temporal and processual nature, and the way the physical reality of the illness led R. to construe it as an 'it', a 'thing' with an almost objective and factual 'life of its own'. 'Career' also enables me to perceive that R. felt she was a stigmatised and unwittingly deviant social being because of 'it'; that she had a 'front' maintained by performances of various kinds, and 'passed as normal' by these means alone.

Taking R.'s utterances as my raw material I can, in Goffman's (1961) terms, take as my main concern the moral aspects of R.'s career, for she underwent changes influenced by her external relationships with other members of society, but also by her view of herself. This 'definition of the situation', whether constructed from 'within' or 'without' or from both, assumed the proportions of a moral (that is, an 'objective' and constraining) judgement, for the changes that R. underwent affected and altered her social fate. This career was not just interesting sociologically for you, the reader, and myself, the analyst and participant: it matters very much because it was immensely consequential for R. herself.

There are, of course, 'the facts'. R. had an operation in which a breast was removed; subsequently she was discharged from hospital and returned home. These facts merge into the background if, as Dorothy Smith (1978) has suggested, I illuminate certain aspects of R.'s career so that there is a 'figure-ground' effect: now you see this aspect and now you don't.

One picture that emerges from the figure-ground is of emptiness and silence. The images and symbols that are available are inadequate to express R.'s feelings and the emptiness is created by all that R. cannot say. Throughout the entire transcript the word 'cancer' is never mentioned. We can only surmise what 'it' was, or is, or may be. This gives 'it' the appearance of a taboo or scandal; it certainly adds to the picture of R.'s cancer growing within an institution of sickness rather than health. R. explains how 'it gives you a secret' and how she feels compelled to hold on to it (in all the following extracts, the references are to line numbers in the original transcript):

R. Well what it is with me ... I tend to brush it all under the
   carpet.... I won't bring it out into the open. (786-8)

and

R. I just can't cope with the situation er – here – really you know I
   can't talk about it.
A. No.
R. To anybody.
A. You can't?
R. No – no. (199-204)

Another emerging figure-ground effect is of R.'s career situated along a continuum. This processual image is temporally located and has three main stages. In the first stage R. becomes aware of her symptoms and searches for a diagnosis; but even these events are not clear cut, for R. cannot define what the initial symptom was and somehow 'it' becomes lost in the agony of the search. She can merely recount how with her friend she managed to get 'it' noticed (but not by her doctor), and then talks about the frightening way 'it' had 'blown up':

R. ...it wasn't through my doctor – because he said there was
   nothing wrong – it was through the family planning ... and I
   didn't know for myself – I went with a friend – and er – she
   just said show them.

A. D'you think your doctor was a bit surprised?

R. Well he was – you know – when he came to see me ... I'd been home two days – it came up like a balloon – you know.

A. Oh – did it?

R. My husband was frightened so he called him out –
... he (the doctor) was quite surprised – he said it was mastitis or something. (766-77)

But R. already had strong suspicions as to what the diagnosis might be and the vivid picture of the mysterious and fast-growing cancer – undiagnosed and unchecked – produces anger in her. She sums up her attitude to her doctor:

R. So erm – he said to me oh don't you worry he said – you're going to be fine – you know but when people say that – oh don't worry you're going to be fine – it's a ridiculous statement I think. (777-80)

The problematical presence or absence of 'it' in her body and the length of time 'it' might have been there in her pre-diagnostic past produces the frightening thought:

R. ...you're not going to be fine and you do worry – so no matter what anybody says to you – it's going to happen. (782–3)

This dark hint of a definite doom is, like the circumstances of her diagnosis in hospital, shocking to her:

R. You've only got to think ... save your life and you shouldn't neither and – but it – it's all wrong .... when they first told me I had a terrible shock – I mean – I didn't know.

A. Yes.

R. And I went into hospital on the Monday morning and of course they did the operation the next day ... so it was all –

A. I remember very well about you – because you didn't want it did you?

R. So I mean of course the first time they told me when he said that to me – I just wanted – I just said no – I'll die – I don't want I'll stay as I am – you know – you think this you see ... (448-58)

So R. now locates herself in the second stage of her cancer career. She is reaching forward into the future and likely end of early death:

R. I didn't think I'd ever – get to this far you know.
(78)

She emphasises this and the poignancy of possible premature death when mentioning the lady she had been introduced to in the clinic:

175

R. She introduced me to this lady – but she was ... me all over
again – you know – and she'd had her operation seven months
ago – and of course she was ... only young like me – well I say
young.

A. Yeah – young. (23-27)

However, R.'s horizons also extend back in time in her search for
causality and meaning. She muses on the possibility of her cancer
growing unseen and unfelt, and of the pervasive and intangible nature of
cancer generally:

R. Marvellous really – how this could have been going on for
years and it never –

A. Yes.

R. Actually knew what it was – you know.

A. I know.

R. You hear so much of it now – don't you?' (759-64)

It becomes clear that this 'it' is equated with death. R. had not wanted
the mastectomy even though she felt that if not treated she would die.
However, having the operation does not remove the fear of premature
death. The problematic nature of her career becomes more evident as
she describes the terrible uncertainty that is now always there but
quiescent until rudely brought to the surface by the everyday reminders
of mortality and disease:

A. ... you were saying it isn't really on your mind until somebody
like that mentions it –

R. Mentions it – and then I read about – that upsets me – that –
actress that died – you know erm –

A. Who was that? Did I miss that?

R. ... I know her name is B. – and er she died the week I went to –
back to hospital – and I think that must have been in my – now
she had – she'd had her breast off – and of course – nobody
knew this 'til the write-up in the paper – that she'd had her
breast off – and it didn't stop the disease from spreading – and
of course she died with it two years after – and that played on
my mind – you know ... well it makes you wonder – like erm –
you've gone through all this – and you're still going to er – not
get better. (673-92)

These doubts about the efficacy of treatment remain as pivotal in R.'s
career; reassurances from others, professionals or lay people, do not
help. R. knows she will not be fine though she also knows that her views
on this can vary:

R. If I'm busy – I'm pretty good at erm – forgetting things. (702)

And

R. ... and I keep thinking oh – well – probably in another couple of months – or another couple of weeks – I'll be better – and – ... (814-16)

She can construct some vestige of hope, for in relation to others she may have a more hopeful prognosis. The doctors told her that she was 90 per cent sure to be all right, but much more important to her was her shrewd observation that some ladies in the clinic were 'having needles', for she had not been required to undergo such treatment:

R. ... I was talking to a lady outside of course and he (the doctor) said something about she had an eighty per cent ... so I said to her what does that mean? So she said oh – they can't give you a hundred per cent.... I was asking him – you see – curiously – and erm he said no – we're ninety per cent sure you're all right – it appears that he gives some ladies needles though or something er –
A. Yes – some ladies do have treatment alternatives.
R. That must be er – there must be something wrong if they give them treatment for something. (735-46)

In the third and final stage of her cancer career R. shows how 'it' has become more integrated into 'life' but also 'life' is conceptualised around 'it'. When she comes across the objective statement of the final bit of the 'cancer career' – death – she is very upset. She recalls how someone she met following her discharge from hospital had 'broken her heart':

R. This friend – well – she's not a friend really....I met her when I was shopping last week – and erm – she went on and on – that she – I came home and broke my heart – you know...
A. What about?
R. It wasn't about the breast – really – it was about the disease you know – and erm – (I think that was the first time).
A. What did she say?
R. She kept saying – ooh – you're only young – and it's a terrible thing – and they'll all miss you when you're gone – as if I was dead and buried you know ... and then you start thinking – well all day – it was last Thursday it happened – and all day I was thinking erm – well – if I don't get better and I – so it brought something else on then – you see.

A. Yes – yes – yes.
R. And it it's er – if it comes back.... (644-69)

R.'s views on her cancer career have led her life to be conceptualised around how she thinks others feel. She is constantly confronted with uncertainty and fear, wondering how 'others' she meets will react. This agony of her sensitivity mobilises her to action so that 'they' won't notice.

The 'terrible feelings' associated with R.'s views on the reactions of others, to both the cancer and the breast loss, illuminate the third figure-ground effect. This has a force that can knock her sideways, so to speak, whenever her mirror image is reflected. Goffman (1963) writes that there are two stages in the process of becoming stigmatised. First you learn (and in R.'s case remember) the normal point of view:

R. We used to do a lot of dancing. (178)

And

R. You see I like holidays – and this is where I'll feel the pinch more than ever.
A. Because you wear bikinis.
R. Well I always have done – but I can't now can I.... (30-3)

And

R. I've always had that little bit of self-confidence when I've gone anywhere – you know. (611-12)

Second you learn that you are 'different' and disqualified from being 'normal':

R. I don't think it's that you're vain or anything like that – I think it's erm – you feel abnormal – you feel like a freak. (890-1)

In R.'s case she certainly had times when this feeling seemed intrinsically personal, but it also seemed as if her new identity was very much a concern of others:

R. But erm – you see going to this dance – there'll be a lot of friends that I've not seen – and there you've got to face again – you know – they say er –
A. They know you've had the op?
R. O – aye – well – news travels – really. I wasn't going to tell anybody – but erm –
A. D'ya think they ( )?
R. – people just find – whether they know or whether you just think they know – you know – you don't know – but – all the

time you're thinking – oh – they're feeling sorry for me and er
– and it makes you withdraw yourself.... (220-9)

For R., the challenge of coping with her pre-cancer, pre-breast loss,
pre-stigma friends seems to be much greater than coping with strangers.
R. acknowledges that 'whether they know or whether you just think they
know' actually makes no difference to their ability to reflect her
different image and her own deep sense that she is different. The picture
of R. as a 'different' woman is illuminated by R.'s ever-present but
hidden space adjacent to her chest wall. This empty space at times
becomes the centre of R.'s world and assumes the proportions of an
overwhelming and gaping void. Like 'the disease', this space has no
name. R. explains the lengths to which she will go to hide 'it' from
herself and others:

R. It's only this that upsets me – it upsets me because for one
thing it's changed my life in a lot of ways – because I've never
never slept in a bra in my life – and I would not take it off.
A. You won't?
R. No – I can't bring myself to. (103-7)

Some comfort is extracted from A. telling R. that her reactions are
'normal'. R. can now notice that she is advancing in her career as a
stigmatised person and can see herself as presenting not a category
specific to her but the category of breast cancer patients generally:

A. But then – they're normal changes – really – at this stage.
R. Well other people are like that – aren't they?
A. Yes definitely yes.
R. Oh – well – I'm glad to hear I'm not the only one.
A. No – you're not – you're not alone – it's extraordinary how
many people do have these feelings. (1204–9)

She found it helpful to meet another patient:

A. You probably feel you're the only one to feel like this – really –
but a lot of people are very upset – when their breast is...
R. Well – that lady I spoke to seemed like that – she said – I was
terrible – you know.
A. Did you find it at all helpful to speak to her?
R. Yes in fact she gave me a number and said if you ever feel –
because she notices I've got over it marvellous... (365-7)

Though nameless, this empty space has the power to separate R. in
practical as well as metaphysical terms from the rest of the world. She is
isolated in a prison of her own making:

R. I've never kept myself secretive when I'm getting dressed or anything –

A. No – No.

R. But now I do – I close the door – but I go upstairs to change.

A. Yes.

R. Or I close the door and I lock it – the bedroom door so that nobody can come in – and this is something that – I've never done – so you change – it does change you in a way. (294-301)

Much of R.'s construction of her womanhood comes from how she senses that her husband views her body. She cannot take the risk of allowing him to see what she feels is such an abnormal and different self, and yet she longs to reach out from her apparently self-imposed retreat:

R. ... I can't bear it at all – I feel so inadequate –

A. Who else has seen it? Has your husband seen it?

R. Nobody.

A. Your husband hasn't seen the scar?

R. No.

A. Does your daughter know you've had the operation?

R. Well – when I came home – the little girl – of course she's only ten we've always been close – because from being little – I mean – we've never – she came into bed with us – things that I – (I'm very broad-minded with children).

A. (I know) – I remember you saying that.

R. And of course when she came home – she kept saying ... have you had your tummy done ... so I showed her the stitches.

A. Has your husband seen it at all?

R. N-oh he's asked and he'll say you're so silly – you know – er – but I can't – you know I just cannot take it off – it's terrible – you – but it – it builds a barrier – I think. (124-40)

R. creates a wall of silence between herself and her husband, her sadness at what she has lost in the sense of a 'glamorous life' brought home by the perpetual reminders of the media:

R. I'll perhaps be sat watching the television – you see advertisements for bras and lovely underwear – and then I start crying –

A. Well it brings it home to you all the more – doesn't it – it must be awful.

R. Things like that – or – you can just be watching something and it er – you think well – I'm not like that – and it does erm – but with my husband we never mention it and this worries me too

you know – 'cause we'd –
A. He doesn't talk about it?
R. No.
A. He doesn't tease you or anything ( )
R. No nothing.
A. Do you think that's because he feels so upset about it – that he doesn't want to bring it up.
R. Yes I think so – though really – it does build a barrier.
A. Yes – you feel that whereas before – you were completely open about anything –
R. Oh – yes – yes – and in every way – you know – er – we've always been very close – and er – but now – I'm not – I tend to think er – oh – well – er – he's feeling sorry for me – or something – and things go through your mind – and er – you just shut him out completely – you know –.... It's so silly because in a way – he's the main one. (788-812)

The barrier that R. mentions is a reflexive construction creating and being created by her 'differentness'. With her husband, F., she felt discredited because really he 'knew', and so she had to manage the tension of knowing he knew; but she was also potentially discreditable because she would not let him see or talk to her and managed just how much information she felt he should have:

R. Oh he's very good – I mean he never mentions it – he – and he never even – you'd think it never happened with F. – he never mentions it.
A. What about – can you make love – even without –
R. Well we've not been too bad – but I'm not the same.
A. You're not – you can't enjoy it?
R. No – it's –
A. – Can you relax?
R. No – he's tried to put me more at ease – and er in fact he's been very very good – really – but you think erm – well er – is it sympathy – or –
A. I know I'm sure you're bound to feel that –
R. It's awful you know. It's really erm – it's all in your mind – really it's all psychological in your mind you know – you –
A. D'you – d'you feel it happens as much, that you can make love as you used to?
R. Oh – no ( ) – no – I think it's –
A. No. I mean – has it hap – you have actually managed to since the op – have you?

R. Yes – yes – well – that was only through a lot of erm – and then again – that was in my mind – that er – that was probably – for me to feel better – you see what I mean. (306-35)

Much of what R. felt made her into a 'desirable woman' to F. has gone with the loss of her breast, and that any sexual advances he now makes are seen as being kind and 'helping' so she might feel better. These feelings are made worse by her guilt at 'leaving him out' of how she constructs her relationship with him.

For R. 'passing as normal' is crucial and her 'face' can be easily damaged if she is teased:

R. Because it is noticeable.
A. Yes.
R. No it's not noticeable dressed – no – but you do get people that do know – erm – even my daughter – I mean – she says it in the nicest possible way – but you know – she'll say you've got a better figure now than you had before – you know – joking – you know.
A. Yes yes.
R. But erm – you think – well – they're looking and they're thinking erm – well one of them isn't real – and this is going through my mind – you know. (255–64)

R.'s concern with 'passing as a woman' is therefore in part dependent on the status of the beholder:

R. Well – she's going on ten – she's a sensible child ... she'd notice because I – that I wear a bra in bed – you know – because er – but then – I think if she asked me I'd tell her – and I'd show her – more so than F really – it's silly isn't it? – 'cause I think with a child there's no deceit. (941-6)

Thus it is not merely R.'s breast cancer career that is a reflexive construction: so too was the very nature of R. as a woman in the pre-cancer everyday world. In some ways R. felt that 'being a whole woman' rested on 'unquestionable axioms' such as the possession of two breasts, and in particular this was so in relation to F., a man, although interestingly not in relation to her daughter.

For R., and probably for all of us, a woman is not a completed reality but rather a becoming: less an incontrovertible fact of biology and more a complex and negotiated relationship that takes account of social interpretation and reaction. What seems to matter most, though, was that R experienced 'being a woman' in such a way that her cancer and her 'career' were experienced as a painful and objectively constituted reality.

The organisational basis of breast cancer

R. had a 'career' as a breast cancer patient. However, although it seemed clear enough that R.'s career was indeed problematic, the process by which I came to characterise her in the previous section was not. Although I saw R. as in part a constructor of her social world, I failed to go much beyond the question of what that world looked like to her. I felt no responsibility to give particular weight to the means by which I pieced together my understanding of what was going on. That is, I did not try to 'unpack' my own research process. What I did was to define, retrospectively, how R. had constructed and managed her breast cancer career. Although I wrote about her in particular, I was also making generalisations – that a breast cancer career was indeed 'like that'. This puts you, the reader, and myself, the 'expert analyst', into a relationship of power over R., or rather over her account and so her experience. 'She' has become the object of our interest and we define what we think life was like for her.

Dorothy Smith (1974, 1978, 1980, 1982, 1987) writes that telling what is happening, as I did with R., is a constitutive element in the relations of ruling. The 'knower' is cancelled from the act of knowing by the procedure, for instance, of objectifying and separating R.'s experience by defining it. I have taken it for granted that the theories, concepts and methods I have used do not require any examination of the organisation or conditions of the existence of my knowledge and understanding.

However, if R. and I are to have an equal relationship within my analysis, and if you, the reader, are to decide whether how A. made sense of R. is valid for you, then it is important to see what my 'methods' were. In other words, how is A.'s understanding done? The researcher's understanding, which is my own, must be made explicit.

This is important in making available ambiguities and contradictions within accounts and between individuals in the research process. Most importantly, though, it makes available for ethical scrutiny the 'intellectual autobiography' of the researcher. This should be a fundamental concern of those researchers who are concerned to combat, in whatever way, the oppression of women, for it relocates a resource – the data 'out there' – so that it becomes the central topic: how the researcher uses the data. Here I explicate the institutional basis of breast cancer for R. and myself in relation to its temporal setting and the place of 'markers' within this.

Despite the division of the research project's assessment structure into physical, social and psychological aspects, it was clear that these were irrevocably enmeshed each with the other. For instance:

A. How soon are you planning to go back to work?

R. Well I saw the doctor last week and he said to me erm – I'll
leave it up to you Mrs – there's nothing wrong with you – he
said and if you think you can cope –

A. Yes.

R. Of course he knows I'm a bit – erm –

A. No I don't think there's anything wrong – I just think you're
quite normal in your reactions – but I think they are ( ).

R. Well as long as I am normal because sometimes you think erm
– er – it's sending me round the twist you know – you do –

A. Yes I'm sure you do.

R. But I think I'm getting better.... (545-56)

Getting back to work was one of the 'markers' in a patient's
rehabilitation. Resumption of social and sexual relationships was
another. The organisational framework of having breast cancer was also
dependent on formal temporal arrangements – the discovery of
symptoms, presentation of symptoms, diagnosis, treatments and
check-ups. For some, it was also dependent on recurrence of symptoms
and the circle of discovery, diagnosis and so forth starting again.

R. and I used a temporal timetable to give meaning to our actions.
From the first page of the transcript we were engaged in establishing
when R. left hospital, when she had her first check-up, when she had
been fitted for her prosthesis and when she had seen her GP. Obtaining
such information and thus establishing R.'s timetable was part of the
reason for my visit, but the visit was also part of R.'s and my own
timetable. Julius Roth (1963) has discussed the importance of institutional timetables, and also that a patient's progress is to a large extent
determined by organisational practices; and this is borne out by my
experience.

In the case of the women undergoing mastectomy there was considerable variance in the advice given by surgeons on the timing of a
woman's post-operative return to work. The younger surgeons tended to
make suggestions such as 'it's only a simple op', while the older
surgeons were more cautious. However, as younger surgeons gained
experience, they were likely to moderate their advice and start advising
women to have a longer convalescence. So these social practices
accounted for a 'normal (with variance) timetable'.

In R.'s case, even reaching the stage of a definitive diagnosis of
cancer was very much the result of a negotiated outcome. Her GP
thought there was 'nothing wrong', but the family planning doctor
clearly thought otherwise. Also, ambiguity concerning cell structure of
malignancy had surprised me, as I came to realise that as knowledge of
such matters increased, so 'objective diagnosis' was a movable feast.

When R. voiced doubts about her survival there were practical, organisational reasons for suggesting that the outlook 'looked hopeful'. Though her tumour was not small, at least the lymph glands under her arm were free of cancer. It looked as though the cancer had been confined to the tumour and this, it had been hoped, had all been removed. Also, because I had a job to do it was important that she had confidence in me and perhaps I hoped that my apparently optimistic attitude would infect her with a more hopeful outlook so that she would 'get herself together' and soon be 'rehabilitated'. Although at this point the research of Stephen Greer *et al.* (1979) on the possiblity of a woman's life expectancy with breast cancer being influenced by psychological attitude had not been published, the existence of Greer's research team was known to me (Morris *et al.* 1977). Further, my own nursing experience suggested that patients who exhibited a fighting spirit, rather than turning their faces to the wall, 'did better'.

Also, I and the mastectomy patients I worked with had to manage the actual moment of our interactional encounters. Time and again I hear myself on the tape recordings made over the years finding 'good reasons' for the situations which the women and I discussed. These were attempts to cope with the moment – not coming too close to matters of life or death, which frightened me as much as R. and others. Being outwardly hopeful was a useful mechanism for making myself almost believe that R. and others were free of cancer. They and I knew we could not be certain, but by being (with some justification in R.'s case) hopeful, perhaps she and I could summon the necessary emotional mileage to carry on:

R. And then you start thinking – well – all day and all day I was thinking erm – well – if I don't get better and I – so it's brought something else on then you see –

A. Yes – yes.

R. And if it's er – if it comes back – and er.

A. You do know how hopeful the outlook is now though, don't you?

R. Well – they say I'm pretty well – all right you know which I suppose erm ....

A. So I mean it's not really – you were saying it isn't really on your mind until somebody like that mentions it –

R. Mentions it – and then I read about it – that upset me – that – actress – that died – you know erm. (664-77)

R.'s despair because someone else had died was perfectly under- standable. The meaning of her breast cancer was dependent on her shared experience with others and her definition of their situation. When describing R.'s career, I showed how she observed that some women had treatment 'needles' and some, including herself, did not. She asked me questions about such treatments. When she did this, a part of the organisational basis of breast cancer (as R. and I experienced it) became apparent. Even now I cringe at the hypocrisy and confusion of my reply and can remember the acute discomfort of having to work within the hierarchical constraints of the organisation from which I came. It was hard enough to know R.'s suffering, it was worse to toe the party line and mislead her about the research that was going on:

R. It appears he gives some ladies needles though or something.
A. Yes, some ladies do have treatment alternatives and there – yes.
R. That must be er – that must be something wrong if they give them treatment or something?
A. Well – no – each patient is treated individually – it doesn't necessarily mean that – really honestly – truly – there are a whole lot of factors they take into consideration – it's quite a complicated thing deciding who has the treatment and who doesn't – and it doesn't mean to say it's an advanced case or anything – because a lot of treatments are drugs – and they are not radiotherapy – which people used to have – well instead of saying no – we'll have treatment – or everybody must have radiotherapy – which is what they used to do in the old days – and they really didn't have definite ways of deciding it – now they really look at each patient as a whole person – and their whole make-up and their blood – and everything else – and they decide then.
R. Marvellous – really – how this could have been going on for years – and it never – (747-61)

It was not surprising that R. ignored my garbled message. In fact the organisational basis of selection for chemotherapy treatments following mastectomy was based on the sacred cow in medical scientific circles of the randomised controlled trial. In this, women who had 'positive' lymph nodes under their arms at the time of mastectomy were randomly selected for 'adjuvant' treatments. I had found this difficult to cope with emotionally, because knowing a particular treatment was toxic I would be fearful as to how certain patients would cope with it. Some surgeons told me I was unscientific. I would be better thinking that patients were fortunate to have the opportunity of treatments that, it was hoped, would prolong their lives, or at least the time in which they were 'disease free'. So I tried to believe them.

The worst aspect of the situation for me was that patients were not told of these experiments. Because of training needs, the junior surgeons rotated jobs quite frequently. Also, the top consultant surgeon was rarely in the follow-up clinics. Consequently information about treatments and prognosis was often inconsistent. Some patients were given percentages about their possible prognosis. If a woman had experienced someone dying of breast cancer or was feeling down in some way, even if she was told she was 80 per cent likely to survive, the chances were that she would mentally associate herself with the 20 per cent who would experience a recurrence. Most of the patients were told that the treatment was an insurance – just in case, to stop anything nasty happening. Such euphemisms rarely fooled the patients, but they did, as with R., make it difficult for them to think through what was happening to them.

Postscript

A few months after the 1983 tape was made R. died. R.I.P., dear R. and your sisters.

© 1990 Ann Tait

References

Garfinkel, Harold (1967) *Studies in Ethnomethodology*, Englewood Cliffs, NJ: Prentice-Hall.

Goffman, Erving (1959) *The Presentation of Self in Everyday Life*, Harmondsworth: Penguin.

——(1961) *Asylums*, Harmondsworth: Penguin.

——(1963) *Stigma: Notes on the Management of a Spoiled Identity*, Harmondsworth: Penguin.

Greer, Stephen, Morris, Tina and Pettingale, Keith (1979) 'Psychological Response to Breast Cancer: Effect on Outcome', *The Lancet* (Oct.) 13:785–7.

Maguire, Peter (1976) 'The Psychological and Social Sequelae of Mastectomy', in Judith Howells (ed.), *Modern Perspectives in the Psychiatric Aspects of Surgery*, Edinburgh: Churchill Livingstone, pp. 391–421.

Maguire, Peter, Tait, Ann, Brooke, Mary, Thomas, Christopher and Sellwood, Ronald (1980) 'Effect of Counselling on the Psychiatric Morbidity Associated with Mastectomy', *British Medical Journal* 282:1454–6.

Maguire, Peter, Pentol, Anne, Allen, David, Tait, Ann, Brooke, Mary, Thomas, Christopher and Sellwood, Ronald (1982) 'Cost of Counselling Women Who Undergo Mastectomy', *British Medical Journal* 284:1933–5.

Maguire, Peter, Brooke, Mary, Tait, Ann, Thomas, Christopher and Sellwood, Ronald (1983) 'The Effect of Counselling on Physical Disability and Social Recovery After Mastectomy', *Clinical Oncology* 9:319–24.

Morris, Tina, Greer, Stephen and White, Patrick (1977) 'Psychological and Social Adjustment to Mastectomy', *Cancer* 40:2381–7.

Quint, Jeanne (1972) 'Institutionalised Practices of Information Control', in Eric Friedson and James Lorben (eds), *Medical Men and Their Work*, Englewood Cliffs, NJ: Prentice-Hall, pp. 220–38.

Rosser, Jane (1981) 'The Interpretation of Women's Experience, a Critical Appraisal of the Literature on Breast Cancer', *Social Science and Medicine* 16:315–22.

Rosser, Jane and Maguire, Peter (1982) 'Dilemmas in General Practice, the Care of the Cancer Patient', *Social Science and Medicine* 16:315–20.

Roth, Julius (1963) *Timetables: Structuring the Passage of Time in Hospital Treatment and Other Careers*, Indianapolis: Bobbs Merrill.

Smith, Dorothy (1974) 'Women's Perspective as a Radical Critique of Sociology', *Sociological Inquiry* 44:7–13.

——(1978) 'K is Mentally Ill', *Sociology* 12: 22–53.

——(1980) 'No-one Commits Suicide: Textual Analysis of Ideological Practices', Unpublished paper, Department of Sociology in Education, Ontario Institute for Studies in Education.

—— (1982) 'The Active Text: an Approach to Analysing Texts as Constituents of Social Relations', Unpublished paper for World Congress of Sociology, Mexico City (Aug).

——(1987) *The Everyday World as Problematic: a Feminist Sociology*, Milton Keynes: Open University Press.

Tait, Ann (1986) *The Mastectomy Experience*, Studies in Sexual Politics No.10, Sociology Department, University of Manchester.

Tait, Ann, Maguire, Peter and Brooke, Mary (1980) 'Plan into Practice', *Nursing Mirror* 150(4):19–21.

Wilkinson, Susi, Maguire, Peter, Tait, Ann, Brooke, Mary, Faulkner, Anne and Sellwood, Ronald (1983) 'A Comparison of Three Methods of Counselling and Monitoring Women Who Undergo Mastectomy', Proceedings of the Edinburgh Nursing Research Conference, Edinburgh University.

Chapter fourteen

At the Palace

Researching gender and ethnicity in a Chinese restaurant

Chung Yuen Kay

Beginning research

As an undergraduate I had been involved in various Chinese or Malaysian groups and increasingly my academic interests centred on issues of race concerned with the Chinese in Britain. I also became a feminist. At the same time my sociological stance moved from a structural to an interactional one. As a graduate student, I decided to do research on some aspect of the local and large Manchester Chinese community. However, and as Chung (1985) discusses in detail, focussing on something more specific than this took time and work, for gaining access to my chosen 'field' was no simple matter either practically or intellectually.

I decided that I wanted to explore the interactional components of the actual work of Chinese restaurant and take-away staff; however, my lack of practical experience meant that finding employment was not easy. Finally and in quick succession, I obtained a two-nights-a-week job in a take-away and then the owner of the Palace restaurant (all names of persons and of restaurants in this chapter are pseudonyms), whom I had contacted earlier, offered me work in his restaurant.

I was enthusiastic about working in both a take-away and a restaurant. The family at the take-away were from Malaysia, whereas the people at the restaurant had come from the New Territories in Hong Kong; and I thought about a comparative study. But I had not been prepared for the volume of business in the take-away; also tasks which, from the outside and on paper, seemed easy, in practice involved much skill. And there were hazards for the uninitiated, including scalding fat, boiling sauces, steaming puddings and pies, and greasy floors and paths. Competent practitioners do their tasks easily, but the uninitiated have to learn to accomplish the correct way to cook and turn out chips, how to assemble funnels for chips, how to wrap food, and how to work out the cost of complicated orders and give change.

At the end of each working evening I felt washed out and would usually have a massive, throbbing headache. The unexpected physical strain affected my research capabilities. Because I was always tense about doing the wrong thing I wasn't in a state to make observations, to be consciously aware of what was going on and therefore able to record it mentally. In a way the matter was taken out of my hands. After the third week I became ill; I had a history of chronic anaemia and I decided it would not be sensible of me to carry on beyond what I could physically manage. So I left the job at the take-away; I was asked to work one more night at the Palace, and I now concentrated on the restaurant.

Learning to labour

The 'forgotten whatness'

My 'career' in the take-away, though short-lived, provided experiences which highlight the crucial importance of 'the job' and its skilled accomplishment. I was forced to revise my initial, rather arrogant opinion about the simplicity of the tasks involved in being a part-time worker in a take-away. There is a taken-for-granted attitude about 'work itself' in sociology. The world of employment is one of the most pervasive aspects of everyday life, in some sense almost synonymous with adult status, and yet we do not have much knowledge about the most fundamental details of how members routinely construct organised events in work situations. Traditional studies in the subject area of employment have focussed on labour and industry, division among management and workers, professionalisation and specialisation of labour. But there are very few data to show how work routines of the most mundane sort are accomplished as interactional phenomena.

Occupational ethnographies may expound lengthily on roles, status systems, labelling, but seldom on 'work itself'. For example, Becker's famous study of jazz musicians tells us everything we may want to know about jazz musicians – except the details of their playing music (Becker 1951). Garfinkel calls this the 'forgotten whatness' of work (Schwartz and Jacobs 1979:243).

As a stranger to the Palace restaurant I did not know what was going on there; but I was also the waitress who had to be practically involved and competent in her new setting. I was subject to the same practical conditions and situations as other members, but without their competences. Hence I had to learn things from scratch. I soon became aware that waitressing was a job of great interactional as well as practical skill; these skills are now briefly outlined as the *kung fu* or 'body of expert knowledge' of being a Chinese waitress at the Palace (and the Appendix provides a 'who's who' of the people who worked there when I did).

The skills of a kei toy

The job of the waitress or *kei toy* involves two types of skills. The first involves the specialised skills she has to learn to be competent at her job, the basics of waitressing which become routinised in the technical competencies of the job. The second involves the management of interaction with customers, among staff, and between staff and the boss.

One of the first things a novice waitress learns is to use the abbreviated Chinese terms and simplified characters for the items on the menu (in English at the Palace) and how to make an order correctly. A common pitfall is not to make allowance for extra portions that a customer might want after ordering their main meals so that there is no space left on the tiny order sheet. Also the waitress will have to write clearly or else the wrong dish might be cooked:

> Q. (the manager) tells Hing (a new waiter) to learn from us how to clear and lay tables for tonight and not to take orders when we are busy. ... Hing takes an order with me standing behind him. His 'beef' looks like pork instead, and I later pointed out to him that the order must be correct, or Cook might do the wrong dish.
>
> (Fieldnotes, 1 December)

It is important to see that customers' orders are taken swiftly. It creates the feeling they are 'getting service' and it soothes them to feel that, busy though we are, they have got their orders in. Then too the waitress has to learn to manage at least three plates on her left hand (and the crook of her arm). It took me quite a while to accomplish this and I slowed up the delivery of meals by my incompetence.

A waitress is also expected to know about drinks. I found the various combinations and their abbreviated names rather bewildering at first. It also took me a while to figure out the 'correct' glasses for different sorts of drinks. Skill with drinks was also one area in which Q. liked to 'do power' over us. In this instance Q. deliberately used the situation as a resource to emphasise the novice status of the waitress concerned, which in turn underlines his status as boss (and indeed this was his favourite means of status-marking new waitresses):

> Q. 'tested' Siow (a part-time waitress) by pretending that he was a customer ordering. He deliberately asked for 'Rum and Black' which she couldn't know really. He rather dramatically made a fuss about it, saying that it was a good thing that he was not a real customer. Siow was rather embarrassed by this. He just wants to show up her incompetence I think.
>
> (Fieldnotes, 9 November)

Another task-oriented skill is that waitresses have to be aware of the 'progress' that customers are making with their meal, both in terms of her own actions and to alert kitchen staff. They should also keep an eye on other customers. For example, I may be vaguely aware that each time I walk round, Table 4 doesn't seem to have any plates in front of the people there. Even though I was not the one to take their order, nevertheless I would try to find out from the kitchen if their order had got 'lost' and set about remedying the situation.

'Tipping' was, at the Palace at any rate, seen to be an indicator of the amount of skill that a waitress had shown. The waitress took pride in the amount of tip she got; and if it was a particularly large amount she might 'casually' publicise the fact. This was rather ironic because none of the waitresses got a penny from the *ngap jyie* (or 'ducky', which for some obscure reason referred to the box in which tips were kept): the management kept all the tips. It was not the monetary aspect which mattered – it was seen as a symbol of good service and so of skill.

The specific skills of waitressing were part of the *kung fu* that Q. mentioned to me when I first started work. The central skill I developed as a strategy and as a persuasive device in my interactions with customers was through speech. I drew on my fluency in English as a resource for repairing a 'performance' that had been faulty in some way as well as in accomplishing the actual performance. A smile, which Goffman discerningly calls the 'ritualistic mollifier' (Goffman 1976: 48), was also extraordinarily useful to me. Thus I was often sent by kitchen as an emissary to persuade:

> Chap at Table 10 wanted Crab and Mixed Vegetables, and kitchen did not have any crab. But they did not want Customer to settle for a less expensive meal, so they asked me to persuade him to have scollops instead, which is also one of the more expensive dishes. Well, I persuaded him and he agreed.
>
> (Fieldnotes, 15 December)

I had to attend to a complex set of details, contexts and systems of relevancies to accomplish the doing of the practical tasks involved. If I had been an observer only I could not have attended to the same things; certainly, if I had not actually done the job I would not have structured and analysed matters in the ways I did as a waitress. In Chung (1985) I discuss various aspects of the job and of 'doing ethnicity' in detail. However, here I focus on 'gender' as a topic for explicating further dimensions of the skills, here the interactional skills, of the *kei toy*, although in doing so I also note its similarities and differences as compared with ethnicity.

The problem of gender

Looking for gender

If I had thought I would uncover ethnic phenomena at the Palace restaurant, then I was even more sure I would observe 'phenomena relating to gender'. Gender can be conveyed fleetingly in any social situation and is seen to indicate the most basic characterisation of the individual. I therefore believed I would witness instances of sexism, sexual overtures and sexual stereotyping accomplished in and through talk in the restaurant as I did elsewhere in social life. Yet when it comes to discussing gender here, I have been most sorely tried. In my attempts to 'write gender' I came to the realisation that my difficulties and problems in doing so are in themselves a topic that needs to be discussed. Therefore I use my experience of these difficulties as a basis for discussing gender in customer–staff interaction and then amongst the staff.

When I went through my notes I was shocked at the pitifully small number of 'observations' that had direct relevance to gender. To pronounce that sex has been a relevant factor here or there can be immensely problematic, because the element of gender in customer–staff interactions is often not clear-cut and overt, but more subtle and shaded into other circumstantial factors, including one's interpretation of the event or happening at the time. I found it easier to identify instances of ethnic phenomena. For example:

> Q. told us of a fight that Koo's (a part-time waiter) brother had with some of the customers when he was working here. Q. said he had to bring down his shotgun which scared the hell out of the customers. Apparently, the customers had 'teased' Koo's brother for a discount on their bill, and when he refused to joke along with them, they got racist and called him a 'fucking Chinese rat' which had made him see red and he had lunged out at them. Afterwards when the customers dashed for their car, Koo's brother rushed out after them and slammed his fist into the car. As he had a black belt in judo, the car was dented.
>
> (Fieldnotes, 19 October)

The obviousness of the ethnic phenomena here cannot be easily overlooked. I instantly identify that the customers 'got racist'. To call someone a 'fucking rat' would be insulting, but to call someone a 'fucking Chinese rat' is to use the actual membership category of race so that it becomes clearly racially insulting.

It is often much more problematic to draw the boundaries for defining an instance of gender:

Table 4 was being troublesome. Wanted extra portions of rice, curry sauce, etc. And then one of the men wanted chopsticks too. And each time they wanted something, they would wait until they caught my eye or beckoned to me. I just about managed to be pleasant. When they were paying the bill, one of the men patted my hand and said 'Thank you, you have been very nice. You have got a sweet smile.' And he sort of leaned closer. I backed away a little, but still keeping on my 'sweet smile'!

(Fieldnotes, 12 January)

The element of gender here is introduced elliptically and has to be 'worked out' as tied to gender by the person interpreting it. The man's remark that I had been 'very nice' brings in my membership category of waitress; and as for my 'sweet smile', that too could be read along lines that I had been a pleasant waitress, instead of being an outright 'gender' remark. Thus it is possible to interpret this exchange as one in which an occupational categorisation, rather than a gender categorisation, was applied, but a female transformation of that categorisation.

Gender, although actually more prevalent than ethnicity accomplishment, is often less 'noticeable' because more ambiguous. It can often be expressed in 'non-sexual' ways as through female transformations of forms of categorisation; and thus it can be taken for granted in a way that ethnicity is not. I now look at gender 'out front' in customer–staff interactions to make these points more concretely.

Gender out front

One way of looking at gender phenomena would be to analyse turn-taking sequences in customer–staff talk. However, it would be difficult to say whether asymmetric patterns in turn-taking occur in male–female conversations between customer and staff even if I had actual transcripts rather than retrospectively assembled records of conversations. This is because most of the talk between customers and staff follows a ritualised pattern which looks like this:

CUSTOMER: (*enters restaurant*)
STAFF: (*goes forward to meet customer*) Table for four? Please come this way.
CUSTOMER: (*gets seated*)
STAFF: (*hands them menu and goes off*)
CUSTOMER: (*studies menu*)
STAFF: (*returns after a while*) May I take your order now?' (*or*) Yes, please?
CUSTOMER: (*unless indicates not ready, then starts to order*)

STAFF:	(*goes away and returns after a while with meals*)
CUSTOMER:	(*sorts out among themselves whose meal is whose*)
STAFF:	(*goes off then returns after a while to clear plates*) Have you finished?
CUSTOMER:	Yes, thank you.
STAFF:	(*clears away plates*)
CUSTOMER:	(*if had not previously ordered sweet and/or coffee, may do so now*)
STAFF:	(*repeats order as this is not taken down on order pad, goes away and then returns with order*)
CUSTOMER:	(*signals to staff for the bill or comes to the counter to pay on the way out*)
STAFF:	(*brings bill and goes away*)
CUSTOMER:	(*pays bill and leaves*) Goodbye (*sometimes*).
STAFF:	(*smiles*) Goodnight, thank you.

There is thus a formalised framework for the sequential ordering of events, and turn-taking between customer and staff falls within this sequential order. There are deviations, for how else do instances of ethnicity get accomplished? But as far as turn-taking and interruptions in turn-taking are concerned, there are only narrow margins in which such happenings can occur. However, simple interruptions of turns by male customers need not of themselves constitute a means by which 'power' is 'done to' the waitresses. First, as a waitress I am primarily concerned with taking my order, and typically when drawn into a conversation not directly pertaining to the order I respond only perfunctorily. So even if I were denied my 'right' to turn-taking in such a conversation I would not necessarily interpret this as doing 'male power' over me, because typically I choose to miss such turns. Second, I sometimes deviated from the ritualised structure of customer–staff interaction by my greater effusiveness. This does not invalidate the general point that waitresses are not interested in conversation with customers, for here my 'deviant' behaviour was usually a device for covering slips, errors and accidents that occurred in the performance of tasks by myself or a fellow waitress: they were purpose-oriented rather than friendly communications.

Another area of gender phenomena might be in terms of address, but this too proved ambiguous. For example, I and the other waitresses were often called 'love', 'poppet', 'my pet' or 'my dear' by male customers. But then quite a lot of women customers also addressed us as 'love' and 'poppet' and the like. And, after all, being called 'love' in the North of England is a very common pleasantry or term for establishing informality. Pleasantries in address are therefore ambiguous and it is perhaps safer to say that there can be elements of status power incipient in terms of endearment which customers confer on the staff, but not power necessarily or entirely related to gender. That is, this familiarity on the part of customers of both sexes is not one the staff has.

In addition, an element of ethnicity can be carried in these pleasantries. We are seen not only as waitresses but as *Chinese* waitresses, something different and perhaps more amenable to familiarities. This might explain why I have sometimes been revoltingly called 'my little oriental flower' or 'my little lotus blossom'. The gender aspect is present, but it shades in with other factors such as status and ethnicity and it is difficult to separate the different shades from one another or say which, if any, is the dominant reading of these remarks.

What about more overt sexual elements in customer–staff talk? I recorded only a few instances when direct sexual remarks were made by customers. One such incident I recorded thus:

> Customer at Table 16 asked for Chicken Curry. So, as was customary, I asked, 'breast or leg?'. At which he laughed and looked at me and said, 'Breast, eh? Why not? I like a good breast. Give us a breast, then.' I did not quite catch on at first, but when I did, I got quite flustered, and quickly took down his order for chicken breast without mentioning the word again.
>
> (Fieldnotes, 19 January)

The elliptical reference to 'breast' here was an interactional resource drawn on by the customer; and the same sort of incident occurred a few more times during my work at the Palace. Otherwise I cannot think of other similar incidents, unless I did not realise the sexual overtones because these occurred so elliptically or in particularly obscure slang.

Staff being chatted up by customers was so prevalent it was taken for granted. We did not like it, but felt we had to put up with it. For example, many male customers would give their order to a waitress and tag on, 'And what would you be doing on Saturday night, my lovely?', accompanied by a laugh or a nudge. I learned to accept mild flirtatious overtures with resignation as an occupational hazard. This could perhaps be another reason for 'not noticing' and categorising gender phenomena: they occurred routinely and so were classified as 'other' in nature.

Also it is not easy to decide when a male customer is trying to 'chat up' a waitress and when he is being merely friendly:

> There was this creepy young man at T12, though he didn't seem like that at first. He was alone, very pleasant, smiled at us and said 'Hello' when he first came in. I think he was that local policeman who came in with another policeman to get a take-away late one night. When I went to take his order he said 'charmingly' that he

would put himself in my hands and that he was relying on me to help him choose a good meal with soup, main meal and sweet. I did not mind that at first, but he took such a time ordering, asking a lot of questions about the various dishes, and in the end choosing something entirely different after all. I began to feel rather impatient with him and when he complimented me rather fulsomely on first my spoken English, and then how clever of me to know how to write Chinese, etc., I had a vague suspicion that he was being more than just friendly. Then while he was drinking his soup, he called me over and said, 'Oh, I forgot to ask you, may I know your name please? I feel that it's so important to get to know the staff in a restaurant when I eat there. It creates for a more friendly atmosphere, and I enjoy my meal more' and gave what he thought must be a winning smile, I suppose. I was beginning to get annoyed, but at that moment I didn't know how to refuse and merely said foolishly that it was Kay. Afterwards I thought rather regretfully that I should have invented a false unpronounceable name, something like 'Auyang Luk Wan' that would upset his smarminess. As it was, he had the cheek to call out to me, quite unnecessarily, that he had finished what he was eating then. Also during his meal, he would from time to time try to catch my eye, and smile at me. He was giving me the creeps. I told Giny and Siow about him and warned them not to be caught by him. Siow took over his table after that and I studiously avoided catching his glances. He really got up my nose! And he had seemed so 'ordinarily pleasant' at first.

(Fieldnotes, 15 December)

To outward appearance this man was only being friendly. He had made no overt sexual overtures, nor had he touched me 'casually'. So, even though I felt threatened, I also felt that the situation was sufficiently ambiguous for my 'subjective' interpretation to be 'objectively' refuted. Hence I did not know how to refuse his 'request' (Goffman 1956). Even for me, the 'victim' of the situation, the gender aspect of it was not clear from the start. And even when I concluded he was being 'over-friendly', I felt what was happening was sufficiently ambiguous to submit to his questioning. The reality of gender as an interactional phenomenon in staff–customer relations is not as something simply 'there' to be described; it is almost always complex, often ambiguous, something to be adjudicated and compromised and puzzled over retrospectively (and this is of course not to say that it does not sometimes take entirely unambiguous forms elsewhere in social life).

There can be other occasions when customers who may seem to be 'getting off' with waitresses are not however accredited with that intention by us. This is often the case when the customer/s in question are young boys or teenagers whom we know as semi-regulars. The membership categorisation device we select to read their behaviour is 'stage of life' rather than 'gender':

> Some late customers, mostly boys – semi-regulars – came in after 1.30 a.m. They were exuberant and in youthful spirits. They asked Tina (Q.'s brother's fiancée, a full-time waitress) for a jug of water when she took their order. (They had made the same request last time they were here.) Tina told them pertly, 'Bring your own jug next time.' They were very taken with that. When I handed them their water, they asked for her name. I retorted they could ask her themselves. They then wanted to know mine. I went off. They teased us a bit, but they were not unpleasant. When paying their bill, one of the boys said to me, 'You are very nice, I like you', but he said it in a cheeky and disarming kind of way which I did not mind. One of the other boys, a gangly youth, went down on his knees – meant to be a teaser about his height and my tinyness. I asked him if he had weak knees.
>
> (Fieldnotes, 18 January)

It is clear we did not perceive this as gender phenomena. At first I could not explain to myself why, but now I feel the main factor is that we do not perceive 'domination' to be operating in these comments and behaviours: they permit reciprocity. We feel that the usual publicly observed rule of the customer as superordinate and staff as subordinate no longer applies and we relax our formal public demeanour. Thus Tina, who is usually rather expressionless with customers, unbends to exchange good-humoured remarks with them; and I too respond to their antics.

I have tried to show the complexities and intricacies involved in seeking out, analysing and defining gender phenomena in everyday interactions. It is there, but its routine prevalence typically shades in with other aspects of interactional dynamics. Only atypically, in so far as my research is concerned, was it expressed as overt, direct attempts to downgrade women as women.

Non-verbal interaction – the new 'forgotten whatness'?

Many non-verbal aspects of gender are present in my observations. For example, in my fieldnotes I describe a man as giving me a leering look, a drunk 'pushing his face towards me', and even my observation of a youth's 'exuberant spirits' is not one deduced from speech but rather from the lad's demeanour. As for the smarmy policeman, part of his 'creepiness' derives from his excessive smiling, again a non-verbal cue.

In the realm of the sexual, non-verbal cues are an important resource although, as Nancy Henley (1977) has suggested, non-verbal communication is still very little studied by social science.

I paid little attention to this while working in the restaurant. Yet there is no doubt that touching frequently cropped up in customer–staff encounters. Thus I can cite numerous occasions when 'regular' and some 'not so regular' customers have grasped hold of my hands, or patted them, thrown an arm round my shoulder or waist. But I do not perceive all such touching by men as undilutedly sexual. Whatever the intentionality, quite often it was done in a way calculated to be avuncular or jocular and thereby diffuse whatever overt sexual content it might otherwise have had.

There are clearly status connotations in touching. These customers, superior in status as customers and as men, may touch us as waitresses and as women. The status difference, with its implication of a differential power distribution between customer/waitress and man/woman, can explain the differences in touching behaviour that I observed. We waitresses are expected to accept touching and feeling by male customers as a regular and mundane feature of our work. Whether or not these acts of touching are intended as acts of domination by those who do them, they expect submission in the form of acquiescence. If this is not forthcoming the situation can become potentially or actually violent, as the male who has 'lost face', as we Chinese say, tries to reassert his former position of dominance:

There was trouble between Table 3 and Table 6. I came out to see man at Table 6 going through the motions of taking off his jacket and saying, 'Any day of the week, any day of the week, I am ready for you'. His female companion tried to placate him. At the other table, people were trying to stop the other man. Q. says he's going to call the police. Repeats this a number of times. Finally man at T3 leaves. The other chaps at T3 stopped at T6 on their way out, talked things over, and apologised for the 'aggressor' by saying that he had had a few to drink, and they all shook hands and wished each other Merry Xmas! Man at T3 then left. I overheard man-who-wanted-to-fight at T6 say to his friend (they were discussing the affair), 'But he shouldn't have said that to a girl'. Soon after, they too left. I tried to get the story from Mye (Q.'s wife, who usually worked in the kitchen but sometimes as a waitress) when we were clearing up. Apparently, man at T3 had felt Tina's bum a number of times when her back was turned to him. She then told him to stop doing that and he got ugly, swore at her and told her to 'piss off'. Mye went away at that stage, so I did not get the full story. But I gathered that the man at T6 had then stepped in.

Afterwards I heard Tina saying to kitchen staff that Q. did not like her scolding his customer.

(Fieldnotes, 21 December)

Various things here demonstrate touching as a male prerogative. First, Tina endured his touching her bottom a number of times before she finally spoke to him about it. Second, her resistance must have been seen as unexpected, for the man isn't abashed as someone caught doing something 'not normal' might have been. Third, although the man at Table 6 intervened in a manly fashion by offering physical violence, it seemed that what he objected to was less that the man had sexually assaulted Tina, more that he had sworn at her: sexual assault is permissible, swearing is not! Fourth, the molester leaves the restaurant, his manly image untarnished by having to apologise to Tina. As for his male companions, they feel that an explanation is called for, not to Tina, the victim, but to him who would act as her protector. Then they all shake hands; male camaraderie rules. And to cap it all, we have it from Tina that Q. as manager was displeased that she 'scolded' his customer and caused the uproar. The happening almost 'speaks for itself'.

Gender out back

Gender in staff interactions is more distinct, direct and more obviously chauvinistic. Amongst the staff there is not the 'ritual' structure which informs customer–staff interactions and which inhibits overt or obvious manifestations of sexism. Here too the dimension of sex is tied to power and status. There is also a great deal of resistance, although this takes quite subtle forms, as indeed does 'power', which can be typically described in these interactions as acts of subversion, of discrediting women's versions of 'reality'. When I arrived to start work, the restaurant was usually thinly populated with customers and the staff was often gathered round a corner table, chatting to while away the time. At the beginning of my time at the Palace things were often quite lively, because Koo's (a waiter) brother (a former waiter) and Q. were quite chummy; after he left and Koo took his place Q. was less chatty as he was less familiar with Koo. These talks between Q. and Koo's brother contained views about the nature of the sexes. Attributions about the sexes were made as 'objective fact' which transcends the situational and is true for all time. These included things like: men to work, women in the home; women shouldn't want much education because they end up as housewives; it is OK and 'manly' for men to have extra-marital affairs, but for women to commit adultery – unthinkable!

At first I used to argue hotly over these and similar ideas but I soon gave up, they were so predictable. Also when I started work at eight,

rather than the earlier time, there was less occasion for arguments
involving 'conceptual' ideas about the sexes. Generally speaking, the
other women did not participate in the 'ideological debates' about the
role of the sexes with the men, though they would listen to anecdotes
relating to relationships between people they knew. On the one hand it
seemed the women acquiesced in the men's version by being silent
when they passed comment about the female sex. But on the other I
could interpret their silence, not as passivity, but as refusing to rise to the
bait. Refusing to reply to these goads can be seen as the women
disaffiliating from the situation rather than allowing themselves to be
'done down'. And in our own circle the women sometimes subverted the
version of reality about women that the men built up. Although the men
may have the power to present a dominant version of reality, the women
voiced dissatisfaction, discussing it among themselves and subverting
the male version of events:

> Mye, Tina and I sat round the table talking. Got on to the topic of
> sex. Tina said that it seemed men were 'naturally dirty minded'.
> They seemed to see sex in everything. And the dirty jokes they tell,
> as if it were so clever! Why, she could tell a few good ones herself,
> and she proceeded to tell us a few sexual jokes, but in a
> self-mocking manner. We all laughed a lot. Q. came over and
> wanted to know why we were so gay. He often gets suspicious
> when he is being left out of things. Anyway, Tina said, 'Nothing',
> and Mye retorted, 'Nothing of your business'.
>
> (Fieldnotes, 2 February)

What exists among the waitresses is a kind of solidarity, not as
'oppressed women' perhaps, but as waitresses. At first this solidarity
existed among the three female part-timers, because after all Mye was
Q.'s wife and therefore 'on the other side', while Tina as the sister-
in-law was also 'them'. Later on, however, the situation changed. Given
Mye's difficult relationship with Q., she felt it was easier talking to us
part-timers than to Ah Soh, who was Q.'s sister (and worked in the
kitchen) and therefore more likely to take his side, or to Q.'s mother
(who also sometimes worked in the kitchen). Also she was genuinely
quite fond of me and so there was quite a lot of communication amongst
us. Later, when Tina felt that I was 'trustworthy' and had proved myself
to be a good worker, she thawed towards me and by the time she left we
had become quite friendly. Even Tina and myself, who were not that
close, supported each other in our working relationship and showed
concern for each other.

The symbolic symbol of authority at the Palace was Q., as its
manager. While not flouting Q.'s authority to his face, we part-timers
especially would devise strategies to avoid carrying out the more

unreasonable of his demands:

> Q. again tells me that when I take an order for 2 at a table for 4, I
> should take away the other two sets of cutlery to prevent theft. This
> is really a nuisance, especially when we are busy. First, there is the
> extra bother of taking away the cutlery to the racks. Second, this
> means that when we lay the table again, we would have to lay 4
> places again when we need have laid only two. Directly after he
> told me this, I avoided taking the order for Table 5, a couple at a
> four persons table. Siow (a part-timer) took the order instead,
> without knowing about the new dictum, and so she did not take
> away the two extra sets of cutlery. So he had to repeat his words to
> me to her again. We just didn't bother about it afterwards.
>
> (Fieldnotes, 23 December)

For Q. successfully to 'do power' over us depends on the amount of
effective resistance we put up. As for our resistance, this in its turn is
affected by other circumstantial factors such as: if I disobey him how
much backing do I have from the other waitresses, is his request within
reasonable demand, will I be testing his patience too far having just
resisted him over something else, and so on? The two aspects of power
accomplishment and resistance thus feed into each other. Sometimes he
had his way, at other times by a policy of muteness we could simply treat
his 'power' as though it was not there. While it is difficult to sift out how
much of the 'power relationship' with Q. is due to gender and how much
is derived from differential status between him and us, I also feel that the
two are interlinked and are integral aspects operating on the same level
simultaneously.

Gender or 'gender'?

I have utilised my difficulties in pinpointing and analysing gender as a
topic for consideration. Gender is indeed pervasive in the restaurant as
elsewhere, but precisely because it is everywhere, paradoxically, its
everyday forms are 'unseen' as such. It is not a self-evident presence but
is rather interwoven with other aspects of interaction and can be
meaningfully studied as such.

I found that, while in interactions 'out front' at the Palace the realm
of the sexual is more shifting in nature, in the 'back' region of the
restaurant there are more distinctly 'ideological' portrayals of gender in
conversation. This is because of the ritualised framework which
structures interactions with customers and the perceived necessity to
maintain 'personal front'. Hence gender 'out front' is much more
ambiguous and elliptical and therefore complex and difficult to trace. In
the back region where there is only staff, however, 'suppressed' opinion

and behaviour occurs. Hence the more clear-cut and accentuated nature of gender 'out back'; but here too, of course, distinctions about what stems purely from gender and what from factors such as status are blurred, the blurring often itself being an accomplishment of situated negotiation.

Some last words

In analysing the 'methods and resources' by which everyday life at the Palace is socially organised, practised and accomplished through becoming a waitress myself, I am rejecting the view that studying everyday life requires a position termed 'detached' and 'objective'. I have used myself as a prime source of data because I considered my own activities and understandings as irreparably part of what I was studying. Rather than pretending that my own experiences had not 'intruded' on the research, I have utilised them. In doing so I am also rejecting the opinion held by many sociologists that data obtained from observing oneself are in principle inferior to those obtained from observing others because self-observation is differentially subject to bias, distortion, value-judgement and the like. I do not agree.

I am not denying that what I am offering is a version of the reality I explored while working and researching at the Palace. Doubtless other alternative interpretations can be supplied for all I have reported on; indeed, at various points I have said I have pointed out other possible readings of what I discuss. I have attempted to show *why* my preferred reading is indeed my *preferred* reading, by providing an explication of the data and how I examined and analysed them. And as for the data, I do not consider them a domain of 'established findings'; rather, they are to be seen as integral features of the contexts from which they emerged, and I have always tried to locate them in this context.

© 1990 Chung Yuen Kay

References

Becker, Howard (1951) 'The Professional Dance Musician and His Audience', *American Sociological Review* 57:136–44.
Chung, Yuen Kay (1981) 'An Ethnography of a Chinese Restaurant', Unpublished M.A. thesis, University of Manchester.
——(1985) *At the Palace: Work, Ethnicity and Gender in a Chinese Restaurant*, Studies in Sexual Politics, No.3, Sociology Department, University of Manchester.
Goffman, Erving (1956) 'The Nature of Deference and Demeanor', *American Anthropologist* 58:473–502.
——(1976) *Gender Advertisements*, London: Macmillan.

Henley, Nancy (1977) *Body Politics*, Englewood Cliffs, NJ: Prentice-Hall.
Schwartz, Howard and Jacobs, John (1979) *Qualitative Sociology: a Method to the Madness*, New York: Free Press.

Appendix: *Who's who at the Palace*

Q.: In his mid-twenties; he was the manager and part-owner of the Palace. He married Mye in late September 1979.

The Father, the Mother, the Brother: They were the parents and brother of Mye, Yen and Fey. The Father was the chief cook, the Brother was the assistant cook and also the one who assembled the meals, while the Mother fried portions of spare ribs, meat in batter, chips and so on. When Mye married Q., her family sold their share in the restaurant to Q.'s Sister and Brother-in-law (Ah Soh and Cook, as they are referred to in my fieldnotes). And so they left the Palace in early 1979.

Mye: Sister to Yen and Fey. Also Q.'s wife. Generally she worked in the kitchen but sometimes she stood in as a *kei toy*.

Yen and Fey: Sisters to Mye. They were waitressing at the Palace until about mid-October 1979, and left not long after their parents and brother. They were *kei toy* from whom I absorbed the skills of the job.

Ah Soh and Cook: Q.'s Sister and Brother-in-law who took over from Mye's parents in the kitchen.

Ah Sum: The mother of Q. and Ah Soh. She lived above the restaurant (as did the others) and did not come down very much, although sometimes when we were busy she would help out in the kitchen.

Tina: She was the fiancée of Q.'s brother, who did not work in the restaurant. She came as a full-time waitress in mid-November 1979. She was seen by the part-timers as 'one of the family'.

Giny and Siow: Part-time waitresses.

Koo: Part-time waiter.

Hing: He started off waitering, but was later transferred to the kitchen.

Chapter fifteen

Counter-arguments
An ethnographic look at 'Women and Class'

Sue Webb

Introduction

In writing this chapter I had no wish to add to the theoretical controversy which has occurred in British sociology over the past few years concerning whether women have 'a class of their own'. Doing so seems to me fairly pointless, for I don't believe that any amount of data or sophistication in argument will persuade the male sociologists concerned that there is a problem with their approach to contrary analytic opinions as much as to the data they comment upon. Instead I look at the question of 'women and class' in a different way, explaining how a particular group of women understand and use ways of seeing hierarchy, authority and control in the workplace (however, interested readers are referred to Goldthorpe 1983; Heath and Brittain 1984; Goldthorpe 1984; Erikson 1984; Dale, Gilbert and Arber 1985; Abbott 1987; Erikson & Goldthorpe 1988; Leiulfsrud and Woodward 1988; sensible overviews are provided in Crompton and Mann 1986, and Abbott and Sapsford 1987). My chapter explores my changing ideas about what class is by locating and analysing women's class within an ethnographic study of a particular workplace (and an extended version can be found in Webb 1985).

The processes by which I conceptualised and analysed these women's class position developed as I attempted to understand their different workplace actions and responses in the context of the large department store they worked in, Dep-Sto. Broadly ethnographic research was appropriate because it enabled me to give due recognition to the complexity of women's experiences. I chose this approach because I wanted to situate consciousness and identity, and felt this would have been difficult if not impossible with more formal methods such as survey research or interviewing. I wanted to study a workplace in which women were *typically* employed. I had also noted that there were few sociological accounts of shop assistants. I therefore decided upon an ethnographic study of shop assistants – and thus the title of this chapter, *counter*-arguments to the conventional male view of women and class. The department store in which I carried out my fieldwork is one of a chain of retail outlets situated in a large industrial conurbation in the North of England. The beginning of my fieldwork coincided with the decline of opportunities for full-time permanent work for women in general; and the experience of women in Dep-Sto was no exception.

Class and the Dep-Sto labour process

An issue that immediately arose in my fieldwork was how to conceptualise the divisions that exist within the store and which cut across the class divisions that can be recognised through an application of Marxist conceptual categories. Work in the store was divided into departments predominantly along sex lines. Female assistants dominated the floor in most departments, but as one moved physically through the store and the goods sold became more expensive and bulky, so male assistants predominate; and as one moved behind the scenes away from the public arena of 'the floor' and into office areas, so here too women were concentrated in clerical roles and were absent from most others. Consequently, notions of differences between, and thus a hierarchy of, departments constitute an important conceptual framework held and used by the assistants and managers. For example, to work 'in the canteen' or 'on wet fish' was a threat frequently and effectively used by managers to keep assistants in their place in other departments.

However, within departments there were further divisions of authority and control between personnel into managers, sales assistants and demonstrators. Using formal class categories such as place in production, clear divisions in work position emerge between the managers on the one hand and the assistants on the other. Such felt-divisions certainly existed and informed the behaviour of members of the workforce. Therefore cutting through departmental solidarity was some evidence of worker solidarity against management. In addition, another division cross-cuts this. Some of the sales assistants were called 'demonstrators' and worked for outside companies which operated concessionary shops within the store; and direct employees of Dep-Sto (that is, both managers and assistants) recognised and often acted upon a common bond which set them apart from the demonstrators.

The problematic here was how to conceptualise the class place of Dep-Sto women in ways which recognised these multiple divisions within the workplace. I found little to suggest that these differences derived solely from factors external to the work situation, like who they lived with. This affected their lifestyles, but it does not necessarily follow that derivative notions of class and identity are appropriate means of conceptualising such effects, nor that they are one-way (from men to women) only.

To explore these issues in more depth, I then initially considered the shop assistants from the viewpoint of Marxist approaches that focus on the work position of the individual (that is, take a non-derivative approach to the class position of women). By doing so, shop assistants can be seen as all receiving wages from revenue and therefore as part of the new petty bourgeoisie (Poulantzas 1975), or all occupying a working-class place in the global function of capital (Carchedi 1977), or all as deskilled, non-productive members of the working class with little control over day-to-day work (Braverman 1974). Considering the appropriateness of these classifications to the empirical setting of Dep-Sto required me to examine the labour process and thus the work position of shop assistants in the store.

The labour proces

The Dep-Sto labour process is divided into different modes of operation such as selling, pre-selling, welfare, catering and security, and the training and administration of all sectors. Here it is selling that is dealt with, focussing on saleswomen's experiences of their work. The sales assistant is clearly differentiated from other positions in the organisation, not just by the nature of the work done but also by sex, spatial location and dress. Male assistants predominate in non-selling departments and appear in the selling departments that deal with high-quality, bulky goods like furniture and electrical equipment; elsewhere sales assistants are overwhelmingly female. Different forms of work are demarcated by different 'uniforms' and were especially clear following a directive for all sales staff to wear either black or dark blue which was put into effect during the period of my fieldwork.

Most people are familiar with the more obvious aspects of the work of a shop assistant; but perhaps what is not noticed is its physical nature, the lifting of boxes, moving of stock, and the dirt that all this entails coming into contact with. At 10 o'clock one morning Immy was on her knees, a bucket at her side and a cloth in her hand washing down all the fixtures and plastic wrapped articles; she remarked that 'it's a really dirty job ... that's why I never wear black to work any more'. Three months later the staff directive concerning the wearing of regulation colours was put into effect, in spite of what was a widely accepted feeling that such coloured clothing prevented the recognition of how dirty clothes had become during the course of a working day.

Along with the hard physical nature of the work goes low pay. Not surprisingly, then, it was several months before most of the assistants were to be seen wearing the new regulation colours. On their net take-home pay, and despite staff discounts, just coping with basic needs like housing, food, clothing and transport was a complex financial balancing act in which changes in the price and variety of food offered in the staff canteen brought with them a severe worsening of the assistants' conditions of employment. It was not surprising, then, to hear Jessie encouraging Tony to go to the store's centenary party, for 'You might as well get your free meal here ... it'll save you having to get something at home.'

On entering the store a new assistant is told which department she will work in, what she is to wear, how to conduct herself in the store, and she is trained on a computer terminal. The formal training lasts half a day and covers the techniques required for using the computer point-of-sale terminal or till; and this is coupled with the allocation of a number to her, so that all the financial transactions that assistants conduct are stored in the computer memory and can be traced back to individuals.

After this induction, weekly half-hour sessions before the store opens are organised in each department following the outline of a training manual which covers the whole store. However, rather than training, these sessions tend to be meetings for the managers to convey the latest piece of managerial policy to assistants, or, as sales time approaches, some managers use them to move stock around the department without the interference of customers. As one assistant commented after a training session, 'They're a real insult ... assume you haven't got any intelligence.' This was despite, or maybe because of, the concluding remarks of the manager, 'Well, I'm sorry, but it does make it a bit more interesting doesn't it. Gets your brains working.'

Sales assistants have very little control over their work: 'Look out, there's Mr K., if he sees us standing here he'll find us things to do' (Edna). 'Looking busy' is an important part of being a sales assistant and 'spreading out' is the main technique for accomplishing it. Assistants discuss arrangements of the stock, display shelves and the positioning of terminals, not just in terms of attractiveness or sales potential, but also in terms of possible seating arrangements that might hide them from managers and in terms of the distance they will have to cover in order to keep up friendships with other assistants or do their work. All these arrangements are imposed on them; and the assistants get used to the frequent visits of men in dark suits who start measuring fixtures in front of them but never explain or discuss what they are doing.

In Dep-Sto all women over 60 and part-time staff lost their jobs in this period. Doreen, an interior designer, talked to a colleague about why she felt her job was insecure. Whilst her colleague argued that it would cost the firm more to have outside contractors to do her work, Doreen responded that, 'Well p'raps not my bosses (that is, those who would want to make her redundant), but it's those at head office who decide and all they're concerned with is saving a wage packet.'

These redundancies increased the work load for assistants in some sections. In one department demonstrators work with the store's assistants, and the prevailing feeling is that 'we work as a team'. On certain Saturdays there are no store staff on this section, but the manager knows that customers will be served and new stock priced and displayed by the demonstrators. As Immy says,

> F. knows the work'll get done so he doesn't help us but he'll get down on his knees to help that lot [that is, meaning a different section of his department]. He relies on the goodwill of C.'s and B.'s [that is, two outside companies operating concessionary shops] staff whereas in the other section the dems only do their own work. Dep-Sto is saving on staff.

Alongside this lack of control, the assistants are excluded from knowledge of the work process. Part of the work involves the ticketing of goods and, while many assistants do understand the codes used and have a good practical knowledge of prices, it was not their job to allocate these to the products. Their job was simply one of putting the labels on to the goods. Consequently when, as often happened, the managers and pre-selling clerks allocated the codes and prices incorrectly, the assistants did not rush forward to sort the problem out. After a hard week of re-pricing all goods following the New Year's increase, Connie recognised that certain articles seemed rather expensive; she said, 'These are the wrong price, aren't they?' Immy measured the goods and realised that they had been wrongly priced, and she said, 'Put them back, forget you saw them, we'll do it tomorrow.'

Similarly, when it came to stock-taking the assistants' job was to help the manager arrive at the figure considered by managers to be appropriate. On this Miss B. said, 'So if you're over any time we put them somewhere and then find them again if we're down ... we put them in someone else's stockroom and they put theirs in ours.... We don't actually take them home, you see, it's not our own doing.'

Most assistants and even trainee managers, if female, recognise the limited chances of promotion and were reluctant to take on extra duties for their basic gross wage, or to aspire to become an Assistant Department Manager (ASM) to gain extra responsibility for very little more money: 'I could do the ASM's course but it's not worth it. My boyfriend S. did and he was an ASM at 18, but where can you go after that? If I became an ASM at 22 I'd be stuck there till I was at least 30, how are they going to have me over someone like Betty at 22? All the trainees who started with S. have now left' (Immy). Other trainee managers echoed the same thoughts on promotion: 'It's not much only to ASM' (Olga); 'And not many women get to be manageresses ... just look at us, most of the trainees are girls but only one or two of the managers on fashion and the ground floor (in the perfumery) are women' (Olga).

As women, they felt they would have to work harder than men to achieve the same position. For example, during the discussion the Assistant Training Manager informed the group that the entry requirement of two O-levels had been lowered for males in their year, in order to boost recruitment following requests from managers for more male trainees: 'Managers want a porter really but they'll settle for a trainee, so they really want some males though I shouldn't say it.'

These women also recognised indirect discrimination against married women if they were competing with men for promotion. In order to gain promotion and be accepted as a manager, they had to use different methods from their male colleagues because they were operating in a male-dominated field with all its resentments and fears that 'masculinity' was being undermined. As Sharon put it to her male counterparts on the course, 'We get you to do what we want by letting you think it's your idea.' In this particular store there was a definite basis for these understandings, because there was clear differentiation into place in the hierarchy and also physical location in the store according to sex.

Various of my fieldwork data provide insight into the attitudes of sales assistants to staff recruitment and turnover. For example, Connie emphasised that 'I never believe these married women who say they work because they're bored at home. They work because they have to.' And to this Connie responded that 'They say they don't need to work because their husband's got a good job, they're just bored. Well if they really had money they could do all sorts, join voluntary organisations, they needn't be bored.'

Fundamentally, then, it is money that keeps these women in their jobs. Betty said, 'I wish I could just stop working', while later, following her fifty-ninth birthday, she sang, 'Oh eleven more months and ten more days and I'll be out ...'. And it is money which encourages most of the Dep-Sto women to change their jobs, a point recognised explicitly by management: 'About a third of the women are in their fifties, working for a bit of extra money and if they can save on the bus fare or get a few bob more at X's they'll go' (Training Manager).

This recognition was expressed by the sales assistants themselves; and their knowledge is reflected in the advice that Betty, who was nearing retirement, gave to Immy, who was young and single: 'There's a good job going in the new Co-op up C.H....on the checkout, it pays well, more than here'. Immy did not take this advice because she had other ideas and thought that the job 'would drive me mad'. Instead, she was accepted on to a different store's training scheme nearer her home, where she thought she had a greater chance of rapid promotion. Her reasons for doing so show a keen insight into the nature of sales work, in particular in the context of Dep-Sto. She said,

> I couldn't stand it here any longer.... I need something to get me teeth into, some sort of challenge ... apart from coming here and talking to Carol there's nothing here ... even Carol's a bit better off, she goes away, meets her managers. I never see mine and the stock control goes straight to them.... I haven't told anyone yet except Carol.... Betty'll go mad when I tell her, she thinks I ought to be here till I die ... get married, have children and come back to Dep-Sto's. I just couldn't stand that.

Even when there is no concrete evidence of someone having left Dep-Sto in order to improve their work position, stories abound to this effect: someone who used to work at Dep-Sto and had now gone on to better things was the most frequently told 'leaving story'. However, concrete evidence of this actually being the motive for and the effect of leaving are also to be found. For example, one young man went to a jeans boutique as an assistant the year before and is now its manager; he comes in regularly to see how everyone is, have a few laughs and so on. Another example is the work-experience girl who now has a job in an office and looks well dressed and has had her hair done. These and similar examples are told as success stories in which the people who left Dep-Sto are now better paid and freer to do as they please.

Work experience and class identity

The Dep-Sto assistants held, and used in analysing and understanding their work and other experiences, clearly non-derivative interpretations of their class position. For many of them, this is well illustrated by the notion of their 'trade', for occupational history was an important, indeed a key source of self-identity for these women. Their own qualifications and experiences were prime, and they took no analytic cognisance of their husbands' work/class positions in producing descriptions and explanations of job identity and class location.

Jessie, who works in the glass and china department, frequently refers to herself as a machinist. When a new cash-point was installed, she hounded floor controllers and the manager of the fabric department for some brown material to make a curtain screen to hide the inside of the counter. Despite the doubts expressed by the controllers as to whether a sales assistant should use the sewing machines in the store's alterations room, Jessie was able to convince them that, as a trained machinist, she would be perfectly safe in doing so; and the curtains and

Jessie's part in their making featured frequently in conversations over the next few weeks. On other occasions Jessie explained her involvement as the works trade-union convenor in relation to her experience in other workplaces as a machinist, where she had been a shop steward, and as a result of management: 'You have to watch them you know, they'd steal anything off you if you don't.'

Betty had worked in towels and linen at Dep-Sto for the last seven years and before that in other shops, and is now nearing retirement. In spite of this she very definitely sees her trade as a quilt-maker. She had worked in factories making continental quilts until made redundant; and she sees shop work as a poor alternative to this: 'It's not as much money ... we was on piece work and I could get quite a lot on bonus and overtime. There's nothing like that here.' Describing herself as essentially a quilt-maker occurred frequently when meeting new assistants and seems partly to explain her placement in this particular department. It was also an identity often used to structure her interactions with customers. For example, in reply to a phone enquiry about the revamping of ordinary bed quilts into duvets, Betty explained that the store did not do this but, as it was her trade before coming to the store, she could give the customer the names of several factories that would undertake this process.

On ladies' suits, Miss B. was a tailoress by trade and had worked in the store off and on for about forty years. This acknowledgement of her trade actually reflects the past nature of store work, where assistants were trained in particular skills such as tailoring, hat-making and so on; but Miss B. had not let the identification of herself as a tailoress go when the job itself was de-skilled. Her practical experience, as well as such an identity for herself, was carried through into her daily work so that she would talk knowledgeably to customers about the material content of clothes and proudly explained to me that 'We'll be missed after January (when she and the two other women over 60 in that department were being forced to retire) when they try to do their stock controls and they've no idea what there is, like on dresses where they were once £2,000 down ... no one knew what had gone so they couldn't claim on the insurance.'

In chinaware, Carol had always worked with this product both in Dep-Sto and in another local specialist china shop. She knows all the company patterns and designs and is the acknowledged expert in this area; and she is consequently frequently called upon by other assistants to deal with customer questions about the past and present china stock. For example, on one occasion a customer wished to buy a piece of china to match some purchased several years earlier. The assistant she had spoken to called upon Carol's expertise, asking her 'Carol, what's this from (holding up the piece of china), do we still stock it?' Carol replied,

'That's blankware, it's not in this year's catalogue but I'll go and see if we've still got some of it (that is, in the stockroom).' And yet another example is Jerry in the staff canteen. She acts as cashier and occasionally stands in as a waitress in the managers' room, and she described herself to me as someone who has 'always been in catering ... waitressing ... used to work in the Bistro (a public cafeteria in the store)'.

The fact that the Dep-Sto women hold these identities could be an important factor in placing them in various departments in the store, for, as I have said, there was often a close fit between the identity held and the particular product handled by the women. However, it should not be taken as a causal connection that, for example, Betty who once worked in a quilt factory now sells quilts and sheets. Certainly some women's expressed trade identities distinguished them sharply from the product they worked with, and indeed from the position of shop assistant altogether. For example, in the bed linen and towels department, Susan held an art degree and distanced herself from some of the duties of a sales assistant, using her time to design displays and so on. Also Connie, in the same section, had been an office worker; and her slowness at manual work like labelling goods caused Betty to remark that 'She'd be no good on piece work. We'd still be on the first batch if Connie were here.'

What this suggests to me is that an expressed trade identity says more about an assistant's understanding and acceptance or non-acceptance of their place in the store than it does about their full occupational history. For example, a number of the women's expressed identities often reflected their view of the high point in their occupational experiences; and becoming a shop assistant is implicitly (and sometimes, like Betty above, explicitly) presented as a lowering of their status, pay and conditions. Nevertheless, that these trade identities were so widely expressed and utilised provides an interesting empirical counter to derivative notions of women's class identity.

Class as an explanation of social behaviour

Gender and class identity

The Dep-Sto women have radical understandings of the workings of capitalist society and their place in it; and an ideology of scepticism and resistance to authority. It is frequently apparent that their criticisms are also applied to male authority: 'He can't cope with working Saturdays so he gives us a party, while we women have to work every day of the week.' It has been suggested that when women resist dominant ideologies and assert that the women's world is superior, they thereby insulate themselves from working-class influences and collude with the dominant ideology. In my fieldwork, these are the women who turn away from the union and towards their departments to sort out workplace problems even though they are very critical of management. There are, however, alternative ways of understanding their actions.

The Dep-Sto women, like many other – male well as female – workers who hold apparently inconsistent ideologies do so because they use different reference groups in different situations. In the Dep-Sto case, the women use *women* as their reference group. At times they develop ideas that are critical of the organisation and at other times ideas that are critical of the union; and in both situations they turn towards their immediate women's reference group, which is their department. The notion of 'inconsistency' here is founded on two rather shaky assumptions: the assumed primacy of 'class consciousness' over 'women's consciousness'; and the implicit assumption that male workers have class consciousness and are the norm, and women workers do not and are therefore deviant. Both assumptions suggest a greater homogeneity in male and class identity than seems to be the case. Within any workforce not everyone will possess the same belief system, and certainly there are few signs of a complete overlap between male and class identities.

I now focus on the actions of women active in the Dep-Sto union and how these are variously understood by other women in the store.

There are a number of women who regularly attend union meetings and are particularly dismissive of the idea that married women could not attend branch meetings after work because of family commitments. They argue that if these women could work late (the store stayed open later on Thursday nights), they could organise their family commitments in the same way one Wednesday in four. But it was the single women who are most heavily reproached by them: 'There's plenty of single ones but even they don't go and it's not that they've got families' (Jessie).

The influence of these activists on members of their departments can, however, be understood as an essentially women's/departmental solidarity and identity. For example, during a union meeting on a pay claim, the most vociferous opposition to acceptance of the management's offer came from a woman who was a Communist Party member; and in the ballot most of her department voted with her. Anne said that 'Jessie dropped a big hint by telling us that this would be all we'd get till this time next year and just to think about it, what with inflation and everything ... most of those on toys including my sister voted against.'

The explanation for this voting pattern is not simply that all members of a department come to hold the same political views, but rather that there is a daily stress on departmental consciousness and solidarity. This produces general lines of agreement and boundaries for workplace talk which are progressively constructed in workplace interaction and which affect patterns of behaviour. This is by no means a simple process. For example, the CP woman who had gained the support of the rest of her department over the pay offer had previously been removed from another department because the women already working there disliked her political views and also her attitudes towards work.

Members of this other section asked me how I liked working in 'china' and who I was working with. I told them I was with Jessie, and they responded: 'Not with Jessie!' (Carol); 'Oh we had her sister on here, we soon got rid of her' (Betty); 'She was all union' (Betty and Carol together). I said, 'Don't you agree with the union?'; Betty replied that 'It's not that, it's just that all she did was stand with her hands on her hips, stirring it up all the time. She never did a bloody stroke.... I told her when I was off for me lunch there was a pile of tickets to be done and she might do a few while I was away. When I got back the pile was still on the bloody floor untouched.' Carol added that 'We went up to Mr F. ... yes, we said we wouldn't work if she stayed, so they soon got rid of her.'

This woman did not fit her department's notions of how to work, and this was seen as tied in with her political views. Underlying the strong sense of pragmatic departmental solidarity against management, and sometimes against other departments, can be deep conflicts and tensions. This may be at the level of conflicting lifestyles, as when Carol and Immy do not talk about sex in front of Connie except occasionally to embarrass her or because they are fed up with her assumption that they'll get married and have children and return to the store. The conflict may be at the level of attitudes towards management and the organisation and to strikes and unions. And it may also result from very different ideas about how assistants should engage with the work process itself. And of course two or more of these sources of tension and conflict can and often do feed into and off each other, as in the above example.

Class as a workplace specific

The Dep-Sto women's similarities or differences in consciousness can be related to their everyday work experiences. Dep-Sto is a city-centre store, and consequently there was a great variety among the women who worked in it in terms of age, previous experience, educational qualifications and lifestyles. It was this diversity in objective experience, coupled with their orientation to the work process itself, that led to differences in the Dep-Sto women's class identity. It was not something that could be read off from the class identities of the men with whom they were connected.

Differences in class association were clearly visible and very important in affecting workplace behaviour, and certainly the placing of people in departments, or as assistants or demonstrators, relied on commonsense notions of class in which definitions of the kind of people who would work in the 'dirty, mice-infested canteen', with 'wet fish' or in 'fashion and high-class furs' are constructed and used. This can be seen clearly in the personnel manager's statement about how he conducts interviews:

> a sixth sense tells you whether you're going to employ them ... dress, speech, mannerisms, would you like to be served by them ... a woman came in here reeking of alcohol, there's no way ... you get some coming in who haven't shaved or washed for a week, and that's only the women! ... you can tell when they walk in the door where you can put them. ... For instance, there were two girls from Manpower Services, I put them in catering. There's no way I'd put them on selling, they're not the type. It sounds as though I'm a terrible snob but it's not that, we're trying to raise standards. If someone leaves we try to put in someone better.

As the raw material of Dep-Sto, as of any organisation, is people, members of its workforce are likely to develop definitions of types of persons as an essential part of their everyday involvement in the work process. In Dep-Sto a conception of what selling is, how it should be done and to whom it should be done, was perpetually discussed and applied to people and behaviours. These concern, for example, what a 'good assistant' is like, what her daily practice should be and what a normal customer is like. Such definitions are in no way abstract classificatory schemes, for they develop in specific circumstances and have application to specific locations and contexts. What is meant by a 'good assistant' is not bound by factors such as appearance or dress or even by specific items of behaviour: it is contextually defined by others, as the following example demonstrates.

According to Betty and her department, a good assistant is one who takes trouble to be helpful to customers and never just points to goods saying 'it's over there', but takes the customer to the articles in question. None the less, if Betty and the others are in a hurry or they are fed up, they do point. However, this action does not become a determinant of their identity and make them bad assistants; but it would be a determinant for someone they wanted to exclude from their group, as the incident outlined earlier shows.

Just as the organisation is divided administratively into different sections, so these divisions are visible in terms of how one dresses, what

space one occupies in the store, and which doors, stairs, toilets and canteen one uses. Towards the end of my fieldwork I was invited to meet
the training manager for lunch but could not find him. So, after making
enquiries, I was sent through to the managers' dining room from the
door connecting with the staff canteen. Heads turned towards me in
surprise and dismay, as I had broken the rules of position and place that
operated within the store.

Another example concerns how such divisions are constructed, used
and mediated by the various sales assistants rather than by management,
in relation to the demonstrators. 'Look at her, you'd think she owned the
place,' Elsie said about a demonstrator who walked past arrogantly
trying to get a cheque signed. 'Well it's all Dep-Sto's fault, they won't
call them managers,' Jessie replied. In doing so she was referring to the
generally accepted fact among the assistants that the demonstrators may
be treated as assistants but, because they do not experience their work
like this, they distance themselves from this role by acting like managers.

The demonstrators occupy a management-oriented place in the store
compared with the other assistants. They are able to arrange their own
daily routines, days off, holidays and the timing of tea breaks, and they
also have greater flexibility about the length of these breaks. On one
particular floor, all the demonstrators take their morning tea breaks a
half-hour after the store break and use the public cafeteria. This group
has some autonomy to take breaks under different circumstances from
those of the other staff; they thus constitute an informal group, but one
that is none the less part of the structure of organisational control. That
is, by having this autonomy they feel they are successfully differentiating themselves from the other assistants (as indeed they are); but
this differentiation is limited, for they still have to adhere to various
organisational rules. They do set time limits, they do go back to work,
and they do not all arrive and leave the cafeteria at the same time but
make sure that there is adequate staffing of the floor: the rules are there,
and they impose them on themselves.

Demonstrators' work is generally more skilled than that of the
assistants, in that they have to keep records of goods sold and take part
in the re-ordering of stock. Because of this they have more reason to be
sitting and writing and using telephones, all of which are work processes
more typically associated with management; and this means that they do
not have the perpetual problem the Dep-Sto assistant has of needing
continually to 'look busy'.

Economically, demonstrators are in a somewhat different position,
for their pay is often greater than that of the other assistants and made
up by commission or bonuses. This itself can create divisions between
staff over the necessity for the correct use of production codes so that

demonstrators are credited for goods sold by them. Through their control of stock, demonstrators also experience more perks, like free samples, meals out with their area managers and more in-service training. Along with this, they have a concern for the total volume of sales and stock lost by theft, and this too aligns them more with management. The demonstrators still physically chase shoplifters, while the Dep-Sto assistants have learned their lesson the hard way and tell many stories about threats of violence by shoplifters and lack of support given by the store.

Thus the demonstrators' work situation continually differentiates them from the other assistants and aligns them with management. The divisions in identity are most acute when the department is spatially divided between Dep-Sto and non-Dep-Sto staff, and this may obviate the development of section and departmental solidarity and anti-management consciousness. Yet the division is frequently not recognised in this simple way: in some departments all sales staff 'work as a team', as I have already indicated. In the department I referred to earlier, the different types of assistant are located by the same terminal, and the extra control that the demonstrators have over their stock is used to the advantage of all the department's assistants. Goods are sold to assistants in this 'team' at negotiable prices, so emphasising their common identity as waged employees and providing evidence of an underlying informal economy operated by and for the sales assistants.

Examined thus it becomes clear that the workplace division between sales assistants is an incredibly complex one. This complexity is derived from the contextually specific knowledge-in-use which the different kinds of assistants derive from real material differences in their work experiences. The demonstrators have confirmed for them every day that their job and that of the Dep-Sto assistants is different; and this also happens for the Dep-Sto assistants. And it is only when these real material differences are breached that a common identity and departmental solidarity can come into existence.

Conclusion

In considering the extent to which the Dep-Sto women form stable collectivities based on their work position, I identified elements in the store's labour process which gave rise to similarities in their class place. These women occupy low-grade, de-skilled manual work in which they have little control over their work time, little formal knowledge of the work process, and little chance of upward mobility within the store. Furthermore, the way in which management utilised the women's expressed work identities and occupational histories (their 'trades') when placing them in different departments in the store, and the meaning and use that this perception of trade had for the women, suggests that more attention should be paid by class theorists to women's own work position than to the conjectured effects of sexual divisions in households.

Once we accept that these women do form a stable collectivity in their own right, the next consideration is the extent to which this forms the basis for their class identity and action. My data revealed a rich variety of anti-management views expressed both verbally and in actions which were carried through into the minutiae of how the assistants organised their working day. This suggests clearly that the workplace was at the very least as important an influence on the identities and behaviours of these women as other external factors, and probably a great deal more so.

The next consideration is the extent to which variations in the Dep-Sto women's social behaviour can be attributed to other than workplace factors. In other words, did the women display variations in identity and class action because their prime orientation to the class structure is through their families and thus structured by their relationships with men? Far from needing to resort to derivative notions of class on the one hand, or to any uni-dimensional and trans-situational notion of 'gender' on the other, I found that differences in the material conditions of the work process perfectly adequately accounted for divisions in identity and action between departments, and within departments between Dep-Sto and non-Dep-Sto employees. These differences in identities and class action are thus traced to the women's own work experiences unmediated by their men's class position. There may indeed be a coincidence between their place in the store hierarchy and the men's class position, but this is precisely a coincidence from which no causal relationship can – or rather should – be deduced.

My chapter has not denied the importance of sexual divisions, but I would suggest my data demonstrate that sexual divisions should not be raised to the level of a determinant of women's class position. My fieldwork suggests very strongly the need for a theory of women's class that is sensitive to the effects of gender in placing men and women in paid and unpaid work, but which does not treat gender as a structurally imposed determinant of contextually specific behaviour, including class-related behaviour. Instead such a theory would, just like any other adequate class theory should, incorporate the complexity of the 'material reality' that can be found in the work process, indeed even in one single workplace.

© 1990 Sue Webb

References

Abbott, Pamela (1987) 'Women's Social Class Identification: Does Husband's Occupation Make a Difference?' *Sociology* 21:91–103.

Abbott, Pamela and Sapsford, Roger (1987) *Women and Social Class*, London: Tavistock.

Braverman, Harry (1974) *Labour and Monopoly Capital: the Degradation of Work in the Twentieth Century*, London: Monthly Review Press.

Carchedi, George (1977) *On the Economic Identification of Social Classes*, London: Edward Arnold.

Crompton, Rosemary and Mann, Michael (eds) (1986) *Gender and Stratification*, Oxford: Polity Press.

Dale, Angela, Gilbert, G. Nigel and Arber, Sara (1985) 'Integrating Women into Class Theory', *Sociology* 19:384–409.

Erikson, Robert (1984) 'Social Class of Men, Women and Families', *Sociology* 18:500–14.

Erikson, Robert and Goldthorpe, John (1988) 'Women at Class Crossroads: a Critical Note', *Sociology* 22:545–52.

Goldthorpe, John (1983) 'Women and Class Analysis: in Defence of the Conventional View', *Sociology* 17:465–88.

——(1984) 'Women and Class Analysis: a Reply to the Replies', *Sociology* 18:491–9.

Heath, Anthony and Brittain, Nicky (1984) 'Women's Jobs Do Make a Difference', *Sociology* 18:475–90.

Leiulfsrud, Hakon and Woodward, Alison (1988) 'Women at Class Crossroads: a Critical Reply to Erikson and Goldthorpe's Note', *Sociology* 22:555–62.

Poulantzas, Nicos (1975) *Classes in Contemporary Capitalism*, London: New Left Books.

Stanworth, Michelle (1984) 'Women and Class Analysis: a Reply to Goldthorpe', *Sociology* 18:159–70.

Webb, Sue (1985) *Counter Arguments: an Ethnographic Look at 'Women and Class'*, Studies in Sexual Politics No. 5, Sociology Department, University of Manchester.

Chapter sixteen

Using drama to get at gender

Vivienne Griffiths

Introduction

Adolescent girls until recently have been neglected by researchers. This gap is now being filled: studies of gender and schooling have proliferated over the last ten years. However, there is still a lack of research into the social, as distinct from the educational, experience of adolescent girls. I undertook the research reported in this chapter and in Griffiths (1986) as a response to this need. Angela McRobbie and Jenny Garber (1975) suggest that girls experience adolescence very differently from boys, forming a 'distinctive culture' of their own. One of the main purposes of my study was to identify some features of this culture.

I worked with 13–14-year-old girls (black, Asian, white) using drama to focus on important areas of concern to them. I chose to study 13–14-year-old girls (that is, those in their third year of secondary schooling) for several reasons. First, this age group has rarely been concentrated on in recent research. Second, I wanted to assess how important different aspects of teenage culture are to girls in their early adolescence. Third, subject options are chosen during the third year of secondary school; it is therefore a crucial time for both girls and boys in relation to future plans about jobs or further education.

As a feminist, it was important to set up and conduct my research from the girls' point of view. The research and my choice of methods – drama and informal discussion – were also influenced by my previous teaching experience. I also brought my feminist perspective to the evaluation of the findings, presented in Griffiths (1986) in the context not only of the girls' sex and age, but also their class and ethnic background. However, in this chapter my discussion focusses on the role of drama as both a research technique and a particularly successful means of 'getting at gender'.

I carried out fieldwork in two co-educational comprehensives in the North of England: a three-week pilot study at Millbridge High School (this and all other names of institutions and persons in this chapter are

221

pseudonyms); and the main study, which lasted for seven weeks, at Newton High School. I returned to Millbridge High six months later for a further three weeks' work with a different group. All the girls in the study were aged between 13 and 14; those in the main study were working class and from a range of ethnic backgrounds: Asian, black and white.

Role-play and dramatic improvisation were my main methods of working, with informal discussion forming an integral part of each session. I chose themes which I thought would be relevant to the girls' present concerns and also involve some consideration of their future lives. The pilot study helped me decide what topics to concentrate on in the main study. For instance, I had made 'school' a special focus at Millbridge, but at Newton concentrated on 'families' instead. I presented open-ended themes which would allow the girls to express their own ideas and experiences. Many issues were in fact introduced and developed by the girls themselves, as I had hoped. Most of the discussions and improvisations were recorded on either audio or video tape in order to facilitate later analysis.

Using drama as a research method

Many researchers (McRobbie and Garber 1975; McRobbie 1978; Llewellyn 1980; Cowie and Lees 1981) have written about the particular difficulty of working with adolescent girls. Dramatic role-play and informal discussions were my main methods of working with the girls. Open-ended discussions have been used with valuable results by other researchers working with girls (Sharpe 1976; McRobbie 1978; Jamdagni 1980; Cowie and Lees 1981). I favoured these over individual interviews because I felt that the girls would be inhibited by being interviewed alone. Discussions also fitted in well because I could compare what the girls expressed through their dramatic improvisations with what they said in discussion. Together the two formed an integral process. Because drama has rarely been used as research method, I explain the reasons for my choice and describe my methods of interpretation. Central here has been my experience as a provider of drama in schools prior to this research: for three years I was a school-based drama teacher; for a further six years I worked with drama-in-education groups.

By 'drama' I mean an extension of children's play, a creative process which, at its deepest, can be an aid to child development. Gavin Bolton (1979:38) refers to this as 'Drama for understanding'. In practice, drama of this kind might range from the creation of imaginary situations, derived perhaps from myth or legend, to the re-creation of actual incidents drawn from the children's own experience. This type of drama provides a safe context through which attitudes and feelings may be revealed which might not be easy for pupils to express in classroom discussions or written work. In my experience, participants very quickly reach levels of feeling and expression that might otherwise only be expressed after lengthy periods of discussion with a trusted teacher. This factor has a particular advantage as a way of gaining the trust of adolescent girls, who may be especially resistant to intrusions into their private lives.

I used role-play to maximise this effect. As an introduction to each theme, I took on a role; for instance, in the first session at Newton I became the mother of a teenage girl who asked the girls advice about her daughter. The advantage of this technique with adolescents, particularly if they are new to drama like the girls at Newton, is that they become involved in a dramatic situation without realising it, since at all times they remain as themselves. I found the girls quickly became involved in the situation, revealing their own attitudes as they talked to the mother. They were then ready to improvise their own scenes where they took on the roles themselves.

Another advantage of drama work is that it is a practical medium: the members of the group enter into and experience a concrete situation and react to it spontaneously as they improvise the scene, rather than simply thinking in the abstract as they might in discussion or written work. In this way, feelings and attitudes may be revealed that might not be openly admitted or even recognised by participants if asked directly. It is also invaluable when it comes to a topic like 'the future', which 13–14-year-old girls find quite remote and difficult to envisage; in my research, the dramatic process made this theme much more immediate and accessible to the girls.

Drama work often brings out different aspects of people – for instance, children normally lacking in confidence often become much more forthcoming in drama, even taking the lead on some occasions. This is particularly relevant to any study of gender. In my experience of using drama with mixed groups, the girls often become more assertive and dominant in relation to the boys than they might be in other lessons. This can occur even when the drama is not focussing directly on gender, though it seems to be a prerequisite that the drama is set up in a non-sex-typed way. Working with girls by themselves can enable them more easily to break through the stereotype of the 'quiet' girl.

Drama has rarely been used as a research method, so there was some problem in finding satisfactory methods of evaluation. Although role-play is used extensively in therapeutic settings, and is widely reported in studies of children's play, the methods of interpretation employed were not altogether appropriate to my research. Similarly, although drama is now being used quite frequently with adolescent girls by teachers and youth workers, the purpose of this work is rather different from mine. Here I consider role-play and collective story-building, together with the question of my own influence and the girls' commitment to the drama, and assess how relevant these are to an evaluative approach.

My influence

My influence in the drama work cannot be ignored. I was interested in the girls' lives and using a medium which by its nature involved me fully. At the same time, I did try to minimise directly influencing the girls' attitudes by not expressing my own views unless directly asked. Drama has potential as a consciousness-raising agent and I hope that it may have, incidentally, increased the girls' confidence and encouraged them to question aspects of their present and future lives, but this was not my particular intention.

As I was working alone I set up the drama sessions myself, usually introducing each session with a short scene enacted by me. The purpose of this was to encourage and maintain interest and commitment from girls who had little previous experience of drama. I knew that the direct representation of a role by an actor has a strong impact; because of this I tried to keep my own input to a minimum, and I thought hard about what roles I would adopt and how I would present them. For example, in the opening session at Newton, I played the role of the mother of a teenage girl. Mother and daughter have had a row the night before, and now the daughter is refusing to return home. In presenting this situation, I was careful simply to set the scene, and included no explanation as to why the row had taken place. This made a 'concrete' way into discussion about what things might lead to arguments with parents, and subsequently into the girls' own improvisations.

I tried not to present traditional stereotypes; at the same time I wanted to portray characters to whom the girls could relate in a fairly immediate way. Retrospectively, I am aware of how much my own class attitudes influenced how I interpreted those of 'the working-class' from the outside and contained precisely stereotyped, and not necessarily valid, portraits. For example, my 'working-class mum' says, 'Wait till your Dad gets in', whereas many working-class women utilise authority and dispense rewards and punishments without waiting for anyone else, as the girls made clear to me. The girls certainly brought their own attitudes to the roles they played. In the case of the mother above, the girls criticised me for being 'too soft' on my daughter. The mothers they presented themselves were highly authoritarian in my terms.

Another example seems less problematic in retrospect, although I was more concerned about it at the time. When I introduced the theme of 'the future' at Newton, in a short scene where I received a letter from an old friend I was anxious not to present myself as a particular type of traditional woman (married with children, not working outside the home) whom the girls might then use as a model. As I could not easily present two different types of women myself (at Millbridge with the second group, I enacted the same opening scene with a friend, Marcia Spring), I implied that the woman I was portraying had a job – the letter arrived as she was leaving for work – but left everything else ambiguous. The girls' own scenes in fact covered the whole range of possible futures: unmarried working women, mothers at home with small children and working mothers. I felt that my own role on this occasion had neither encouraged a particular result nor inhibited alternatives.

Collective story-building

The themes I introduced were elaborated on by the girls in discussion and then incorporated and transformed into their own scenes. These stages, which I have called 'collective story-building', were fascinating to follow through, seeing how particular ideas might be taken up by the whole group, or changed and adapted by the smaller groups in the course of their improvisations. Through this process it could clearly be seen what themes seemed important to the groups as a whole, and what were special interests for the smaller working groups.

It is also interesting to see how particular phrases occur in more than one scene. The most striking example of this concerns 'coming home late'. The first version of this was enacted by me, in the role as the mother, and a black girl, Irene, who played the part of my daughter Sharon:

Extract 'Coming home late', Newton (black/VG)

MUM:	What sort of time do you call this?
SHARON:	Half past eleven. (*Much audience laughter*)
MUM:	What time are you supposed to come in in the week?
SHARON:	Half ten.
MUM:	You know don't you? Well why are you so late?
SHARON:	Didn't have me watch on. (*Audience laughter*)
MUM:	But you've got it on now. Oh Sharon!
SHARON:	If it works.
MUM:	Let's have a look. It's working now all right. It says the right time as well.
SHARON:	Yeah, but I hit it. (*Laughter*)
MUM:	Sharon, it's no use making up stories. Look, I've just about had enough.

225

At the time this caused great hilarity, which I read intuitively as not only pleasure at daughter cheeking mother, but also at the 'out-of-drama' dimension of pupil cheeking teacher. Irene was setting new bounds as to what was allowable in the drama with me, a stranger to the girls, and I think this gave it added significance. The pattern of the opening of that scene (especially the first two lines) became ready-made dialogue for many of the girls; such phrases were used in a similar way to the dramatic props like the telephone: they provided part of the framework to which they then added their own individuality.

Understanding role-play

One possible approach to interpreting the girls' scenes is to 'match them up' to their real lives. The fact that I chose realistic themes about family, relationships, school, makes this approach seem attractive. However, the presupposition that there is, or may be, a direct match between drama and real life experience seems highly questionable to me. Even in such an everyday occurrence as recounting an anecdote, the story-teller changes events slightly depending on whom s/he is talking to. The original episode may be altered out of all recognition according to the need it has fulfilled in the retelling. Similarly, in the drama process an actual event may be heightened and transformed without the participants being deliberately aware of the changes that have taken place.

Attitudes to any subject are derived from a complex mixture of sources – upbringing, education, the media and so on – which interact with one another. The resulting attitudes may of course contain a stereotyped element, depending on the individual. But there are considerable problems associated with such a reading of a role-play. For example, my initial assessment of the Newton girls' role-playing of mothers was that they were stereotyped. However, this depended on bringing my own middle-class perspectives to the girls' working-class experience, so I was not in a very good position to judge.

There was more evidence of stereotyped role-play at Millbridge than at Newton. This seemed to occur when middle-class girls tried to portray working-class people (and myself when portraying a working-class mother, as I said earlier). It also seemed to reflect a certain kind of drama teaching (which I have used frequently myself) around the acting out of stereotyped sitations (for example, the bus queue, the doctor's waiting room). This tends to produce 'types' such as 'the business man', 'the posh lady', 'the nagging wife' and so on. At Millbridge, this kind of stereotyped role-play was evident; at Newton, where the girls had no previous experience of drama, it never occurred.

Reading commitment

Various levels of interest were evident in the groups of girls I worked with. It is important to take this into account when analysing their scenes, in order to judge how far the drama may have had personal meaning to the girls, and how far they were simply 'going through the motions'. I tried where I could to move the drama beyond the play level to a deeper involvement, by presenting my own improvisations in a serious manner: for example, by asking them to show their scenes (if they were willing), thereby bringing them back together in the common enterprise of watching. For some of the girls, however, the play-acting level did emerge strongly, although it usually coexisted with or alternated with other deeper levels.

Whatever value there may be in the play-acting level, it is easy to judge when this has been replaced, even momentarily, by a deeper level of involvement. There may be an intensity, evident both physically and verbally. If the girls were enacting a scene in front of the others, for example, complete involvement was sometimes evident in their becoming oblivious of the audience. This happened in 'The Two Terrors', when the two black girls, Rosamund and Suzanne, became totally immersed in a conversation about boys which formed part of their scene. In quite a different way, involvement could show itself in a girl's reluctance to show anything because it was too personal. This showed itself when Frankie, the group's tomboy, took the part of a young mother in a scene set in the future. Frankie was usually enthusiastic about showing scenes; on this occasion she was reluctant to appear in this unexpected role, and I felt that this showed that she wanted to be taken seriously in it, or perhaps that she felt particularly uncomfortable in it.

With short scenes in particular, it was often possible to identify intense moments where the drama rose above the play-acting level and there seemed a heightened significance. This may or may not have been part of an interaction between actors and audience, but seemed to arise more from the interaction of the participants in scene. For example, in 'Not Allowed Out', improvised by some of the Asian girls at Newton, the intense moment occurred when Michelle said 'I wish I was a boy', to which her mother replied, 'Well you wish everything don't you?' (extract). I wrote in my fieldnotes at the time:

> This was the 'nub' of the scene, the moment where feelings were at their most intense. Trying to identify what gave that moment its quality and significance, part of it was a stillness and quietness as the mother said, 'Well you wish everything don't you?', and afterwards, for the daughter had no reply and there was a pause –

complete quiet ... meaning emerging in what wasn't being said, in how they looked etc.

(Fieldnotes, Newton, 17.11)

In showing how drama can be used analytically to discuss gender, I focus on the themes of 'families', while in Griffiths (1986) I also deal with 'likes and dislikes about being a girl', 'girlfriends', 'boyfriends' and 'futures'.

Families

Family relationships played a dominant part in the discussions and improvisations at both schools. This was partly because I made them a particular focus for certain sessions. It also reflected the relative importance of family concerns over, for instance, school issues, for most of the girls. Many issues related to family life concerned the girls' perception of lack of freedom and independence, owing to their age, gender or both. In the presentation of parents in the scenes, mothers were the dominant figures, particularly at Newton. The interaction between mothers and daughters was generally shown as stormy but close. In contrast, fathers were scarcely included at all.

I used a family situation as the starting point for my opening session at Newton. In a short improvisation, already tried out in my pilot study at Millbridge, I played the role of a mother of a 13-year-old girl. The mother and daughter have had an argument, and the daughter Sharon is now refusing to come home. The scene largely consisted of the mother finding that Sharon is not at home and telephoning round to see where she might be. After the discussion, I asked the girls to create their own follow-up to the story of Sharon by working out scenes in small groups. At both schools, the issues related to teenage culture took precedence over school concerns in the subsequent improvisations. This is a strong example of the way in which the girls took up ideas only if they reflected their own concerns.

At Newton, I deliberately tried to confirm ideas which the girls had raised by including them in intermediate scenes which I improvised on the spot, resuming the role of the mother, and with two girls in turn taking the part of the daughter. In one of these scenes I concentrated on the school issues which had been introduced; in the other, boyfriends and coming in late were the focus of concern. The school ideas were largely dropped from the girls' own scenes, apart from the Asian girls, whilst boyfriends and going out were prominent issues for a number of weeks. The other related issues which were mentioned as causing arguments within the family were clothes and spending money.

In most of the scenes improvised by the girls around the theme of family relationships, the parents' underlying reason for a particular prohibition is their daughter's age or 'femininity', or a combination of these. Similar undercurrents to an 'apparently trivial' argument about clothes are also evident in this extract from 'The Broken Window', a scene by some of the Asian girls at Newton.

Extract 'The Broken Window', Newton (Asian)

MUM:	Now look at this new jacket I've got you.
SHARON:	I don't want a new jacket, I want a new pair of jeans.
MUM:	Well I can't afford it yet....And you're too young and all, and you dress up –
SHARON:	I'm not too young.
MUM:	– like you're a real old girl.
SHARON:	Well I am aren't I?
MUM:	No you're not.
SHARON:	I'm not a big baby you know.

This is part of a larger argument about a boyfriend, and depends on the mother's judgement that her daughter is too young: to have a boyfriend, to come in late, to dress the way she does. The extract reflects what some of the Asian girls told me – 'We can't choose any of our own clothes' – but this idea was reflected in scenes by the other ethnic groups too.

The matter of money also seems important – 'Well I can't afford it yet' – and this is mentioned as a source of conflict in relation to clothes in other scenes. For instance, in an improvisation by white and black girls at Newton, 'To the Disco', Sharon and her friend Maureen are talking about some recent purchases when Sharon's mother overhears:

Extract 'To the Disco', Newton (black/white)

SHARON:	I bought a skirt and some mascara.
MAUREEN:	I bought some material.
MUM:	Where'd you get the money to buy it with?
MAUREEN:	Mum gave it to me.
SHARON:	(*to Mum*) You gave it me. (*Laughter from audience at Mum's horrified expression*)
MUM:	(*to Maureen*) You're not wearing them jumpers to our school (*corrects herself*) house thank you.
SHARON:	I want a dress.
MUM:	You're not having a dress.

It is interesting how Mum reacts from her shock at discovering how her money has been spent by turning on Maureen and criticising her for her unsuitable clothes.

Mothers dominated the family scenes at Newton. All the girls either portrayed a mother themselves or were in a scene which involved a mother, at some time over the seven weeks. Because I introduced the subject of mother–daughter relationships myself, I may have contributed to the dominance of this theme. However, I do not feel that I influenced the presentation of the mothers themselves, except in so far as the girls may have reacted against my own role-playing.

In the presentations of mothers at Newton there was great variety in terms of whether they work outside the home, as in 'Pregnant', or whether the home is their domain, as in 'To the Disco'. Whatever the case, these features are presented as normal and unremarkable, often forming the framework of the scenes. This suggests that the portrayals were based to some extent on the girls' own experience. Information obtained from an information schedule filled in by the girls as part of the dramatised careers interviews supports this idea.

The portrayals of mothers at Newton have in common an authoritarian attitude to their children, which in turn responds to and provokes rebellious behaviour in their adolescent daughters. Important clues to the girls' own attitudes emerged before they worked out their improvisations, when they advised me as Sharon's mother what to do in relation to my daughter. This provided an intermediate stage, where the girls were involved in a dramatic situation, but remained themselves throughout. The girls were responding to a scene which I had just improvised on the spot with Annette (white) taking the part of Sharon and myself as Sharon's mother, Mrs Walker.

Extract Discussion/Drama, Newton

IRENE (*black*): You were too soft.

LINDA (*black*): Yeah.

ANNE (*white*): You should have punished her.

MRS. WALKER: Should have punished her? What – ?

PENNY (*white*): Yeah, slapped her.

Mrs. Walker: You can't – now she's 13 I do try not to.

ROSAMUND
(*black*): Give her more spending money.

MRS. WALKER: What?

ROSAMUND: More spending money.

MRS WALKER: That's partly what the argument was about – well, not that particular argument, but you wouldn't – ?

LINDA: She might want more choice.

IRENE: Keep her in until she stops that arguing.

MRS WALKER: But if you were Sharon would you think that was fair?

IRENE: No. (*Laughter*)

PENNY:	Keep her in at nights.
ANNE:	Yeah.

. . .

MRS WALKER:	What about this Gary?
IRENE:	I'd stop her from seeing him.
TRICIA (*white*):	No I wouldn't.
ANNETTE (*white*):	I wouldn't either.

What struck me most strongly were the dual attitudes the girls expressed. On the one hand, they were asserting that I, as the mother, had been 'too soft' in the way I had treated my daughter ('should have punished her'; 'should have slapped her'), and advocating harsh punishments ('keep her in until she stops that arguing'; 'keep her in at nights'). At the same time, they were horrified when Mrs Walker said (earlier) that Sharon had to be in by 10.30 p.m. in the week, and there were some suggestions like 'Give her more spending money', 'She might want more choice'. It seemed to me that the girls understood the mother's predicament and had definite ideas about how she should act in relation to her daughter. At the same time, being girls of the same age as the fictitious 'Sharon', they could understand and sympathise with what she wanted.

In their own scenes, the girls who played the part of Sharon's mother put into practice the advice they had given me as Mrs Walker. In many of the scenes the mothers punish their daughters, not just with verbal rebukes but by slapping them. They also frequently stop the very things their daughters want most – money and going out. In 'To the Disco', for example, when Sharon's mother finds her at the disco with Gary, her reaction is: 'I'm not having none of this. You're coming back home and I'm keeping you under lock and key like it or not.' Later, when Sharon has escaped to the disco again, this time with Maureen, her mother says: 'You're going back home and you're not coming out again, you, and you're not having no money for three weeks.'

In 'Pregnant', the character of Sharon's mother dominates the play; she is a commanding rather than an obviously understanding mother and does not invite confidences. However, there is evidence of her underlying concern for Sharon. In the first scene Sharon's mother seems to want to pick an argument with Sharon and put her in the wrong, which Sharon resists. Sharon obviously feels that she cannot confide in her mother about being pregnant; she has told her best friend Maureen and her boyfriend Gary, but her mother is the last to find out. The news eventually reaches her through Gary:

231

Extract 'Pregnant', Newton (white)

GARY:	Didn't she tell you then?
MUM:	Tell me what?
GARY:	Went to the doctor's yesterday, 'stead of the disco last night. She told you a lie.
MUM:	Oh no. What do you mean?
GARY:	(*grinning*) Pregnant.
MUM:	(*knocks on the chair*) Sit down. Sharon!
SHARON:	(*from upstairs*) Comin'.
MUM:	Hurry up now. (*Gary grins and shuffles. Sharon comes in. Mum stands up*)
MUM:	Come 'ere. (*Gestures her over*)
SHARON:	What? (*Mum sits down*)
MUM:	(*to Gary*) Just tell her what you told me. (*Gesturing*)
GARY:	I told your Mum about last night.
SHARON:	You silly sod. (*Mum looks at Gary who is grinning*)
MUM:	(*to Gary*) There's nothing to laugh at you know. (*Gary nods at Sharon to go on*)
SHARON:	But –
MUM:	(*to Gary*) You just better go home.
SHARON:	(*untranscribable*) – now, Mum.
MUM:	He'd just better go home, 'cos I don't want to see his face in this house again.

Mum's reaction is one of shock. There is also an element of hurt that Sharon has not only failed to confide in her but also lied to prevent her from finding out. When she demands that Gary repeats the information in front of Sharon, it is as though she is daring Sharon to deny it to her face. Her immediate blame of Gary shows traditional attitudes but also a desire, I feel, to protect Sharon, even at this late stage. In the final scene at the hospital, where Sharon is taken after she starts to miscarry, it seems as if Sharon's mother is trying to show that she really cares about Sharon.

Extract 'Pregnant', Newton (white)

MAUREEN:	She's been ages.
MUM:	I know.
MAUREEN:	(*tearful*) What's happened to her?
MUM:	It's not my fault you know. I'm just as upset as everyone else.

. . .

(*Sharon comes in crying*)

SHARON:	I've lost it.
MAUREEN:	Oh Sharon.

MUM:	(*hugging Sharon*) All right?
SHARON:	Yeah.
MUM:	Come on, let's get home.
MAUREEN:	Come on.

The interchange with Maureen seems to touch a raw spot. Sharon's mother seems to want to justify herself to Maureen, to prove that she really does care for Sharon even though she may not always appear to. Her most direct expression of feeling to Sharon herself is the hug she gives her at the end. It also seems as if Sharon herself turns to her mother for comfort here (this is more obvious on the video recording).

Similarly, in 'To the Disco', the mother only shows direct evidence of caring when Sharon starts quarrelling with Maureen about who is going out with Gary. Then she leaps to her daughter's defence, even though she has been reprimanding Sharon for going out with Gary a few moments before:

Extract 'To the Disco', Newton (black/white)

MAUREEN:	He's going out with me.
MUM:	Away!
(*More arguing*)	
MUM:	Don't start arguing with my Sharon. He's not going out with you, he's going out with her. He don't like you.
MAUREEN:	How do you know?
	. . .
MUM:	(*to Maureen*) Get on home. Get out.

This changing of sides when an 'outsider' threatened her daughter brought out a family solidarity which was amusing to watch but also had a powerful impact. In spite of the heavy sanctions she imposes on her daughter, you felt that this mother would do anything to defend her daughter. Irene, who played the part of the mother, was a strong presence throughout, not only because she was physically large, but because of this aspect of her presentation as a character.

Conclusions

The girls I worked with at both Newton and Millbridge showed a remarkable awareness of the limitations faced by adolescent girls, especially of restrictions on their freedom arising from their gender and age. They expressed particular dissatisfaction with the differential treatment they received at home and school compared with boys. The strongest feelings concerned the common experience of not being allowed out as often or as late as their brothers. These feelings were expressed by all the ethnic groups, though not as strongly by the black girls, and are similar to the findings of previous studies of adolescent girls.

Some of the girls also felt that boys were considered more important than girls. Given this rather bleak outlook, I was surprised that most of the girls said they preferred being girls, especially as they could think of so few things they liked about being a girl beyond clothes and appearance. At Millbridge, where the girls in the second group had a somewhat low regard for boys, more positive aspects of being a girl were mentioned.

I was somewhat depressed by the lowness of the girls' aspirations and the way some of them seemed to be narrowing their future plans in order to accommodate what they saw as their expected roles as wife and mother; for instance, in the stories at Millbridge, the girls generally gave up promising careers when they had children. From what the girls themselves said, it seemed that they did not totally endorse these traditional roles, and would have welcomed alternatives, such as role-sharing, had these seemed possible to achieve. There was also a degree of realism in the girls' awareness of limitations on jobs open to women. These findings were also in line with many previous studies of girls' aspirations.

Some of the dissatisfactions expressed by the girls would be difficult to change directly; for example, those concerning relationships at home. However, girls at both schools mentioned the non-availability to girls of certain subjects such as woodwork before the fourth year; and here pressure can be applied to bring schools in line with the Sex Discrimination Act.

At several stages in my work, particularly at Millbridge, the girls expressed the view that opportunities for change might be blocked by boys' or men's attitudes and expectations. For example, this was suggested at Millbridge in relation to women staying at home with children. Boys' sexual attitudes also seemed to reinforce the Millbridge girls' sense of being considered less important. This suggests a need for action which could be taken in schools. Discussions of gender roles could usefully be undertaken by teachers, questioning traditional attitudes where they limit opportunities. I feel strongly that boys' attitudes need changing as much as girls' if any improvement in girls' situation is to be effected.

The most positive aspect of being a girl which emerged from the research was the importance of friendships between girls. This was an unlooked-for finding, which in itself validated the use of drama to me. The improvisations showing friendships build a clear picture of the type of supportive interaction girlfriends might have. This is an area which I should certainly like to pursue in future research, especially as there are some discrepancies and gaps in the findings of existing studies.

I feel that the use of drama was successful. It certainly had the effect of gaining the girls' interest and involvement. At Newton, in particular, some girls who contributed little to discussion work were able to express ideas through the drama. The drama also gave me entry into the private world of girls' experience outside school, by the concrete enactment of scenes at home or with friends. The use of drama together with discussion was crucial on several occasions, building a broader picture of the girls' attitudes than could have been obtained by one method alone. On the basis of this research, I certainly feel that drama is worth developing as a research method.

© 1990 Vivienne Griffiths

References

Bolton, Gavin (1979) *Towards a Theory of Drama in Education*, London: Longman.

Cowie, Celia and Lees, Sue (1981) 'Slags or Drags', *Feminist Review* 9:17–31.

Griffiths, Vivienne (1986) *Using Drama to Get at Gender*, Studies in Sexual Politics No. 9, Sociology Department, University of Manchester.

Jamdagni, Laxmi (1980) *Hamari Rangily Zindagi: Our Colourful Lives*, National Association of Youth Clubs, Leicester.

Llewellyn, Mandy (1980) 'Studying Girls at School: the Implications of Confusion', in Rosemary Deem (ed.), *Schooling for Women's Work*, London: Routledge & Kegan Paul, pp.42–51.

McRobbie, Angela (1978) 'Working-class Girls and the Culture of Femininity', in Women's Studies Group (eds), *Women Take Issue*, London: Hutchinson, pp. 96–108.

McRobbie, Angela and Garber, Jenny (1975) 'Girls and Subcultures: an Exploration', in Stuart Hall and Tony Jefferson (eds), *Resistance through Rituals*, London: Hutchinson, pp. 209–22.

Sharpe, Sue (1976) *Just Like a Girl: How Girls Learn to be Women*, Harmondsworth: Penguin.

Chapter seventeen

Becoming a feminist social worker

Sue Wise

Introduction

This chapter reconstructs changes in my theoretical and practical understanding of local authority social work. I started out my job as a social worker with a problem: that of marrying my feminist beliefs with a job that some feminists see as fundamentally anti-feminist, given that social work as an institution is seen by some feminists as 'by nature' sexist and anti-woman. Over a five- to six-year period my ideas about social work, what it is for and how to do it in a feminist (that is, non-oppressive) way, changed quite dramatically.

Initially, working as I did with a basically structural analysis of social work as an institution, I was concerned to discover whether 'feminist social work' was a realistic possibility or not. Later on I came to the conclusion that analysing social work as an institution in a conventional structural way was unhelpful, indeed actually misleading, in understanding the day-to-day experience of the work that 'being a social worker' involves: I concluded that it was possible, on an individual level, to work in a non-oppressive way with women. But later still I came to think I had set myself the wrong problem and that feminist social work, as I had defined it in terms of working non-oppressively with women, was a fantasy based on a fundamental misunderstanding of what local authority social work is about. That is, I see 'social work' now as the policing of minimum standards of care for, and the protection of the rights of, the most vulnerable members of our society – some of whom are women, but most of whom are not. Moreover, this 'policing' and 'control' function of social work is one I feel happy with, as I explain later.

Such changes in my thinking occurred over a long period. It is impossible to know exactly *how* and *when* the changes occurred. However, the changes have indeed occurred and have emerged from the complex relationship between 'theory' and 'everyday experience' that exists in doing generic social work and from the way in which I tried to match one against the other.

Time past and time present

Where I started from

I am able to look back fairly precisely at the way I started out thinking about feminism and social work because of things that I wrote about it at the time. The start of my social work career coincided with the opportunity to get down some of my thoughts and feelings about it on paper, in an M.A. dissertation on a small piece of research and writing which followed my professional training for the Certificate of Qualification in Social Work (CQSW). I was a feminist before I went into social work, and so from the start of my training I was concerned with sorting out how to be a 'good feminist' and at the same time a good social worker. Indeed, if feminism and social work proved to be incompatible, then I was clear that I wanted no part of it and would find myself another career.

When I joined the CQSW course, I already had some experience of grappling with the issue of how to relate political conviction and everyday practice outside of a social work setting. I had had to work out such things as an 'out', publicly open, lesbian feminism from early 1973 on. I had for some years been involved in gay self-help groups and, in particular, in helping other women, as I had been helped, to come to terms with their own, and societal, reactions to their sexuality. All of this took place within a broadly feminist framework, one which changed as my feelings about many things changed and matured. This framework provided both the political rationale for being involved in such an activity, and also some of the tools for doing it. Thus consciousness-raising and small groups were used, in the lesbian group I was involved in, to enable participants to explore their (usually) negative self-image and begin to regain their self-respect and feel good about themselves. Once this happened they, in turn, were able to help others in similar small groups – thus challenging and overturning the concepts of 'sorted-out' experts and passive recipients that 'helping' usually involves. Feminism therefore provided both the means and the ends in this mutual helping activity.

Although perhaps naïve, I assumed that social work could be like this and that it should be possible to use an overall feminist framework within which to do the work. That is, I somehow thought that I could work 'with' women clients, that I could dismantle the inevitable power barriers which social work would involve, and that I could somehow evolve a 'self-help' structure by which they could come together and help one another.

At this stage my ideas about feminism and social work were based on very little practical experience, since I had never worked as a local authority social worker, but as an assistant housemother in a local authority children's home. They were, rather, based on feminist structural analyses of social work (see, for example, Weir 1973; Kravetz 1976; Wilson 1977). Such analyses see social work as fundamentally sexist as well as racist and classist, and this ideology is seen as reflected in all the workings of the agency. Thus working-class and ethnic minority clients are seen to suffer a power imbalance within middle-class and white-dominated agency provision; and in a broadly similar way so too are women, the main consumers of social work, seen to suffer from its sexist ideology. Social work is seen to be 'women's work' in a double sense, in that not only are most social work *clients* women, but also most social *workers* are women too. In a structural analysis both sets of women suffer the same inequalities and injustices because both live within the same social structure with its sexist ideology enacted through equally sexist institutions and agencies. Moreover, although women account for the vast majority of social workers, there are disproportionately few women in top jobs or indeed in social work management at all. Thus women social workers should 'recognise their unity with women clients' (Kravetz 1976:167). Social workers should identify with their clients, and also fight alongside them to alter what is, in reality, a common oppression:

> Both social work and women's domestic labour within the family are concerned with ensuring the efficient reproduction of labour power...they are both engaged in similar types of labour...there is a real unity of interests between these two groups of women and many issues on which we can fight together.
>
> (Weir 1973: 217)

Although I recognised that this argument was problematic (what about non-feminist women social workers? how do oppressed but 'arm of the state' women social workers relate to oppressing but 'passive' male clients?), it was just the kind of thing I needed to hear at the time. Armed with such a feminist perspective on the nature of social work as an institution and thus on the social problems I was about to encounter, coupled with my multi-faceted street credibility empathy kit (ex-working class, woman *and* lesbian), I felt well equipped to embark on becoming a feminist social worker. However, five or so years and many experiences with clients later, I now have a different view of this.

Where I am now

I now question whether feminist social work is *possible*, but also whether it is even *desirable*. The answers to this question depend on what one thinks social work is and what it, ideally, should be; and this requires a recognition that there is a real distinction between what the agency is for and is supposed to do (according to the 'boss', the 'worker' and the 'consumer') and what it *actually* does in real, everyday life.

One of the things that perpetually annoys me, and many other practising social workers, is that much of what passes for 'expert writing' on social work fails to show what it is that social workers actually do. Continual reiterations of 'social work is the long arm of the state' tells us *nothing* of what this job entails for the average social worker, nothing about what kinds of people and problems you have to work with, nothing concerning what kinds of powers you actually have and even less about how these are mediated by circumstances and other people, nothing on what 'a case' looks like; and, equally, it tells us nothing at all about how it is experienced by the client on the receiving end of it. As far as I am concerned, one kind of person and only one kind of person really knows 'what social workers do': those who experience it, as workers or as clients.

There is a dearth of writing that could give readers an insight into what doing social work is like; therefore I now examine in detail some of the things that have been involved in my own 'doing social work'. I discuss some case studies in such a way that people's identities are heavily disguised and all unnecessary detail is omitted. The focus is upon *me*: what I did, how I felt, what the issues were for me. My purpose is a simple one: to show that the feminist critique of social work and social workers is a vastly over-simplistic one. My conviction is that feminism deserves something better than this, as do all the many social workers who, like me, try to do their best in full knowledge of the difficulties and contradictions.

Case study 1

Mrs G. became involved with Social Services after the breakdown of her first marriage. In her early twenties, she was left to care for children aged 1, 2 and 3 after the separation. An acrimonious divorce and concern about arrangements for the children led to a Matrimonial Supervision Order being made. This therefore gave supervision responsibilities to Social Services.

Mrs G. is a large, loud, aggressive, difficult woman who is described by her psychiatrist as suffering from 'personality disorder'. She is a law unto herself – literally, sometimes, when, in court appearances, she will argue loudly with the magistrates about the level of her fines and defy them to send her down when she thinks they are asking too much. She is a hard worker, who provides well for her children and knows more about the DHSS and its workings and fiddlings than most welfare rights officers. She is deeply committed to her children, and would walk through fire for them, and crush without mercy anyone who harmed them. She also suffers from depression and needs hospital admission regularly.

If Mrs G. had never had children, she has enough power within her to have been more or less anything she wanted to be. She is exceptionally bright, but has had little education and married at the earliest opportunity in order to escape an unhappy home life which had included physical and sexual abuse. This meant three children at an early age with a first husband who was feckless and pathetic.

The children's physical care is excellent, they are beautifully clothed, fed and clean and live in an immaculately kept house. They are not subject to physical abuse – and although she often expresses concern about the possibility that she might do this, and has certainly no compunction about clouting adults, I have never known Mrs G. to harm them. She is so horrified by what happened to her as a child that she cannot bring herself to slap her own children. They are, however, subjected to destructive and extreme verbal and emotional abuse.

Mrs G. expects her children to have adult responses and rationality, and she holds them responsible for the fact that she is frustrated and miserable. An example of this was when she was feeling depressed, took an overdose, but carefully explained to the children beforehand that she was doing this because of them and when she died it would be their fault; they were at the time aged 5, 6 and 7. Mrs G. is dissatisfied with her role as a mother and feels that the world has passed her by and she has missed out.

Things looked up when Mrs G. remarried, to a man who gradually took over all childcare responsibilities, leaving her free to do what she wanted. However, when given the opportunity, she didn't know what she wanted and she could not get over the basic guilt of not being the perfect, fulfilled mother. The stepfather is a stable, calm person in the children's lives and I hate to imagine what kind of a state they would be in without him.

Not surprisingly, Mrs G.'s treatment has had adverse effects on the children. They suffer from 'nervous' complaints like nightmares, bed-wetting and eczema. They are totally unruly, unpopular with other children and have mammoth temper tantrums. When I last saw Mrs G. she was trying desperately hard to get pregnant and felt that another baby was what was lacking in her life.

My involvement with the G. family was to monitor the welfare of the children, ordered by the divorce court. Such orders are often revoked when things settle down and improve; sometimes, however, they seem to go on forever. The G. family was such a case. I had inherited it from a previous social worker when I arrived, and I passed it on to another social worker when I left.

I got to know this family very well. I saw the children grow from toddlers to schoolchildren, was invited to the second wedding, and became very fond of them all. They learned to trust me and accepted my support and advice (sometimes), and I was sometimes able to help avert crises by understanding the warning signs. Although my rationale for involvement was my authority role, my overriding motivation was much more personal: I cared about them a great deal and wanted them to be happy.

In these kinds of long-term involvements the edges of friendship and formal relationship become very blurred indeed for both worker and client. This can become a real problem when the need to emphasise the 'authority' role arises. For example, whenever I had to produce court reports on Mrs G. she felt upset at the things I wrote in them, not because they were things that I hadn't already said to her, but because she felt betrayed that I said them to someone else. Such a close involvement caused some heartaches for me too. Having to watch as Mrs G. hurt and got hurt, over and over again, repeating the same patterns and mistakes and never seeming to learn by them, was a soul-destroying business. But while my heart bled for her, I had to try and remember that I was there to keep an eye on the children.

This 'care and control' dilemma is, for me, the most difficult problem in social work for both worker and client. It's all very well maintaining a 'properly professional' perspective when you only visit once in a while for ten minutes – anyone can do that. But when you are involved frequently and regularly for a long period of time with the painful and private calamities and heartaches of someone's life, that's a very intimate thing and you would have to be made of stone not to be touched by it. In one family the husband died suddenly and asked me on his death-bed to look after his family. Is it surprising that I found it almost impossible to terminate my contact with them even after, in agency terms, the need for my involvement had passed? This problem of becoming emotionally involved while at the same time being an authority figure is one that receives little discussion in social work. If the worker becomes emotionally involved, it is called being 'unprofessional' and 'bad practice', just as it is in sociology; and if a client becomes emotionally involved, it is called 'over-dependence'. But I would argue that this kind of involvement is a fact of 'good' social work life and relationships as it is of all other human relationships, and we ought to treat it seriously.

Many people couldn't possibly believe that clients would have such relationships with social workers and relate to them as friends instead of as officials. What people who write about the 'stigma' of social work don't seem to realise is that many clients love having a social worker and kick up a great deal of fuss if they can't get one. 'This is my social worker,' Mrs G. announced without batting an eyelid to her wedding guests who, in turn, took it entirely in their stride. Is this the false consciousness of the working classes? Hardly; she knew there were many things that I would do or get for her that she couldn't do for herself, and she also knew that Supervision Orders have no teeth in terms of power.

Mrs G. was trapped in a lifestyle she had chosen when she was too young to make such decisions in full knowledge of the consequences, and now she was stuck with those consequences. Her anger at being so confined was mostly directed at her children, whom she loved and was totally committed to, even though her behaviour sometimes made this hard to believe. A victim of patriarchy, I felt. Well, 'victim' is far too simple, as that is by no means all that she was. For instance, she was at the same time very 'oppressive' and domineering towards others: to her husband, whom she ruled with a rod of iron; to any 'officials' who got in her way (one housing official used to ask me to be present whenever he had to see her, and would insist on my standing between them so she couldn't hit him); to me on occasion, both as 'friend' and as authority figure; but most of all to her children, for whom a day never passed when they weren't told how much they were ruining her life.

To help Mrs G., we can't change society overnight so the only medium for change is Mrs G. herself. If she could begin to see that it wasn't her individual problem, if she could stop feeling guilty about how she felt, if she could find some constructive way of expressing her power and obvious abilities – if...if...if only. But she was one of the few people I have met who seemed to have no capacity for change at all, not with individual help, or through being in groups (she caused a furore in one group, causing everyone else to leave) or through the concrete experiences that she had. I became convinced, after considerable time, there was nothing I as a social worker could do to help her change; and that the best I could do was to give support to her, and later to her husband, in their care of the children. But as the years rolled by, and as the children grew older demonstrating more problems each year, I wondered just whose interests were taking precedence. The situation this woman was in was not her fault and her inability to change was not malevolent, but having said that, what about the children's needs? If this woman lost her children I think it would finish her: but what is staying with her doing to *them* in the meantime? People who criticise social work powers and authority can have little idea of how difficult it is, in practice, to remove a child from its parent. Physical abuse or neglect and, increasingly, sexual abuse are considered suitable grounds for making care orders, but emotional abuse is a very difficult thing to prove. There are no bruises or broken bones, no criminal activity is involved, and yet emotional abuse is just as damaging as every other form of child abuse. There is nothing more heartbreaking than having to stand by and watch a child's spirit be crushed, while knowing that you can't intervene until something absolutely dire happens. And even if a Care Order were possible, how on earth do we measure the known damage that is being done at home against the unknown damage that may result from depriving them of their mother, whom they love dearly?

The detrimental effects of their mother's behaviour on these children may go 'beyond the limit' one day and they may need to come into care. I am very, very glad it won't be me who will have to do it.

Case study 2

The H. family was composed of two children aged 6 and 9, their mother and a stepfather. Social Services became involved when the youngest child received a severe beating from his mother, which led to child abuse procedures being followed. Subsequently both children were registered, and a Supervision Order was made. Becoming involved with the family revealed many problems and difficulties previously 'hidden' by the fact that earlier they had moved from place to place during the children's lives.

Both children were enuretic; they had no friends, and both lived in total fantasy worlds. No overt affection was ever shown within the family. The daughter had from an early age assumed emotional responsibility for her mother and had the air of a child who had never been young and carried adult worries and responsibilities on her shoulders. The children had neither the usual childhood toys nor its pastimes; they spent most of their time doing household chores and were rarely allowed to play with other children. Their parents were very strict, they were expected to do exactly as they were told, to speak only when spoken to, and if they stepped out of line they could expect corporal punishment, either being hit with a stick or shoe or being locked in their bedroom for hours.

Because of her gaucheness and inexperience with other children, the daughter tried to win friends by telling lies to impress them. This always backfired as other children could see through her, so outrageous were her claims (she could fly a plane, spoke several foreign languages ...) and they thought she was tiresome and pathetic. A psychiatrist's assessment of the son reached the same conclusion that I had – he lived in a fantasy world because he had so little pleasure in real life, and what he needed was to be allowed to be a small child.

My involvement was initially to focus on relieving the tensions that had led to the violent outburst towards the younger child; this was relatively easy to do by giving Mrs H. someone with whom to unload worries and pressures instead of letting them build up and burst upon the children following some minor 'misbehaviour'. The emphasis changed as I tried to help the parents examine their over-strict attitudes and to encourage them to allow the children to be more child-like and to let them have playmates. This was an uphill battle as they saw nothing wrong with their discipline.

The situation took a new turn when the daughter accused her step-father of sexual abuse. No 'evidence' was found during the police investigation that followed: it was a case of her word against the step father, and everyone disbelieved her – everyone, that is, except her mother and me. Her mother needed her husband, who provided her with the first real affection she had known and, at the same time, she thought the allegations were true, and loved and wanted to protect her daughter. The daughter refused to stay at home with her stepfather and was received into voluntary care through her own request. Her mother subsequently decided she was lying and, in effect, chose her husband, knowing that it meant that her daughter would probably not return home at all.

My involvement here was a statutory one, following injury to a child; later it also involved aspects of emotional deprivation and 'appropriate' child-rearing and disciplining practices, as well as sexual abuse. It may seem that there were an unusually large number of problems in this family, but when some families go wrong, they really go wrong (I might add that as all families have problems, so they really have to be 'over the top' to get noticed by 'the authorities'). There were other 'minor' problems too – long-term poverty, alcohol dependence, ill-health, marital discord, fraught relationships with the children's biological father. When social workers talk about multiple problem families, they mean precisely 'multiple'.

It's hard in a situation like this to know where to begin, whom to focus on, what to attempt to alter and with what knock-on effects for the other problems and participants. A feminist criticism of social work is that, when there are family problems, it is always the mother who is focussed on. I hold my hand up to that, as I'm sure it is the mother that I usually focus on, but only where it is absolutely clear about why I'm doing it. For example, in this case I began by focussing on the mother, Mrs H., because she was the one who had injured the child and who seemed to be in most need of someone with whom to off-load pressures and tensions. Later, when exploring discipline, I did of course work with both parents.

This was the first child-abuse case of what later became many that I had to investigate and then work with. Before dealing with it, I had wondered how I would react to seeing a child badly hurt and how I would feel about working with the parent who was responsible. The injuries were noticed at school and, after being unable to find the parents to accompany me to the hospital, I had taken the child to the casualty department by myself. He stood there, six years old, naked for examination by the doctor, terrified because he didn't know me or what was happening, covered from head to toe in bruises and hand prints, and stinking from the stale urine that he lay in every night in his bed. I had to fight hard to keep back my tears so as not to distress him any further. And when he himself started crying, saying, 'Mummy will shout!' because he had told us that she had done it, my anguish turned to anger almost instantly. After a full skeletal X-ray had been performed and he had been admitted to a ward and settled down, I went to confront his mother.

I took a colleague with me because by this time I didn't trust myself to be able to contain my anger; although I tried hard I was stroppier than I should have been. After initial denials, she broke down and admitted it, and we discussed the details of how it had occurred and what would happen next. Although some people find some aspects of child-abuse case conferences objectionable (kangaroo courts, one colleague describes them), I do find the application of formal procedures after such an incident very useful. In the heat of the moment, and filled with the emotion of it all, you can't make calm decisions and it's a relief to be able to say, once you have the child in a safe place, that nothing happens and no decisions are made until the case conference takes place. This may take a couple of days to organise and so it gives important time for further investigation, reflection and calming down.

In the event, once I found out more of the details, and realised what appalling pressures this woman had been living with, I was the one who argued most loudly for the child to be returned home. Once I had got over my initial anger, I found what she had done understandable and wanted to try and help her not get into the same kind of state again (many family details have not been recounted here for reasons of anonymity – but this was the most screwed-up family I've ever come across). I suppose you might say I 'forgave' her for what she did and tried to help her forgive herself. This was in stark contrast to my later feelings about the stepfather.

When I learned about the sexual abuse to the daughter, and decided that I believed it even though no one else did, I wanted to rip his head off – although I remained calm and 'professional' in my dealings with him. He kept well out of my way afterwards and knew I believed his stepdaughter and not him. Deciding whether this child was having yet another fantasy was extremely difficult. I know this is the classic put-down used to deny the reality of sexual abuse, but this child really did have the most amazing fantasy life. Not only would she tell absolutely clear-cut whoppers, but she would stick to them come hell or high water. In the end I believed her; and the mother's initial response confirmed my belief. I had also decided it would do more harm to disbelieve her if it was true than it would to believe her if it was false.

I tried hard to put across to her that she was believed and it wasn't her fault, and I encouraged her to talk about it. But everything I did was counteracted by the disbelief of other people, both professionals and others, and by the emotional work her mother did to get her to change her story. The poor girl probably ended up more confused than ever, there were so many crossed messages that she was getting. These problems extended to making future plans for her: whenever there were meetings to discuss her going back home I would say, 'What about the sexual abuse?', only to be told by colleagues that nothing had been proved so it wasn't an issue. To give some credit to colleagues, they were too much influenced by the fact that the child couldn't open her mouth without telling lies about many things.

Another related problem was that this child had never been shown affection and had had some rather bizarre experiences of sex, and was therefore very confused about differentiating between sex and affection. I want to make it absolutely clear that I held the stepfather one hundred per cent responsible for any sexual contact that took place between him and his stepdaughter; and, no matter what she did, he was the responsible adult in the situation and certainly knew better, even though he took advantage of her. At the same time, I thought it likely that this child's perceptions about sex and affection meant that she was going to be wide open to unscrupulous abuse by men who would continue to take advantage of her naïvety and confusion. The problem was, I couldn't raise this without her thinking that I was 'really' saying that the sexual abuse was her fault. So I left it alone.

It is easy to think that the problems of dealing with sexual abuse are because people don't use a feminist perspective and don't generally believe the victim. But I acted always as a feminist actively trying very hard to believe the victim and do my best for her – and I have tended to find that the issue is infinitely more complex than simply 'believing the victim' would suggest to us.

Some overall issues

There are some overall issues that these two case studies (and others are discussed in Wise 1985) raise that I now want to look at more directly. The overwhelming thing that struck me when writing these case studies was how much of my emotions they have in them. Sadness, anger, frustration, affection, empathy, fear, anxiety, powerlessness and despair, to name but a few of my feelings that are expressed or implied in the descriptions. I have made these responses more overt to you the reader than they were to other participants at the time, or than they were to me at the time, for that matter. A necessary block is put on social workers expressing the emotional content of our involvement with clients. As this list of painful emotions shows, who can wonder that this should be so? If we didn't try to gain some control by devising various means of coping we would all be exhausted or nervous wrecks in a matter of weeks, rather than the two to four years it usually takes most of us to 'burn out'.

Responses to these cases were crucially influenced by the limited resources available. And the options aren't governed by the absence or presence of material resources only, but by the clients themselves. The myth of compliant and powerless clients is belied by the reality of the complex process of interaction and negotiation that goes on in defining problems and finding solutions: tell Mrs G. she is a passive victim and see what sort of response you get.

Much feminist analysis of social problems was of little use in helping me to analyse and guide my practice in these and other cases: focussing on a simplistic view of 'women's oppression' and saying little about women and men who fall outside the usual gender stereotypes. Using this framework, how do we understand Mr G., struggling hard to offset his wife's abrasiveness with the children, assuming all practical responsibilities for them so that she can do 'something more rewarding', and loving every minute of it?

Recent feminist work on sexual abuse has been extremely influential in some social work circles and it certainly helped me in my handling of the H. family. Through being aware of some of the basic feminist issues I was able to work out which position to adopt with the child, and was able to stick to it. But the analysis wasn't wholly helpful and in some respects made me more confused. 'Always believe the victim' is a feminist principle that *I did* apply, but it had nothing to say to me about the knotty problem of a child who does lie, and lies about almost everything that has ever happened to her. Similarly, 'the mother never colludes' did not prepare me for the fact that some do, nor help me to handle this when I actually encountered it.

Some 'silences' in feminist analysis are more problematic. Carrying out a literature survey on feminist analyses of family violence, I was staggered to find that these say practically nothing about the physical abuse of children. I can only think that child abuse is not chronicled along with other domestic/family violence because women too are responsible for it, not just men.

All social work involves intrusion by social workers into people's lives, but the form may differ. First, intrusion can be invited by the client him- or herself. Second, intrusion can be tolerated by clients who have it imposed upon them but know that, if they don't want to let you in the door, they can't be made to do so (the situation with Mrs G.). And third, intrusion can be enforced on those on whom it is imposed unwillingly, as in the use of Place of Safety Orders (the situation with the H. family).

Bearing feminist critiques of social work in mind, are these intrusions justified? My answer is an unequivocal 'yes', because they are concerned with protecting the most vulnerable members of society – surely a crucial concern of all feminists. Part of the feminist critique is the argument that social work ought to address itself to women as whole people and not just women as carers, as mothers of children. But does 'the care and protection of vulnerable people' mean that women are vulnerable simply by virtue of being women and therefore need the ameliorative activities of feminist social work? This depends on what you think 'women' need and want and what you think social work can and ought to be for – and also what role you think 'feminists' should have in relation to 'women'.

The reality is that social work is not, and cannot be, about improving the quality of people's lives in a general way. Rather, it is about the social policing of minimum acceptable standards for people who are vulnerable – and in particular the care and protection of children. In my opinion it is right and proper that this should be so; and it is this that creates the fundamental contradiction for me in feminist critiques of social work. That is, how can it be possible to be sensitive and responsive to the needs of both women and children, when those needs frequently conflict? I can think of many examples of clients whom I've worked with, some of whom appear in these case studies, where this has been the case. I can, and do, analyse these women's positions in feminist terms. I find their situations and how they arrived at them eminently understandable; and I understand why it often results in such adverse effects on their children. But while I understand their behaviour with their children, I do not find it acceptable. As far as I'm concerned, children have basic rights which their parents', including their mothers', needs should not be allowed to override.

So, in thinking about feminism and social work, I don't ask 'is social work about social control?', 'is it sexist?' and so on. Rather, my starting point is this: social work *is* about social control and especially the protection of children and other vulnerable people, and this is a morally proper function in feminist terms because feminism is concerned with adopting a moral-political stance to questions of power and power-lessness. Once we accept that vulnerable people need protection, we can then begin to pose other feminist questions, like what feminism can tell us about what should be 'acceptable standards', who should decide what these are, and how they should be imposed. Only when we start to work on these kinds of issues will we have begun to develop a truly feminist social work.

Since this chapter was first written, a number of texts have appeared on feminist approaches to social work (and some useful examples of which include Brook and Davis 1985; Marchant and Wearing 1986; Van den Berg and Cooper 1986; Hanmer and Statham 1988). With very occasional exceptions, however, these writings perpetuate the basic problems I have identified here in the earlier feminist analyses of social work. That is, mostly they are couched in abstract theoretical terms with little reference to the everyday realities of practice, and they seem unwilling to deal with the inevitable aspects of social control of feminist social work, preferring instead to see it only as a tool of empowerment for women.

© 1990 Sue Wise

References

Brook, Eve and Davis, Ann (eds) (1985) *Women, the Family and Social Work*, London: Tavistock.

Hanmer, Jalna and Statham, Daphne (1988) *Women and Social Work: Towards a Woman-Centred Practice*, London: Macmillan.

Kravetz, Diane (1976) 'Women Social Workers and Their Clients, Common Victims of Sexism', in Joan Roberts (ed.), *Beyond Intellectual Sexism*, New York: David McKay, pp.160–71.

Marchant, Helen and Wearing, betsy (eds) (1986) *Gender Reclaimed: Women in Social Work*, Sydney: Hale & Ironmonger.

National Institute of Social Work (1982) *Social Workers: Their Role and Tasks*, London: NISW.

Van den Berg, Nan and Cooper, Lynn (eds) (1986) *Feminist Visions for Social Work*, NASW, MD: Silver Spring.

Weir, Angela (1973) 'The Family, Social Work and the Welfare State', in Sheila Allen, Lee Sanders and Jan Wallis (eds), *Conditions of Illusion*, Leeds: Feminist Books, pp. 217–28.

Wilson, Elizabeth (1977) *Women and the Welfare State*, London: Tavistock.

Wise, Sue (1985) *Becoming a Feminist Social Worker*, Studies in Sexual Politics No.6, Sociology Department, University of Manchester.

Section E

Analysing Written and Visual Texts

Chapter eighteen

Reading feminism in fieldnotes

Anne Williams

Why a feminist reading?

This chapter reflects some of the problems I am now faced with as I try to make sense of notes I wrote while doing fieldwork in a number of ways. Within the chapter I consider some of the implications of making a feminist reading of them.

'Feminism' is not a keyword in my fieldnotes – at least not in the sense of finding it written frequently, nor in the sense that there is anything immediately 'feminist' in the content of the notes. I am not writing about specifically feminist issues, issues that have traditionally been the concern of feminists. My fieldwork has taken me into the world of health care and, more directly, nursing, but I am not focussing on aspects such as the sexual division of labour in health-care work or sexism in exchanges between nurses and patients. Unlike, for example, Hilary Graham's (1984) work on women and reproduction, my work does not seem at first glance to be obviously shaped by a feminist orientation. My work is as follows.

I have written fieldnotes over a period of roughly four years; first, during eighteen months spent in a hospital in London where I was employed as a nurse to work with and give support to first-year student nurses and where it was understood that, as an anthropologist, I would be doing 'research'. Second, I continued to write fieldnotes recording my experiences as a research officer for two and a half years in a nursing research project in Manchester. What then has my research to do with feminism? My experiences of feminism are such that it is unlikely that my research work would remain unaffected. As a postgraduate student I had been strongly influenced by my reading of feminist literature, through people with whom I discussed my work and seminars I have attended, notably the Manchester feminist research seminar. This is not to say that I compartmentalise my life and I am left unaffected in other areas of it, but that feminism has made a difference to how I think about doing research.

How do I describe my research? I sometimes talk about my research as being 'experiential'. What do I mean? When I set out to do fieldwork in nursing settings, my understanding of the word 'experiential' was influenced by my background in social anthropology. At this stage my knowledge of research was connected in a fairly strong sense to the process of trying to understand the experiences of others. I wrote fairly early on in my fieldwork: 'As an anthropologist, I am intrigued at the opportunity being a nurse affords me (ethical issues not withstanding) in gaining access to what goes on behind the scenes' (notes written for thesis supervisor). Here, behind the scenes, I believed that I would be able to move into what Paul Willis (1980) describes as the cultural levels of an institution, where I could understand the subjective reality of the situation for those involved.

Experiential fieldwork or ethnography, in the sense that I am trying to understand the experiences of others, could be considered an appropriate methodology for feminists in so far as it could be used to understand experiences of women which other methodologies, because of their 'scientific' orientations, tend to obliterate. Feminists, however, also use methods which are not experiential in this sense in order to advance understanding. So there is nothing essentially feminist about ethnography where the aim is to try to understand the experiences of others. However, when I started my fieldwork, 'experiential' also meant trying to analyse my *own* experiences in the process of fieldwork. I write:

> But in doing fieldwork ... my work is a cultural performance....
> From the stream of action I encounter, I select bits and pieces. It is
> like Clifford Geertz's (1973) description of ethnography.
> Summarised very crudely, the fieldworker pulls together the bits
> and pieces of the so-called actors' constructions of what is going
> on to create her own constructions. Understanding emerges out of
> interaction between me as a researcher and the situation within
> which I find myself – out of the questions that emerge from my
> response to the situation.
>
> (Williams 1983:2)

This reflexive aspect of fieldwork is where I feel that my research begins to have something to do with feminism or where feminism begins to inform my research. Although the idea of reflexivity within the social sciences pre-dates feminist research, feminism has accelerated its impact. Mike Ames suggests: 'It has only been during the last several years when the women's movement gained an influence in our profession ... that serious anthropological investigations of our own profession began to appear with any regularity' (Ames 1979:23). Reflexivity, in the sense of seriously locating myself in my research in terms of *intellectual antecedents,* was an aspect of the cultural milieu within which I commenced my postgraduate work. Looking back, I find it no accident that most of the people who influenced me in this way were feminists.

One of the substantive ways in which I have put reflexivity into practice is to look at my fieldnotes as artefacts of my experience of doing ethnography. To do this is still to do fieldwork. My notes constitute the field, and my attempt to understand them is in a very real sense fieldwork. So far, I have taken some keywords in my notes to help me 'read' them and to help me puzzle over some of the dilemmas with which I am confronted, such as: where do I draw the boundaries of my fieldwork? or how do I show that something is the case rather than merely to assert that it is? Therefore reading and explicating a word that has meaning for me becomes an analytic tool.

Feminism has meaning for me in the ways I have suggested. So far, however, it seems to touch on my fieldwork in fairly diffuse ways. It occurs in my notes but only infrequently. At the same time it is part of an intellectual backdrop to my research. One way in which I can make it less diffuse is to use it seriously and explicitly as an analytic tool to help me read my notes. What would it mean to commit myself to a feminist reading of my notes? What insights are there to be gained from a feminist analysis? Insights into my experiences and the experiences of those I encounter in the field? Yes, and I think also insights into feminism.

How do I make a feminist reading?

The decision to make a feminist reading of my notes is first of all complicated by wondering how I might start to do this. What constitutes a feminist reading? In puzzling over this question, I am reminded of what Liz Stanley and Sue Wise (1983:162) write about locating one's self and one's emotions and involvements within written accounts of the research process. This raises another problematic: what is meant by self? 'Self' is a complex notion. A step towards making a feminist reading of my fieldnotes might be, then, to elucidate constructions of my 'self' in the sense of looking for my emotions – how I felt about what I was doing and about the people I encountered in the field. And as I look through my fieldnotes, I do find references to how I felt about things. For example, I felt irritation. I write at one time:

> I have learned about my part in the project. 'A' (co-worker) and I are 'tools' of the research project. I have finally grasped that we are going to teach 'the communication skills programme'. 'B' (another co-worker) will be evaluating, Somehow being used as part of the

experiment and being evaluated irritates a little, perhaps because it makes me feel vulnerable.

(Fieldnote book 3:9)

When I read this extract from my notes, I am reminded of Stephen Webster's discussion of Bronislaw Malinowski's ethnography. He quotes the following passage from *Argonauts of Western Pacific:*

> every student of the less exact sciences will do his best to bring home to the reader all the conditions in which the experiment or the observations are made. In ethnography, where a candid account of such data is perhaps even more necessary, it has unfortunately in the past not always been supplied with sufficient generosity, and many writers do not ply the searchlight of methodic sincerity, as they move among their facts but produce them before us out of complete obscurity.
>
> (Malinowski as quoted by Webster 1982:91)

As Webster comments, Malinowski's description of his observations stopped far short of the candour he demanded, and his personal reflections on fieldwork were relegated to a diary in order, as Webster puts it, to discipline himself to objectivity. Webster suggests that an integration of such intimate reflections into ethnographic work would still seem irrelevant to us as well as to malinowski. He continues by posing the following ethnographic puzzle:

> Contemporary ethnography can countenance neither the view that these are a part of the field 'experiment' which Malinowski recommended on the model of the natural sciences, nor the naive positivist assumption that they are simply inconsequential. This is the dilemma we have inherited (mostly directly) from Malinowski.
>
> (Webster 1982:91-2)

One way of starting to think about his puzzle is to ask the question: what are the boundaries of fieldwork in terms of personal feelings about what is happening? Malinowski saw feelings as separate from the field-work enterprise; Webster suggests that to include them is problematic.

When I wrote my fieldnotes, I did not keep a separate diary for recording my personal feelings. Indeed, when I now look at what I have written, I worry that there is so much of how I felt and not enough of how the people I encountered expressed their feelings. And sometimes it seems to me that the problem lies not so much in the decision to include or not to include personal feelings, but rather in the process of elucidating the part they play in marking boundaries. When I now read my fieldnotes, they convey how I felt and they suggest that when I wrote them I believed my feelings might give me insights into the experiences of the people I was encountering. For example, in the following extract from my fieldwork diary I reflect on feeling vulnerable: 'My first foray into role-play. Played the role of a nurse talking to a patient with a colostomy. I felt extremely vulnerable, especially as I do not consider myself as a nurse' (Fieldnote book 3:11). I suggest that this experience might increase my sensitivity to the experiences of others. I write: 'Still, positive aspects were that it gave me an understanding of the vulnerability of nurses who have a generalised knowledge and who are put in situations where they have to deal sensitively with very particular problems' (Fieldnote book 3:11).

The idea that allegiance to a group, whether based on gender, ethnicity, occupation or class, makes for sensitivity towards other members of the group, is a commonly held assumption. It informs, for example, some of the literature on doing feminist research; for instance, Ann Oakley's (1980) deliberations on interviewing women. When I wrote the fieldnotes I refer to above I was subscribing to this idea. However, I also find, if I continue to read, that in many instances there was often complete divergence between how I felt about something and how those I encountered felt, in spite of common experiences of occupation (nursing experience) and sex (most nurses are women).

On one occasion I was talking to a group of student nurses. We were discussing a variety of problems they were encountering in the wards. One particular problem involved a male patient who tried to put his hand up the skirt of a nurse's uniform. I was surprised at the responses of some of the nurses. In their experiences that kind of thing happened fairly often and most of them did not feel angry or upset. I write:

> In discussion the following comments were made: it happens all the time; it's to be expected; it's almost therapeutic. When I asked whether it would be acceptable on the street, the answers were definite 'no's'. Why then, I asked, was it different on the wards? Some, after deliberation, altered their position. One or two who had tended to express outrage in a mild way earlier in discussion said that nurses are people before they are nurses and they should not allow themselves to take this abuse passively. Some, though, said they did not take it as abuse.
>
> (Fieldnote book 3:78)

I continue: 'I felt that they all orientated towards the feelings and desires of the patient, and it came as something of a surprise to be able to say, "No, I find it offensive"' (Fieldnote book 3:79). Later still, I wrote in a paper: 'Afterwards, I felt it had provided arguments for looking at things a different way' (Williams 1983: 23).

I find it tantalising to find that I do not record my 'arguments'. Nevertheless here is an instance where I find women, including myself, thinking and feeling about things in different ways. Simply to write that my experiences give me insights into the experiences of others will not do, because it does not take into account important contradictions and discontinuities in my experience of doing ethnography. For example, in my experience sex alone is not a basis for sisterhood. Looking for how I felt about things in the process of doing research can give me insights into the experience of others, but the process is far more complex than merely making a statement about approximation of feelings.

One thing that strikes me now is how, having started by writing about being sensitive to the feelings of those I was encountering in the field, I begin to separate myself from them. I talk about contradictions and discontinuities of experience. Let me look again at the notes I refer to earlier on: 'I felt vulnerable, especially as I do not consider myself as a nurse' (fieldnote book 3:11). That I say do not think of myself as a nurse is interesting because it is contradictory, in the sense that when I wrote this I knew that I had nursing experience and was even exploiting this experience in order to do fieldwork. In looking for 'my self' in my research, I find a tension between wanting to be with (in the sense of sharing perspectives) those I was encountering and wanting to separate myself. This tension can be explored by teasing out my status as both 'participant' and 'observer' in the field, bearing in mind that these are separations used to think about what was a whole or continuous experience.

I went into the field both interested and disinterested. My role as participant was not confined to a period of research time as with most ethnographers. I had trained and worked as a nurse and was well acquainted with the field from this perspective. Dissatisfied, I had left. Early on in my fieldwork I found myself nursing in order to do ethnography, which meant that I was (like Nicky James 1984) 'really' working and (unlike Nicky James who was working 'for free') actually employed by the Health Authority. Being a participant in this sense affected my experience of ethnography. I felt moved by what I heard and saw to want things changed. And as a trained nurse, that was always a possibility. I could and did comment on what I heard and saw, and my comments were taken seriously because I was a trained nurse and not because I was an anthropologist. And yet, as my notes show, the feeling of being a stranger never left me. I never felt fully a participant.

What did this tension mean in practice? As an observer, one thing that struck me was this: nurses as a group have little or no authority, that is no formal or legal authority. I refer in my fieldnotes to how Helen Evers states this in relation to multi-disciplinary teamwork in geriatric wards. She says:

> For long stay patients, the pervasiveness of the teamwork

mythology and the frequent concurrent withdrawal of other professionals can, at worse, leave the nurses in the invidious position of having responsibility but no formal or legal authority for caring for their patients – work which no other professional is anxious to do.

(Evers 1981:205-14)

As a participant – that is, a person who had worked as a nurse – I could see how this might apply to other areas of nursing. I could draw on my experiences both past and present. After reading Helen Evers' article, I write about the following area of nursing work: 'Look at the question of drug errors. Why do they occur? Can it have something to do with the notion that nurses have the responsibility for giving the drugs but not the authority to prescribe?' (Fieldnote book 1:65). Later I write:

Every week at the Tuesday morning staff meeting, drug errors are reported. There are several reasons for this: (1) Drugs are given *en masse* at certain times of the day and are called drug rounds. This is a very routine procedure and involves nurses in repetitive work of checking and counter checking to see that correct doses are given and to the correct patient. (2) Drugs are constantly changing, are complicated, and it is possible that nurses are not familiar with all the drugs and their dosage. Ideally, if a nurse is unsure, she can look it (the drug) up in MIMS (a reference book), but they don't routinely look up drugs – not each drug (the doctor has gone through this procedure when prescribing the drug, and anyway there is very little time). (3) Doctor's writing may be illegible. In short doctors prescribe drugs and nurses administer drugs. Here is an example of nurses as 'handmaidens' to doctors. They have no say in prescribing drugs. They are not authorised to prescribe what they give. Yet they are accountable for what they give, how much, etc., etc.

(Fieldnote book 1:75-6)

In other notes I comment that how I write these fieldnotes is important. I write these words as someone who has had experience of 'drug errors'. This experience extends into my past. I can recall how I was once very aware and concerned about the possibility of giving a patient a wrong drug. So the words I wrote in my fieldnote book are based on how I remembered the past. The boundaries of my fieldwork experiences are therefore extended back into the past to include feelings from the past. I remember feeling rushed ('there was very little time') and I remember feeling frustrated ('doctor's writing may be illegible'). It was on the basis of these feelings as well as listening in weekly staff meetings to the names of nurses who had made 'drug errors' that I made the following comments:

> It is my feeling that the following should be considered: a) authority of doctors to prescribe drugs; b) responsibility of nurses to administer drugs. If these are considered then the following questions are raised: Is it not dangerous to give something you do not know enough about to prescribe? Is this an underlying factor in drug errors? If you give a drug to a patient should you prescribe it? If you prescribe a drug should you give it? Should nurses, therefore, prescribe drugs or conversely, should doctors give drugs?
> (Fieldnote book 1:77)

Although I am writing here 'as if I were a nurse', it is interesting to note I did not take matters further. I did not write letters to the nursing press as I might have done (the thought did cross my mind), nor did I express how I felt formally to nursing management. Why not? Was it simply because I did not get round to making the effort? Or was there something else constraining me? Did I see myself primarily as an observer and a commentator even if my comments and observations evoke participation, concern and interest?

Implications of a feminist reading for understanding the experience of others

Looking for 'my self' in my fieldnotes gives me insights into the tension between wanting to be a part of a group and wanting to understand the experience of others, but also wanting to be separate and different from others. I refer in my notes to a desire to 'lose myself' in day-to-day events: I become a part of the field. At the same time I can remove myself by seeing myself within a different context; that is, 'doing ethnography' in this way to 'regain myself'. Perhaps, too, this mirrors a similar process in the 'others' I encounter. I am reminded of the discussion following the problem of the abuse of a nurse by a patient: 'It happens all the time; it's to be expected; it's almost therapeutic. When I asked if it would be acceptable on the street, the answers were definite "no's"' (Fieldnote book 3:78). Here, too, nurses appear to lose themselves in the event, and then when jolted into thinking about the event contextually, they see things differently.

A feminist reading of my notes, in the sense that I try to explore the presence of myself in my research, illuminates methodological and epistemological problems in the process of doing ethnography. Further and very importantly, I find links between my day-to-day practice and the day-to-day practice of those whom I encounter. I begin to see how the problems I speak of, particularly in connection with my relationships with others, are mirrored in the relationships of those I encounter and vice versa. It is in this way that I can speak of beginning to understand the experiences of others, by recognising that we are located on the same critical plane of activity and understanding.

© 1990 Anne Williams

References

Ames, Mike (1979) 'Applied Anthropology in our Backyards', *Practical Anthropology 2:1–24*.

Evers, Helen (1981) 'Multidisciplinary Teams in Geriatric Wards: Myth or Reality?' *Journal of Advanced Nursing 6:205–14*.

Geertz, Clifford (1973) *The Interpretation of Cultures*, New York: Basic Books.

Graham, Hilary (1984) *Women, Health and the Family*, Brighton: Wheatsheaf.

James, Nicky (1984) 'Postscript to Nursing', in Colin Bell and Helen Roberts (eds), *Social Researching*, London: Routledge & Kegan Paul, pp.125–46.

Oakley, Ann (1980) 'Interviewing Women', in Helen Roberts (ed.), *Doing Feminist Research*, London: Routledge & Kegan Paul, pp. 30–61.

Stanley, Liz and Wise, Sue (1983) *Breaking Out: Feminist Consciousness and Feminist Research, London: Routledge & Kegan Paul*

Webster, Stephen (1982) 'Dialogue and Fiction in Ethnography', *Dialectical Anthropology 7:91–114*.

Williams, Anne (1983) 'Rhetoric as Cultural Performance', Unpublished paper, BSA Medical Sociology Group Conference.

Willis, Paul (1980) *Learning to Labour*, Farnborough: Gower.

Chapter nineteen

Analysing a photograph of Marilyn Monroe

Denise Farran

Introduction

Marilyn Monroe is overwhelmingly a visual phenomenon: a beautiful blonde with tantalising red lips and voluptuous figure, a sex goddess. This is one view of her, the dominant conventional one, and it is shown in the photograph opposite.

Visual images of Marilyn Monroe are popularly assumed to be 'male things', pictures with just one meaning: sexual. Men are assumed to be 'turned on', to drool almost Pavlov dog fashion at the sight of them. Women's experiences of them aren't usually given a lot of attention, women are not the assumed audience, and neither are men who do not (say they) react in this way. If any assumptions are made about the kinds of critical readings many women make of such 'sexual', pictures, it is usually that they are envious of women like Monroe and so dislike them.

This chapter provides a feminist sociological analysis of how a photograph of 'Marilyn' works: how is the 'sexuality' of this photograph achieved or not achieved? At the heart of my discussion is the idea that this or any other photograph is not an object of fact, but rather meaning and understanding of it is socially constructed. People bring to this photograph of Marilyn Monroe various ideas concerning what are the signifiers of sexuality; and in this way what is 'sexual' is actually a socially achieved phenomenon.

Readers also bring to the photograph certain ideas about the biography of Marilyn Monroe. This picture isn't a picture of any woman, but Marilyn Monroe. The dominant image of her is that she is a sexual woman, not 'Anywoman' but a very particular kind of woman. Ideas concerning her biography are strongly involved in how sense is made of the particulars of the photograph. Many readers will see this as a photograph of a woman who somehow signifies what is (hetero)-sexual, and this information is important in how they construct it as a sexual photograph. For example, would a photograph of Nancy Reagan or Indira Gandhi in the same pose solicit a similar response? Thus a

self-fulfilling prophecy occurs: reading it as a sexual photograph in turn reinforces readers' ideas about the biography of Marilyn Monroe being that of a sexual woman.

However, the importance of context must be emphasised. Photographs are always read at specific times in specific places and moments. Our reading of the 'same' photograph, of what the photograph is about, often changes over time. As the meaning of photographs is socially constructed, so there are always various meanings possible and indeed achieved of a photograph. People often argue about what the 'same' photograph is about. Further, at a single reading of a photograph we can have conflicting ideas about it. For example, the experience a male friend had of this photograph was that, at the same time as he experienced it as 'sexual', he also knew it was a set-up, a construction.

I also take it as axiomatic that this photograph can be read as being not a sexual photograph at all. As a basis for my analysis, I shall explore my own experience and understanding of this photograph. Examining my experience as a socially located and analysable one in this way is the best method of exploring a feminist alternative to the images and understandings of the dominant patriarchal ideology. In doing this I also discuss some analytical ideas concerning photographs.

Photographs as artful productions

The photograph of Marilyn Monroe is an artful production. Its art, however, relies upon hiding the signs of its production so that it appears 'natural': as if there is just Monroe sitting there looking at the camera, as if she exists just for me, the reader. There are no intermediaries, just me and her in this room; and this creates a feeling of intimacy and privacy.

This is one level. At the back of their minds some readers might 'know' or 'think' this is a construction. It appears as something-which-we-all-know-it-is-not: all of us 'know' that Marilyn Monroe was not there looking at us. Yet it could be argued that the photograph is set up for readers to 'read' it as a private photograph – it's just us-subject and Marilyn-object. The private which is thereby hinted at is one of the key ways in which the photograph connotes a 'sexual' meaning. Yet the actual private, the 'real' private of the photograph, is that of props, camera equipment and photographer. The photograph, then, is a version; it is one version, one part of the interactional reality which was the origin of the photograph. What is missing?

First, there would have been the other people in the setting. At a minimum there must have been the photographer. In many photographic sessions there are a whole army of people involved: lighting people, hairdresser, make-up people and so on. But readers do not see outside of the view of the lens, to the surrounding reality. We cannot see what is going on around 'the shot', what the people are doing for whom this is a part of their routine working day. Also what Marilyn Monroe was thinking about, what she had just been doing before the photograph was taken, are not recoverable from the photograph itself; but this does not matter for our sense or understanding of the photograph. Yet when Marilyn looked at this photograph she probably thought of the things which took place 'outside the lens', like items of activities and persons in her life at that time, or more mundane things like, for example, that it was cold sitting there.

Second, as well as not seeing the process of taking the photograph itself, one product, we don't see the process that was the working up of the woman Marilyn, into the version of her which is present in this photograph, as another and closely related kind of product. We do not see the curled hair curled, the red lips reddened, or the flimsy dress provocatively arranged; that is, we don't see the transformation of ordinary self-presentation into 'glamorous' or 'appealing' or 'provocative' self-presentation.

In a photograph such as this there is a popular assumption that the woman in it is an 'object' for other people to view; and further, the inference is that she was the 'object' in the interactional context wherein the photograph was produced. This is an assumption linking the public reality to the private reality. The two main reasons for this seem to be that photographic sessions are seen as situations of 'male control', the photographer more often being a man, and also because of the wider context in which the photograph was produced in the male-dominated film and media industry, with its expectations about how women's sexuality is to be portrayed as stimulating, erotic, for men.

However, whilst I broadly agree with these ideas, they are rather one-dimensional. For example, it is worth questioning the popular idea of 'sexual women' in 'sexual photographs' being sex-objects. This is the case in one sense, for they are indeed objects of the spectator's gaze; but in another we can also recognise that by subordinating herself to a public gaze she thereby gains power over that public: she becomes subject and 'it' an object which reacts in ways determined by her. Relatedly, we can read in biographies of Marilyn Monroe that she was often very instrumental in initiating poses in photographic sessions. That is, she dominated what the sessions focussed on (literally so as well) and thus the form in which 'Marilyn' was publicly consumed as a product. She thus operated as both producer and product of her own public sexual self.

Analysing the photograph

Erving Goffman (1976) analyses a range of gender signifiers in advertising photographs, to see what shared cultural ideas concerning gender and sexuality and thus the 'selves' of men and women are displayed through them. He notes that women are often pictured self-touching, the implications being that their bodies are delicate and precious. In this photograph, Marilyn has her hands clasped across her breasts, perhaps suggesting that her breasts and body are precious; perhaps it is also sexually suggestive: that she may uncover her breasts for just the right person. Her body is slightly lowered as she is bending over. This could be taken as a sign of appeasement, what Goffman terms a 'canting posture'. She is certainly in a non-threatening pose, and the huddled position of her body would add to its sexualness, in that it could be read that she is 'hiding' parts of her body, she is being coy, or that she is being playful.

Smiles are what Goffman calls 'ritualistic mollifiers', which demonstrate friendliness and no harmful intent. Again women are pictured smiling more than men, because it is they who have to appease men. In this photograph of Monroe it can be read as a particular type of smile, a 'sexual' smile that is open and inviting. Goffman also suggests that women are more often presented in child-like and clowning poses, the implication being that women aren't as serious and grown-up as men. This picture presents Marilyn in a child-like pose, and indeed one of the main attractions of Marilyn Monroe is said to be her unique mixture of both woman and child.

Thus Goffman's 'inventory' approach to body posture and facial display highlights the way in which certain poses and representations display current cultural ideas concerning women and men. A similar approach can be used to look at how sexual meaning can be attributed to different elements in this photograph. For example, her skirt has deliberately been arranged so that a large part of her legs is left unshown, teasingly hiding the 'rude' bits; her breasts are emphasised by the low cut dress and the way she is bending forward; her hands clasping towards her chest are signals of coyness; her dress unzipped at the back reveals virtually all of her back; her dress is very frothy and romantic; her hair is bleached blonde and tousled; her mouth is wide open, invitingly; and her eyes have a 'come hither' look.

From detailing these particulars we can 'see' that this is a sexual photograph; that is, this photograph displays current social signifiers as to what is sexual. However, they only display it by readers recognising them and investing them with meaning. For example, I might not recognise her mouth as 'open and inviting' in a sexual sense, but in contrast as 'friendly and playful'. Photographs do not simply 'display'

facts, but rather readers bringing their social knowledge, their ways
of seeing, to 'recognise' these. Further, readers will do this in different ways depending on their particular biography and context of
reading.

Also in an everyday reading we do not produce inventories in this
highly artificial way. Sometimes we just glance through photographs, at
other times we spend longer looking at particular ones. Whichever is the
case, however, we always focus on some particulars and don't notice
others: some are foreground, some are background. Goffman's
approach, then, is a highly 'academic' and non-naturalist one which
presents only one authorised reading of a photograph. However, what
this kind of analysis demonstrates is that 'sexuality' is not an objective
fact, but rather is an accomplished phenomenon.

Some photographs do nothing for a reader, they have no appeal
whatsoever, whilst others arouse a kind of general interest which Roland
Barthes (1984) calls the 'studium' of a photograph. However, some
photographs have elements in them which make us very interested in
them; they contain something which stands out and punctuates our
consciousness, and this is related to our biography, our history and what
kind of things interest us.

This something which strikes us, which punctuates our consciousness, Barthes calls the 'punctum'. For Barthes the punctum is an
incidental to a photograph's composition. Moreover and much more
contentiously he insists that it is 'uncoded', that no socially provided
frame of reference for glossing and categorising and so socially comprehending it exists: if such a frame exists then this cannot be the
punctum. In sociological terms, everything is coded, is socially compre-
hended – even the incomprehensible; and I reject the notion of an
uncoded punctum. My concern is to account for whatever is the
punctum by unpacking the socially available schema for understanding
the part that this punctum plays in our reading of the photograph in its
entirety.

To elaborate a sociological understanding of the punctum of photographs, Harold Garfinkel's (1967) use of the 'documentary method of
interpretation' is of help. One aspect of this concept refers to the process
wherein some particulars stand out, and these influence how we see
other things. In this photograph perhaps at the forefront of interpretation
is the biography of Marilyn Monroe – this is a photograph of a sexual
woman. Thus the biography, 'off frame', is brought into the frame.

My focus of attention is on the face of Marilyn Monroe and I see a
person, a woman, and I think of her biography. For example, this was a
woman who was seldom taken seriously, who was thought of as a dumb-
blonde-cum-joke. I also look at this picture and locate it within what I

know she was doing in 1956 (when I know the photo was taken and by whom it was taken).

Whilst the face is the focus of my attention, in the background I see 'the breasts', 'the revealed back' and so on, and I 'know' that this can be construed as a sexual photograph; but I also know that this isn't for me, that it is for men, for heterosexual men at that. This is my reading; other people may even disagree that it is possible to construct a sexual reading from this photograph in the way I do as a woman-seeing-it-as-(hetero-sexual)-men-do. Also my reading changes over time. For example, when I first saw this photograph I thought, 'It's Marilyn Monroe dressed up in a party frock'. A few months later someone pointed out to me the ballet rail, which I hadn't even noticed. Therefore a new reading for me becomes possible – 'It's Marilyn Monroe in a pose which is like the Degas ballet dancers'.

Different people will read different versions into this photograph. For example, even just among friends, some (both men and women) have read it as sexual and some have said it's pornographic. Also some people (mostly women) have looked at the photograph and, in a similar way to me, ideas concerning Marilyn's biography were conjured up: for example, 'this is a picture of a sad woman who committed suicide'. Other people (men and women) read it as a picture of Marilyn in a playful, not sexual, pose. In talking about the reaction of other people, I do so to indicate that alternative and competing versions are possible. The main point here is that people will have different versions of this photograph and these do not just depend on cultural ideas shared in common (though these are obviously involved). Rather, these ideas are used selectively to form interpretive schemas which are employed in particular situations of reading and by particular people with unique biographies. For example, I read the photograph in particular ways because of my biography: what kind of person I am and what interests me.

The sex of the reader is also important in how a photograph is read, because men and women (through socialisation and its development of 'masculine' and 'feminine' characters and behaviours) have different ways of seeing. Men (heterosexual) see certain things as appropriate to them; for example 'uncovered breasts' are seen as appropriate to them in a sexual sense, whereas women see this as not for them in this way. However, the sex of the reader does not *determine* interpretation, as I noted earlier.

Although in a (sexual) sense this photograph is addressed to men, in another way it is also addressed to women, telling them that she is the kind of woman that men like. It is through such photographs, Annette Kuhn (1985) suggests, that women's sexuality, femininity and indeed 'self' are constructed. This then is an image of woman designed and produced so as to appeal to heterosexual men and their ideas concerning women. Speaking about such photographs, John Berger says, 'This picture is made to appeal to his sexuality. It has nothing to do with her sexuality' (Berger 1972:55), by which he means the ways in which women are presented as passive so that men can have the 'monopoly of such passion' (1972:55). Germaine Greer (1971) suggests that men prefer such a view of women's sexuality as it de-powers women by stripping them of their vitality and demands. It is also notable that men demand and enjoy a portrayal of women's sexuality that is child-like (children being relatively powerless and dependent on adults) – women are preferred stripped of body hair, have tousled hair cuts and so on.

John Berger also argues that men and women have a different way of seeing, not just in attributing meaning to photographs but to all social situations. Women are taught to see themselves as objects, to survey themselves from the position of others – the others being men. Women are used to watching themselves and being looked at by others. Berger says:

> Women watch themselves being looked at. This determines not
> only most relations between men and women but also the relation
> of women to themselves. The surveyor of woman in herself is
> male: the surveyed female. Thus she turns herself into an object –
> and most particularly an object of vision: a sight.
>
> (Berger 1972:47)

According to Berger, when women see photographs like this one of Marilyn, their response is either to survey the woman (that is, to treat her as an object) or to imagine themselves in that position (that is, being surveyed by men). This is in contrast to men, who, Berger argues, have only one way of seeing, that is, to treat the woman as an object: men are always the surveyors, never the surveyed object. Annette Kuhn (1985:31) similarly argues that women can adopt a 'male' position (that is, to see women as objects), look at photographs in the same kind of way as men do and indeed to find such photographs pleasurable; but also that spectators have 'the option of identifying with, rather than objectifying, the woman in the picture' (Kuhn 1985:31).

It is useful to refer back to the concept of the documentary method of interpretation here. All women will not experience this photograph in the same way. In any photograph there are different particulars and as audience we focus on some particulars and relegate others to background focus. It is possible not to see the 'sexual' at all. Or, we can see the sexual particulars but deliberately block them out and concentrate on different things to achieve a different reading. Or, we don't have to interpret the so-called sexual particulars as 'sexual' but as *sexual politics* which we deconstruct analytically. These responses aren't mutually exclusive: we can have different responses at the same time. For example, I might consciously try to block out what I see as sexual particulars and focus on other things, and actually do so; yet in the background I also know that the 'sexual', the woman as object aspects, are somehow 'there' even though I have placed them 'out of frame'. In talking about women's responses to 'sexual' photographs, it is worth pointing out that some photographs lend themselves to a sexual reading from which departures, alternative readings, are harder to achieve. The obvious example here is of hard-core pornography.

There are two main interrelated strands to the dominant 'sexual' image of Marilyn Monroe: the 'goddess' facet, where she is challenging and in a sense dominant; the second is the 'baby doll' facet, where she is soft and inviting and subordinate. The first is symbolised by poses such as her hands on her hips, the upturned pout, the red lips, the glamorous revealing dresses. The second is symbolised through such things as the coy, demure eyelashes; soft, wispy, fluffy clothes; and the blonde, tousled hair. Both these facets are frequently present in photographs and appearances of the 'public' Marilyn, but they are present in differing mixtures unique to each context. For example, in the photograph in this chapter the emphasis is more on the second, 'baby-doll' facet, although the red open lips and glamorous dress are present. The first facet signifies woman's power over men, she is dominant; the second facet signifies woman's dependency on men, she needs caring for. In this way the baby-doll image or facet de-threatens Marilyn: how powerful she would be if represented as purely a 'sex goddess' in the challenging mould, whereas she is flawed by the baby-doll image, for the child-like and dumb blonde attribution makes her less dangerous to men, she is not outside their control.

On one level we can see Marilyn Monroe as breaking the mould of male ideas about women's sexuality. That is, she is a much exaggerated model of what this is supposed to be. Many of her poses are over the top, they tread a thin line between caricature-cum-joke and an object of desire. In some ways she is the female equivalent of a drag queen: a *female* female impersonator, the impersonator of men's stereotypic image of the desirable sexual woman.

Photographs and biography

There is a commonsensical feeling that photographs can capture and summarise a part of a person's life and character. Indeed, there are many books on Monroe which claim to be biographies of her by 'telling' her life in photographs (for instance, Spada and Zeno 1982). Photographs of Marilyn are assumed to be biographical. She is portrayed in them as a sexual woman, not just any sexual woman but a sex goddess. Therefore 'she', the 'real' Marilyn, is also assumed to be sexual in the same ways. This is achieved primarily through processes concerned with the construction and selection of 'relevant' biographical materials: we then bring this biography to the photograph, it informs our reading of 'it'.

There are very few photographs of Marilyn published which show the interactional context wherein 'Marilyn' was produced: for example, photographs showing her surrounded by hairdressers and make-up people. There are also very few photographs of her doing mundane, ordinary things, like bicycling, going for a walk, shopping, being 'on holiday'. Such a selection takes her out of the normal, private everyday world and into the very different one of 'stars', of extra-ordinary and public people.

Some photographs more than others are taken as particularly indicative of the nature of the person's life and character. For example, with Marilyn Monroe, the photograph of her standing over a grid with her white dress being blown up is one such photograph. This exists for other famous people (alive and dead): for example, the photographs of James Dean entitled 'Boulevard of Broken Dreams' and of Winston Churchill's 'V for Victory' pose. This process occurs in paintings too: for example, one self-portrait of Gwen John painted in 1900–5 is used as indicative of her 'true biography' more than any other of her many self-portraits.

It is important to understand that it is not (usually) the person concerned whose choice it is that this picture becomes their dominant image. Rather, it derives from other people's ideas about the biography of the person. For example, the painting selected of Gwen John is of her looking strong and independent. In this way a 'preferred reading' of character can be constructed and then used as a framework for seeing and understanding events and activities in the biographical subject's life.

Recently many women film stars have attracted largely positive feminist attention and admiration (such as Lauren Bacall, Katharine Hepburn, Bette Davis), but Marilyn Monroe has not. The clue as to why lies in the dominant image of Marilyn, for this contains all the attributes seen as despicable by feminists: she was the baby doll who was coy, dumb and weak and dependent on strong, dependable men. However, I feel uneasy about such a view of her and think that a feminist re-evaluation (and see here Steinem and Barris 1987) has been long called for. I also find unsatisfactory the way in which the character traits of the public image are evaluated. Such traits as coyness, girlishness, 'dumbness', are usually viewed as signifying and indeed constituting powerlessness. However, at the same time as they constitute power-lessness, such traits can actually 'do power': it was precisely through the 'dumbness', the 'coyness', that Marilyn was powerful.

Instead of seeing Marilyn Monroe as a victim of the exploitation of men and nothing but, it is more persuasive to suggest that, while this may have been the case, she was also at the same time powerfully exploiting them: Marilyn Monroe did what she did in order to get what she wanted – fame and fortune. The public image of her was a consciously produced product, and a strategy to achieve this. Along the way she was both exploiter and exploited.

It is interesting to question why it is the case that we view sexual women as objects being exploited by men, with the women seen as powerless. To view such sexual women as victims and nothing but is a very 'male' view of the processes involved, one that is comforting to men because by definition it sees what they do and achieve as indicating power and whatever women do and achieve as of course indicating powerlessness. A more complex feminist view argues that women in the process of their everyday lives develop practices and strategies to get what they want out of life – in so doing, some we win, some we lose (Wise and Stanley 1987). However, what is involved is complex, whatever ideological accounts produced by men and some feminists may suggest.

At the same time, Marilyn Monroe and women like her are very problematic for me as a feminist. On the one hand I want to say that the power she had was on male terms, given/achieved because she played their game – portrayed male ideas about women's sexuality. However, the flip side of this is that unless we're talking about absolute power, power is always resisted, negotiated, mediated.

In conclusion I would argue that there should be more exploration of how cultural images are actually assembled and how they have meaning in individual experience. For example, Marilyn Monroe is still a figure strongly present in popular culture: what are the elements of this image? how is this constructed? why is it such a powerful image? and just as importantly, how do people in different situations, with different biographies, experience this image? and what kind of relationship does she have with 'ordinary' women? It is only through analytic examination of the complexity of how such cultural images 'work' that we can fully understand them and the hold they have over us.

© 1990 Denise Farran

References

Barthes, Roland (1984) *Camera Lucida*, London: Fontana.
Berger, John (1972) *Ways of Seeing*, Harmondsworth: Penguin.
Garfinkel, Harold (1967) *Studies in Ethnomethodology*, Englewood Cliffs, NJ: Prentice-Hall.

Goffman, Erving (1976) *Gender Advertisements*, London: Macmillan.

Greer, Germaine (1971) *The Female Eunuch*, St Albans: Paladin.

Kuhn, Annette (1985) *The Power of the Image*, London: Routledge & Kegan Paul.

Spada, James and Zeno, George (1982) *Monroe: Her Life in Pictures*, London: Sidgwick & Jackson.

Steinem, Gloria and Barris, George (1987) *Marilyn*, London: Gollancz.

Wise, Sue and Stanley, Liz (1987) *Georgie Porgie: Sexual Harassment in Everyday Life*, London: Pandora Press.

Name index

Abbott, P. 205, 220
Abbott, S. 31, 47
Abrams, P. 18
Acker, J. 35, 47, 58
Acker, S. 7, 16, 18, 154
Ackroyd, P. 131, 132
Addelson, K. 50
Alavi, H. 72, 78
Alcoff, L. 40, 41, 47
Alexander, S. 25, 47
Allen, Jeffner 32, 47
Allen, Judith 40, 48
Allen, S. 249
Ames, M. 254, 261
Amos, V. 73, 77, 78
Anderson, B. 13, 18, 45, 46, 48
Andolsen, B. 38, 48
Anzaldua, G. 31, 54
Arber, S. 205, 220
Atkinson, P. 146, 147, 152, 154, 155
Atkinson, T.-G. 48

Bandarage, A. 77, 78
Banner, L. 69, 78
Barclay Report 122
Barnes, J. 142, 143
Barrett, M. 14, 16, 26, 37, 38, 41,
    44, 48, 78
Barris, G. 271, 273
Barry, K. 35, 47
Barthes, R. 147, 154, 267, 272
Bartky, S. 22, 48, 125, 132
Bartlett, E. 48
Batsleer, J. 16
Bauman, Z. 10, 16

Beaulieu Presley, P. 140, 143
Beck, E. 57, 79
Becker, H. 190, 203
Belensky, M. 48
Bell, C. 17, 48, 261
Benston, M. 53
Berger, J. 269, 272
Bernard, J. 21, 43, 48
Bernstein, B. 152, 154
Birmingham Lesbian Offensive
    Group 165, 171
Bleier, R. 11, 16, 48, 50
Bolton, G. 222, 235
Bombyk, M. 55
Bordo, S. 11, 16, 38, 48
Bourdieu, P. 7, 16, 17, 152, 154
Bourque, S. 70, 78
Bowles, G. 19, 48, 52, 53, 55, 58
Braverman, H. 207, 220
Brett, S. 16
Bridenthal, R. 78
Bristow, A. 38, 48
Brittain, N. 205, 220
Brock, D. 48
Brook, E. 249
Brooke, M. 188
Bulkin, E. 33, 48, 51
Burden, D. 48, 51
Butler, O. 15, 133

Camden Girls Project 165, 171
*Canadian Review of Sociology and
    Anthropology* 48
Carby, H. 73, 77, 78
Carchedi, C. 207, 220

274

Name index

Rowbotham, S. 69, 79
Rutenberg, T. 6

Saarinen, A. 56
Sacks, K. 71, 79
Sanders, L. 249
Sapsford, R. 205, 220
Sarah, E. 125, 133
Sawicki, J. 56
Sayers, J. 56
SBP 149, 155
SCARS 16, 114, 122
Schutz, A. 42, 56
Schwartz, H. 190, 203
Scott, J. 40, 41, 56
Scott, P.B. 29, 52
Scott, S. 8, 16, 18, 56, 155
Sellwood, R. 172, 187, 188
Shaktani, N. 56
Sharpe, S. 222, 235
Sharrock, W. 13, 18, 45, 46, 48
Sheridan, S. 56
Sherin, S. 38, 57
Sherman, J. 57, 79
Showalter, E. 25, 57
Signs 57
Silveira, J. 79
Simmonds, E. 16
Smart, C. 9, 18, 38, 40, 57
Smith, Barbara 29, 33, 48, 52
Smith, Brenda 57
Smith, D. 5, 10, 18, 20, 24, 27, 34–6,
    43, 45–6, 57 69, 79, 174, 183, 187
Smith, H. 57
Smith-Rosenberg, C. 57
Smyth, A. 6, 18, 57
Sociological Inquiry 57
Spada, J. 270, 273
Spellman, E. 53
Spencer, A. 155
Spender, D. 5, 18, 21, 44, 53, 55, 57,
    69, 79
Stacey, J. 56, 57, 58
Stacey, M. 9, 18, 38, 40
Stack, C. 53
Stanley, L. 5, 9, 12, 16, 18, 19, 20–5,
    34, 38, 40, 42, 45, 58, 59, 113,
    120, 122, 126, 133, 143, 144, 155,

254, 261, 272, 273
Stanworth, M. 220
Statham, D. 249
Steinem, G. 271, 273
Stone, P. 22, 58
Strathern, M. 25, 58
Sydie, R.A. 58

Tait, A. 16, 172, 173, 187
Talbot, M. 91, 102
Tarule, J. 48
Taylor, B. 69, 79
Taylorson, D. 9, 17, 51
Thomas, M. 172, 187
Thompson, F. 155
Thompson, P. 4, 19
Thorne, B. 58

Van den Berg, N. 249
Vetterling-Braggin, M. 48, 58, 132
Vickers, J. 58

Wallace, M. 58, 141, 143
Wallis, J. 249
Ward, K. 5, 19, 21, 58
Warren, C. 70, 78
Warren Piper, D. 7, 16, 18, 58, 154
Waugh, P. 58
Wearing, B. 53, 57, 249
Webb, S. 15, 205, 220
Webster, S. 256, 261
Weir, A. 238, 249
Welburn, V. 140, 143
Weldon, F. 142, 144
Weskott, M. 58
WGSG 146, 155
White, P. 185, 187
Whyte, J. 146
Whyte, K. 59, 155
Wieder, L. 43, 59
Wilkinson, Sue 38, 40, 59
Wilkinson, Susi 188
Williams, A. 16, 254, 257, 261
Willis, P. 254, 261
Wilson, E. 238, 249
Wimbush, E. 91, 102
Winant, T. 59
Wise, S. 5, 9, 12, 15, 16, 18, 19,

Subject index